GOD, CAESAR, AND IDOLS

RICK D.
BOYER

GOD, CAESAR, AND IDOLS

THE CHURCH AND THE STRUGGLE
FOR AMERICA'S SOUL

AMBASSADOR INTERNATIONAL
GREENVILLE, SOUTH CAROLINA & BELFAST, NORTHERN IRELAND
www.ambassador-international.com

GOD, CAESAR, AND IDOLS

The Church and the Struggle for America's Soul

ISBN: 978-1-64960-078-3

eISBN: 978-1-64960-089-9

Cover Design by Hannah Linder Designs

Interior Design by Dentelle Design

AMBASSADOR INTERNATIONAL
Emerald House
411 University Ridge, Suite B14
Greenville, SC 29601
United States
www.ambassador-international.com

AMBASSADOR BOOKS
The Mount
2 Woodstock Link
Belfast, BT6 8DD
Northern Ireland, United Kingdom
www.ambassadormedia.co.uk

The colophon is a trademark of Ambassador, a Christian publishing company.

TABLE OF CONTENTS

INTRODUCTION

This book was written as I attempted to seek answers to my own questions. Why do we live in a land where the gospel is preached every Sunday in churches across the land, on the radio, and on television yet the culture seems impervious to that gospel? Why do we live in a land where the majority of the population identifies as Christian yet there is a wholesale ignorance of Christ's teachings? Why do the cultural markers—our common denominators such as music, movies, and news media—almost uniformly oppose and even mock the basic teachings of the Bible?

Why does it seem the gospel has lost its power to change culture and even to noticeably change individual lives? The problem can't be the gospel. *So what is the problem?*

I finally decided to simply put on paper the questions I've felt and attempt to answer them through Scripture. I make this request of the reader. Don't take my word for the answer. Don't even assume I'm asking the right questions. Go back to the Bible. If you have similar questions, if you too lack wisdom, "ask of God, who gives to all generously and without reproach" (James 1:5 NASB). If the answers in this book—or even the questions—do not square with Scripture, discard them.

But I would also ask this. If the answers do square with Scripture, if the Holy Spirit speaks through the eternal Word of God, let Him speak. Even if the answers are countercultural, even if they are offensive at first blush.

Because the more I come up against truth, the more offensive it seems to modern American culture and, yes, to American cultural Christianity as well.

I hope this book is written with directness but with humility. Because the more I come up against truth, the more it is a "discerner of the thoughts and intents of the heart" for me as well (Hebrews 4:12). The more I see the truth, the more it shows me I fail to measure up.

My prayer is that as you read this book, you would ignore the messenger and simply do as the Bereans—"examin[e] the Scriptures daily to see whether these things [are] so" (Acts 17:11 NASB). And if they are, let us, like Paul, ask the salient question of obedient human existence: "Lord, what wilt thou have me to do?" (Acts 9:6).

Sola Scriptura, soli Deo gloria.
Rick Boyer

CHAPTER 1

JUST QUESTIONS, NO ANSWERS

As I began to write this book, Memorial Day had just passed and Independence Day was just around the corner. Independence Day has always been a favorite holiday for me—and obviously for many other Americans. We watch fireworks, pay tribute to our soldiers, listen to patriotic music, and put our hands over our hearts for the singing of our national anthem.

In our hearts remains the echo of an ideal of human freedom—freedom of worship, of thought, of speech, of political affiliation, freedom to ply a trade and achieve "the American dream" for ourselves and our children. Yet unless we crawl under a rock or anesthetize ourselves with mindless entertainment or drugs, it is impossible not to notice cultural decay, growing polarization, a sense of division, of anger, of rebellion against any semblance of moral restraint, from the White House to our neighborhoods.

In 1991, as a boy of sixteen, I began a career as a volunteer conservative political activist, knocking on doors and putting up yard signs for a friend, Steve Newman, in his first successful campaign for a seat in the House of Delegates in Virginia's legislature. For the next twenty-six years, I put my heart and soul (and thousands of hours) into working to elect candidates who I believed shared my vision of constitutional principles, free markets, individual liberty, and the idea that our rights come from God, not government. All this was in the hope of turning back the tide pushing America ever further leftward politically, theologically, and morally.

Two elections changed my focus. In 2016 I watched as millions of professing Christians embraced the presidential candidacy of Donald Trump, even while candidates remained in the race whose personal lives and public records far more clearly reflected biblical principles. I watched as folks who had roundly condemned the escapades of Democrat President Bill Clinton stood in defense of similar actions by Trump, because "Hillary is worse." I would have understood a "lesser evil" argument, but that's not what I heard. Instead, it was a passionate defense of conduct that had brought censure to a Democrat president from these same people. While the Trump presidency has certainly exceeded my low expectations, the hypocrisy and lack of moral clarity were shocking and chilling.

In 2017 it hit closer to home. I live in Campbell County, just outside Lynchburg, Virginia. Lynchburg is the home of Liberty University, where I received a bachelor's degree in government and a law degree as well. (Liberty is also where I met my wife, Christina, for which I will always be grateful.)

That year featured races in two local districts for both the county board of supervisors (the equivalent of a city council but on the county level) and the school board. In all four races, the local Republicans nominated candidates who were politically conservative, which pleased me, but who were also proudly committed Christians. The key race, as it turned out, was the race for school board in Timberlake District. Republican John Kinchen ran on several issues, but his signature issue was his opposition to the 2016 executive order issued by Barack Obama dictating that local school boards must allow students to use the restroom of their choice or lose federal school funding.

Kinchen's opponent argued that the transgender bathroom issue was not a pressing issue in conservative Campbell County and campaigned on the signature issue of more tax dollars for local schools, while criticizing her opponent for making moral judgments.

With days to go before election and indications pointing toward a Kinchen win, he found a yearbook from the local high school, printed at taxpayer expense. The yearbook featured an article on a local boy whose hobby was cross-dressing for school. Kinchen ran a video ad highlighting the yearbook article as evidence that the transgender bathroom issue had in fact come to Campbell County, and he argued that taxpayer dollars ought not to be used to promote sinful lifestyles. He opened the ad by stating that, as a Christian, he believed that all human beings are created in the image of God and should be valued but that sinful lifestyle choices should not be championed at taxpayer expense. Kinchen's appeal was true to Scripture and sensitive to the boy, who was not named in the ad. What happened next shocked me even more than the Christian embrace of Trump in the 2016 primary.

Social media exploded with condemnation, not of the decision to spend tax dollars to advocate for immoral lifestyles but of Kinchen for "targeting" the student. Kinchen signs disappeared from yards of folks I knew to be professing evangelical Christians. Voters began to tell him he needed to "go to church and repent." Even in church he was told by fellow church members, "I agree with your position, but you shouldn't have targeted a student and made a political issue of it." On election day, as the Republican candidate for governor carried the district with 75 percent of the vote, Kinchen lost by seventy-three votes.[1]

Kinchen's race was lost not because of "the radical left," George Soros, "the liberal media," Barack Obama, Hillary Clinton, or any of the usual suspects. It was lost because professing Christians could not deal with a candidate who was criticized for taking a stand that was the historical position of mainstream Christianity from biblical times until about the past decade. Whether through fear, embarrassment, cultural assimilation, or simple biblical ignorance, a simple, thoughtful defense of a basic biblical truth, devoid of any personal attack whatsoever, was too much for these folks to stomach. And the result occurred in the very shadow of Liberty University, in a town called "the city of churches," in "the buckle of the Bible Belt."

The confluence of these two elections shook me to my core and called for a radical rethinking of twenty-six years of effort. For years I had believed that if I could just get Christians involved in the process of electing leaders and promoting biblical principles through legislation, I would see the tide turn and perhaps I could have a part in leaving a better America for my kids than the one in which I'd grown up.

But in both the 2016 Republican primary and the Campbell County school board race, I had seen Christians defending candidates and positions they could not—and generally did not attempt to—defend with arguments from Scripture or morality. Getting Christians involved had completely failed to superimpose a biblical framework on candidate choices or to move legislation toward biblical morality.

In the backwash of those two races, I began to seek God with a new fervency. I found myself praying Daniel 9, confessing that we and our fathers have sinned and finally realizing that I myself was not taking the time I needed to faithfully instill in my own five kids the biblical principles I had tried to defend in political conflict.

For months following the election, I had only tears and questions. This book is an attempt to encapsulate just a few of the answers I have found in Scripture, to explain what we have lost, and to discern a path through which it might be regained.

In struggling to make sense of it all, I have come to believe that perhaps the answers to our questions are very simple. Not easy, not popular, but simple. Completely unheard in the culture—and almost completely unheard in the American church. But still simple. As we examine these answers in the following chapters, I pray we will be pointed back to the Giver of "every good and every perfect gift" (James 1:17), the Creator, the Savior, the eternal God—without whom all our questions are in vain and our answers can never come.

CHAPTER 2

OUR PRAYERS UNHEARD: "THE LORD HATH A CONTROVERSY WITH HIS PEOPLE"

In my work as an attorney, I handle a large number of court-appointed cases for folks charged with something but without the financial resources to hire their own attorney. The taxpayer picks up the tab for these folks. Some of these are criminal cases; others are related to child custody and support. It's interesting work, but you don't get to pick your clients.

In one child-support case, the client had multiple kids with multiple women and, as far as I know, was married to none of the mothers. He owed support to all the kids and was way behind on the payments. And as I prepared for his case, he had every excuse in the world why he just couldn't pay support.

The court had placed the client in the Intensive Case Monitoring Program. The program helps delinquent parents with job skills, job searches, and transportation issues and generally tries to help better their lives and get an income stream to support the child. The caseworker was a no-nonsense African American lady, sort of a tough-love grandmother type. I walked around the corner and heard her scolding my client, telling him that he needed to quit with the excuses and start supporting his kids. I figured it was just what he needed to hear, so I stopped outside her office and didn't interrupt.

As my client walked out of her office, his words to me revealed how completely he had missed her message. "They oughta make these women get abortions!" he yelled. "Look what they're all doin' to me!"

The words stunned me a bit. This man had been so conditioned to think the world owed him anything he liked that he believed he had a right to do anything he wanted and make everyone else pay for his choices. The women he had impregnated ought to have to pay for his children alone—or better yet, each child ought to be killed before birth so he could go on to the next woman without consequence.

I didn't say what I wanted to say. The court wouldn't have liked it.

Sadly, although that client may be an extreme example, he is the poster child for a culture cut loose from morality and responsibility. And while his degree of heartless hedonism may be extreme, the difference between him and millions of his fellow Americans is a difference only of degree, not of principle.

* * * * *

A CULTURE ADRIFT

Any rational observer of the news in today's America knows that something is far wrong. We are deeply divided—almost at war with ourselves. As athletes kneel in protest at the singing of our national anthem, we are told by one side that kneeling disrespects our troops and by the other side that failure to kneel indicates solidarity with cops shooting innocent civilians. We are so divided that, time and again, one candidate becomes president without winning a majority of the popular vote. And the whole campaign leading up to the election reads like a tabloid front page, with charges of treason, affairs, financial misdeeds, and more.

According to the US Centers for Disease Control and Prevention, 40 percent of high school students responding to a 2017 survey had engaged in sexual intercourse, with 10 percent reporting four or more partners.[2] Among the report's other findings were these:

- "Nearly 210,000 babies were born to teen girls aged 15–19 years in 2016."
- "Half of the 20 million new STDs reported each year were among young people, between the ages of 15 to 24."[3]

- As far back as 1987, former US education secretary William Bennett noted that more than one million teenage girls were becoming pregnant each year.[4]

The 2017 criminal victimization report by the Bureau of Justice Statistics states that twenty out of every one thousand Americans ages twelve or older experienced a violent crime that year.[5] While the national numbers are down somewhat from peaks in the 1990s, America's major cities remain war zones. In 2012 the FBI reported 386 murders and nonnegligent manslaughters in Detroit—more than one a day. In New York City the number was 419, and in Chicago, a staggering 500.[6]

I see it constantly in my own career. As an attorney with a practice heavily weighted toward court-appointed cases, both in criminal defense and as guardian ad litem for children, I see inescapable evidence of cultural disaster. America's heartland is ravaged by an opioid epidemic. Men who are otherwise able bodied and capable are so enslaved by drugs that they are trapped in an endless cycle of drug use, crime, incarceration, probation, more drug use, and more crime. Mothers and fathers are breaking their vows and leaving each other for "greener pastures," leaving the flotsam and jetsam of wrecked, abandoned children, strung out on psychotropic drugs, in their path. The best I can do is point these kids to Social Services. The church has no answers, our people are untrained in social work, foster care, drug counseling and treatment, and we are wholly unequipped to deal with the avalanche of human misery. Time after time I stand in jail waiting rooms waiting to talk to a client, as mothers and babies wait nearby for their turn to talk with an incarcerated dad on the video phone, the closest these kids can get to a touch from their dad.

In 2015, according to the National Center for Health Statistics, a staggering forty percent of babies born in the US were born out of wedlock.[7] According to the National Center on Addiction and Substance Abuse at Columbia University, teens from households marked by divorce are fifty percent more likely to abuse alcohol than those from two-parent families.[8]

And I know from personal experience in the legal profession, even where two parents are involved, kids live in homes marked by abuse of both illegal and prescription drugs.

It seems every week brings another school shooting. Each one inevitably brings a chorus of howls for gun control, echoed by equally loud declarations across the aisle that "they'll have to pry my gun from my cold dead hands." And far too often we find that the shooter was strung out on psychotropic drugs himself.

Social media discourse has been reduced to a verbal barroom brawl. No longer can Americans agree to disagree. We have recoiled into warring camps, college students in "safe spaces" versus echo chambers of libertarians or Tea Party activists repeating old mantras and refighting old battles.

The airwaves are awash in the worst of the worst. The Parents Television Council (PTC) has chronicled a story of cultural rot and defeat:

- "More than 58% of children surveyed (ages 14–17) report having seen a pornographic site on the Internet or on their phone."
- "Nearly 43% of kids have been bullied online."
- The PTC also cited the American Psychiatric Association for the statistic that "by age 18, a U.S. youth will have seen 16,000 simulated murders and 200,000 acsts of violence."[9]

In 2011–12 the PTC conducted a study of US primetime TV broadcasting. Of 238 episodes studied, sixty-three percent depicted females in sexualized situations, and thirty-three percent depicted sexual exploitation of women and girls.[10] Thirty-seven percent of the scenes of sexual exploitation were depicted as humorous.[11]

The United States Supreme Court, in its *Obergefell* decision, decided that the definition of *marriage* as "one man to one woman," which has stood the test of time and civilization for thousands of years, is oppressive and unconstitutional. Justice Anthony Kennedy, who delivered the court's decision, stated, "The right to personal choice regarding marriage is inherent in the concept of individual autonomy."[12] He went on to say, "The nature of marriage is that, through its enduring bond, two persons together can find other freedoms, such as expression, intimacy, and spirituality. This is true for all persons, whatever their sexual orientation. . . . There is dignity in the bond between two men or two women who seek to marry and in their autonomy to make such profound choices."[13]

Justice Kennedy failed to articulate why, if "the right to personal choice" is the standard or if "there is dignity in the bond between two men or two women who seek to marry," there is less right to choice or less dignity in polygamous relationships between consenting adults making "profound choices" as an expression of their "individual autonomy." It is difficult to find a legal argument that would sustain a ban on polygamy under Justice Kennedy's rudderless reasoning.

Nor is the decay confined to "the world." Statistics show that divorce rates in the church essentially mirror rates outside the church.[14] According to a 2016 survey by Barna Group, twenty-one percent of youth pastors and fourteen percent of pastors admit to currently viewing pornography.[15] A 2014 Barna survey revealed that among self-identified Christian men between eighteen and thirty years old, seventy-nine percent view pornography at least monthly. Thirty-six percent look at pornography on a daily basis. For self-identified Christian men between thirty-one and forty-nine years old, sixty-seven percent view pornography at least monthly. Eighteen percent of born-again Christian men admit being addicted to pornography (and another nine percent think they may be).[16]

Whether in the church or without, regardless of party or political affiliation, the cultural news is bad.

Yet the professing church of Jesus Christ in America today, "God's people," we assume, is almost wholly unaware of how desperate our situation is. As long as the Dow Jones keeps going up, the unemployment rate keeps going down, and iPhones keep getting more storage space and longer battery life, we think we're okay. A few scattered souls suggest something is badly wrong. A few books have been written. Robert Bork's *Slouching towards Gomorrah*. Paul Washer's *Ten Indictments against the Modern Church*. Os Guinness's *Prophetic Untimeliness*. But these voices are usually viewed by the church, not to mention the culture, as being on the fringe. Or at most they're talking about someone else, not about me.

THE AMERICAN CHURCH UNDER JUDGMENT YET UNAWARE

One can hardly examine the state of American culture and the role the church of Jesus Christ plays (or does not play) in it without being slapped in the face with Isaiah 1. Isaiah and Micah both prophesied primarily in the land of Judah but also to the Northern Kingdom of Israel during the period of time just before Israel fell to Assyria and while the Southern Kingdom of Judah was also being invaded by the Assyrians. Isaiah foretold the destruction of Judah by the Babylonians, although it happened after his death.

After King Solomon, Israel had never had another righteous king (except perhaps Jehu for part of his reign). The nation was on the cusp of being annihilated by the Assyrians. In both Israel and Judah, corruption was rampant and idolatry was widespread (almost universal in the Northern Kingdom). Yet the people, particularly those of Judah, continued to claim their heritage as "God's people" and assure one another because the temple of God was in their midst, with the ark of God and the Ten Commandments. God would never allow them to fall to the wicked nations around them. Just like today God's people thought things were fine. They lived lives of religiosity—alloyed with idolatry and open disobedience to the law of God. But they were the children of Abraham. The Assyrians were bad. The Babylonians were bad. The Syrians were bad. But not them. They were God's people. Everything would be okay.

In America today we remember the Greatest Generation, D-Day, the moon mission, the fall of the Berlin Wall. We are the greatest nation in history, the richest, the strongest, with the most modern conveniences.

To be sure, there are irritations like over sixty million slaughtered preborn babies, grocery store checkout aisles and an internet overrun with pornography, and cities and schools becoming war zones. But our stock portfolios look great, and medicine is extending our lives to be longer and better than ever. The Syrian refugees are bad. The Mexican illegal immigrants are bad. The Islamic terrorists are bad. The Chinese are bad. But we're God's people. Everything will be okay. We are (or were) a Christian nation. We can live on memories.

But we have forgotten God. Yes, in the church as well. According to a LifeWay survey, "seven in ten . . . women who have had an abortion indicate their religious preference is Christian."[17] Additionally, "36% of women were attending a Christian church once a month or more at the time of their first abortion," and more than half say "no one at church . . . knows they have had a pregnancy terminated."[18]

As mentioned earlier, our divorce statistics mirror those in the world around us almost precisely. We also already discussed the pornography viewing statistics in the church. And according to a 2015 Barna survey, a full forty-one percent of "practicing Christians" agreed with the statement "Whatever is right for your life or works best for you is the only truth you can know."[19] Wherever we're getting our beliefs, it's not from the Bible or the God of the Bible.

The opening salvo of Isaiah hits the American church dead center. The words are stark, brutal:

> Hear, O heavens, and give ear, O earth: for the LORD hath spoken, I have nourished and brought up children, and they have rebelled against me.
>
> The ox knoweth his owner, and the ass his master's crib: but Israel doth not know, my people doth not consider.
>
> Ah sinful nation, a people laden with iniquity, a seed of evildoers, children that are corrupters: they have forsaken the Lord, they

have provoked the Holy One of Israel unto anger, they are gone away backward.

Why should ye be stricken any more? ye will revolt more and more: the whole head is sick, and the whole heart faint.

From the sole of the foot even unto the head there is no soundness in it; but wounds, and bruises, and putrifying sores: they have not been closed, neither bound up, neither mollified with ointment.

Your country is desolate, your cities are burned with fire: your land, strangers devour it in your presence, and it is desolate, as overthrown by strangers. (1:2–7)

Our cities are under fire—their residents routinely gunned down by one another. Our social welfare system is collapsing under the burden of supporting "strangers," refugees from Syria, Mexico, and many other nations—not to mention our own massive welfare class.

And lest we think God was speaking only to the abortion clinics, the casinos, the human traffickers, let's read on:

When ye spread forth your hands, I will hide mine eyes from you: yea, when ye make many prayers, I will not hear: your hands are full of blood.

Wash you, make you clean; put away the evil of your doings from before mine eyes; cease to do evil;

Learn to do well; seek judgment, relieve the oppressed, judge the fatherless, plead for the widow. (vv. 15–17)

God's stark words weren't for the Assyrians, the Syrians, the Babylonians. They were spoken, according to verse 2, to His own rebellious "children." And today they aren't intended for Mexican immigrants, Syrian refugees, or American vice merchants like pornographers or human traffickers. They are a shot to the heart of God's rebellious people—inside the walls of the church!

Let's put what God said here into modern English: "Quit bothering with your tithes and offerings and gifts to church charities. Quit the pretense every

Sunday of darkening the door of 'God's house.' Your Sunday services, your Christmas cantatas, your Sunday school classes, are a sin, an abomination to Me. I am sick of your praise songs. I'm even tired of your prayers. Don't bother with them anymore. I will not hear them anyway. Your hands are full of blood. Start practicing what you preach. Quit taking My name in vain while your lives ooze evil."

"But that's *so* Old Testament," you say. "That was just to Israel. Since Jesus came, everything's different. Of course God hears our prayers."

Really? Jesus Himself chastised the religious rulers of God's people in His day: "You hypocrites, rightly did Isaiah prophesy of you: 'This people honors Me with their lips, but their heart is far away from Me" (Matthew 15:7–8 NASB). Consider 1 Peter 3:7: "Ye husbands, dwell with them according to knowledge, giving honour unto the wife, as unto the weaker vessel, and as being heirs together of the grace of life; that your prayers be not hindered." That's the New Testament. Peter tells us our sins still get in the way of our prayers. That hasn't changed at all.

We would do well to take heed. We dare not consign Isaiah to the fringe. Or Micah, his contemporary. We had better take God's warnings to heart: "Hear ye, O mountains, the Lord's controversy, and ye strong foundations of the earth: for the Lord hath a controversy with his people" (Micah 6:2).

For a follower of Jesus Christ, one who claims to be a product of the gospel of Jesus Christ, it is difficult to escape the questions.

How did we get here? How did it get this bad? Why do we usually not even realize how bad it really is? How can a nation be so thoroughly churched yet so devoid of the Spirit of God? What happened to basic ideas of truth and falsehood, of right and wrong? When did all moral choices become just shades of gray? What happened to the power of the gospel?

It is time we honestly asked these questions. It is time we honestly searched the Scriptures for answers. And it is high time that if Scripture offers answers, those of us who claim the name of Christ submit ourselves to following wherever those answers may lead, however countercultural that direction may be.

In the remaining chapters, we will ask some of these questions and search the Scriptures for answers.

CHAPTER 3

VOX POPULI OR THE WORD OF THE LORD?

Until the last couple of years, I was a huge political talk radio fan. I listened to Paul Harvey report the news and to Rush Limbaugh almost daily. I also enjoyed the local morning radio talk show.

A few years ago, I heard a conversation on our local morning show. One of the hosts, a libertarian, was a decent sort but quite the skeptic of biblical Christianity as a guide for public affairs. The caller, a friend of mine, tried briefly to defend the concept of divine creation. But the host had his trump card ready.

"You're not one of those 'six-day creationists,' I hope," he said with a smile in his voice.

"Well," my friend replied, "I don't know how long God took to create. After all, the Bible says a day with the Lord is as a thousand years."

The host was satisfied. He had gotten my friend to deny the inerrancy of the clear words of Scripture.

In the Old Testament, the Hebrew word yom, *translated* day *in English, is used 2,301 times. Outside of Genesis 1, the word* day *is qualified by a number 410 times. Each time refers to a literal twenty-four-hour day.* Day *is used in conjunction with "morning and evening" thirty-eight times. Each time refers to a literal day.* Day *is used in conjunction with either the word* morning *or the word* evening *twenty-three times. Each time refers to a literal day. And* day *is used in conjunction with night fifty-two times. Every time refers to a literal day.*[20]

What does Genesis 1 say? "God called the light Day, and the darkness he called Night. And the evening and the morning were the first day" (v. 5). "The evening and the morning were the second day" (v. 8). "The evening and the morning were the third day" (v. 13). "The evening and the morning were the fourth day" (v. 19). "The evening and the morning were the fifth day" (v. 23). "The evening and the morning were the sixth day" (v. 31).

If God did not mean a literal day, then He used the word in Genesis 1 completely differently from the way He used it in every similar situation across the entire Hebrew Bible.

God wasn't trying to fool us. He didn't just use the word day. He reiterated for emphasis, "The evening and the morning were the first day" (v. 5). Never mind that God rested on the seventh day and in doing so established the Sabbath as a day of rest for His people.

But "science" (at least according to the majority of scientists) insists that the earth has been around for millions of years. For my friend the Bible had to be forced to fit "science" where the two appeared to conflict. And that was all the radio host needed.

As the radio conversation ended, I made a quick call to my friend. "Buddy, I heard your call and couldn't resist calling you. Don't you realize that surrendering the literal truth of the Bible on six-day Creation surrenders the whole book? Didn't Paul say, 'As by one man sin entered into the world, and death by sin; and so death passed upon all men, for that all have sinned' [Romans 5:12]? If you have millions of years of dead animals before man, before Adam's sin, then death is not the result of the Fall, and the whole gospel Paul lays out in the New Testament crumbles."

"Well, Rick," he said, "I'm not going to get into semantics with you. All I know is that Jesus died for my sins and paid my way into heaven. That's all I need to know." The conversation ended and we parted in disagreement.

But the radio host was right. If my friend gave up a confident belief in the Word of the Lord, in how God said He created, he gave up all certainty altogether. If God can't be trusted about how we got here, He can't be trusted for the hereafter either.

Maybe Jesus wasn't literally born of a virgin. Maybe He wasn't "without sin" on this earth (Hebrews 4:15). Maybe He wasn't literally resurrected. After all, science asserts that can't happen. And if these impossibilities aren't literally true, then the "scientific impossibility" that my soul can live in heaven forever may not be true. As Paul said so clearly, "If Christ be not raised, your faith is vain" (1 Corinthians 15:17).

Either "every word of God is pure" (Proverbs 30:5), "for ever . . . settled in heaven" (Psalm 119:89), or not. If you can't trust God with Creation, your eternity is just a massive game of Russian roulette.

* * * * *

IS THE WORD OF THE LORD SUFFICIENT FOR ALL OF LIFE?

We begin with several foundational presuppositions. This book makes no effort to be other than a direct appeal to the God of the Word and to the Word of God. It makes no effort to offer psychological or sociological solutions to our problems. It is addressed specifically to those who claim to believe the Bible is the Word of God and that Jesus is the only way to Heaven. In that vein, some presuppositions must be considered as nonnegotiables at the outset. Let's consider these:

1. God is the creator of all that is. "Without him nothing was made that has been made" (John 1:3 NIV). As Creator, He has total right to rule over His creation. *All* His creation, including *all* humanity, those who surrender to Him today and those who will only when "every knee will bow" (Philippians 2:10 NASB), are accountable to Him for their actions. He is the one "who is and who was and who is to come, the Almighty" (Revelation 1:8 NASB). People and nations will answer to Him, both in history and at the final judgment.

2. The Bible is the inerrant, infallible, inspired Word of God. It is the record of a holy creator God's demands on fallen, sinful humanity.

3. As such, it contains "everything pertaining to life and godliness" (2 Peter 1:3 NASB). All the answers to human problems are found in its pages. It must be allowed to speak for itself, not interpreted based on our own presuppositions. It must be surrendered to completely; where it speaks, it is the final word. As best as we humanly can, we are to speak its truth merely as messengers of Someone else. As a

necessary interpretive corollary to this, if we in today's society seek His answers on specific issues that are not directly addressed, we must seek to discern the principles that flow from a Spirit-directed and careful study of the nature of God as it is revealed in His Word. Our assumption should be not that God's Word is silent if it does not address a particular issue directly but that principles can be gleaned that can serve as a guide to His people in their every action and choice. Anything less fails to square with 2 Peter 1:3.

4. The entire Word of God is our guide. A careless or misguided devaluation of one portion (e.g., the Old Testament) is a fast path to heresy and misinterpretation of the rest. The source for this claim? The Word itself: "For ever, O Lord, thy word is settled in heaven" (Psalm 119:89). "Every word of God is pure" (Proverbs 30:5). "All scripture is given by inspiration of God, and is profitable" (2 Timothy 3:16). "I did not come to abolish [the law] but to fulfill" (Matthew 5:17 NASB). "One jot or one tittle shall in no wise pass from the law, till all be fulfilled" (Matthew 5:18). If we claim to speak for God, we are bound to speak the whole counsel of God and to consider individual verses and passages in the light of the whole. "The word of the Lord endures forever" (1 Peter 1:25 NASB). The Bible is to judge us; we're not to judge the Bible.

The biblical prophets staked everything on the Word of the Lord. They sought and recognized no higher authority. Yet often in today's church, a plain reading of the Word of the Lord is offensive, rarely preached, and even explained away.

The world looks at the church and has no respect. And little wonder. What the world sees is total schizophrenia. We claim to trust Jesus Christ with the security of our eternal souls in the afterlife. We claim to believe that Jesus is sitting at the right hand of God in heaven and that one day He will take us to be with Him. Although we've never seen Him, we claim to trust Him with something as uncertain and unknown as life after death and to take His word for how to achieve eternal life.

Yet when the same Jesus says something as absurdly simple as His command about divorce in Matthew 19:4–9, we find reasons to do anything *but* take His word for it.

Jesus could not have been any plainer. He did not use the alliterative approach of radio host Dr. Laura Schlessinger and approve of divorce in cases of abuse, addictions, and affairs.[21] He gave a simple command. In the Greek the phrase *let not* is a direct prohibition. When Jesus said, "Let not man put asunder" (Matthew 19:6), He used a command with the same authority as when He said, "Thou shalt not kill" (Exodus 20:13).

The ancient prophets didn't sugarcoat it. I did a rough count and found at least 125 times in Scripture where we are told "the word of the Lord came" to God's man. And most of those times, God's man acted in obedience to the Word of the Lord. The remainder of the times are mostly God pronouncing judgment on people and nations who had already rejected the Word of the Lord.

THE WORD PROCLAIMED SAVES A CULTURE. THE
WORD REPRESSED DESTROYS A CULTURE.

Today the Word of the Lord is rejected—even in the church. No longer is the church calling the world to repentance. To the contrary, the world is calling the tune, and the church is dancing to it. The world sees our faith in Christ for eternal life juxtaposed with our rebellion against His plain commands in this life. And they are repulsed by the hypocrisy. They mock us to scorn.

In 2006 my Roman Catholic buddy Steve Waters and I were regional leaders in the Virginia Marriage Amendment campaign, which enshrined in Virginia's constitution the biblical definition of *marriage* as being between one man and one woman. We engaged in numerous debates on the issue with our opponents in the homosexual community. Their primary attack line was the same: "Your divorce rates in your churches are fifty percent. And you're telling *us* that *we* will weaken marriage? What right do you have to lecture us?"

Our side won fifty-seven percent of the vote that fall. We won the battle. What Steve and I didn't realize was that we had already lost the war. We had lost the moral high ground. The failure of the church to preach the Word of the Lord had exposed the weakness of our foundations. Within less than a decade, *Obergefell* turned our temporary victory into utter defeat.

And the reaction of much of the evangelical church was surrender. In fact, many leaders had surrendered even before the Supreme Court weighed in.

In 2015 a lone federal judge decided that she could overturn the Sanctity of Marriage Amendment to the Alabama Constitution. Alabama's Supreme Court Chief Justice Roy Moore ordered Alabama probate judges to ignore the ruling. Moore's basis was twofold. He argued that a federal judge had no authority under the Constitution to dictate to a state what its marriage laws would be.[22] Accordingly, as the highest judicial authority in the state of Alabama, he ordered Alabama judges to follow their constitution rather than a ruling from a lone federal judge.

In response, Russell Moore, who served as president of the Ethics and Religious Liberty Commission of the Southern Baptist Convention (SBC), criticized the position of Chief Justice Moore (no relation) in the Baptist Press, the official news organ of the SBC. Officials including judges, he argued, must follow federal dictates. He cited Romans 13 (which commands submission to civil rulers) in support of his view, and he stated, "A government employee faced with a decision of violating his conscience or upholding the law, would need to resign and protest against it as a citizen if he could not discharge the duties of his office required by law in good conscience."[23]

Later we will devote a chapter to a more thorough discussion of Romans 13, which I believe is one of the most misquoted and twisted passages in all Scripture in modern evangelicalism. But the story of Daniel contradicts Russell Moore's position on civil servants practicing civil disobedience. Daniel, the number two man in Persia, was under the king's command not to pray to anyone but the king (Dan. 6). And Daniel rebelled against his divinely appointed civil authority. He could have just closed the shutters. He could have just prayed quietly at work without closing his eyes. But Daniel did neither of these things. He opened his window and prayed, out loud, publicly, toward Jerusalem, in an open rebuke of an immoral law that violated the divine law. His was no silent protest.

Because of the American church's unwillingness to take a stand against the pagan influences corroding our culture, a Christian culture has become a pagan culture. The biblical example of Daniel and his three friends stands in direct contradiction to Moore's position. None of these men resigned their position when ordered to bow to the golden statue. They just refused to bow. The rest of the crowd knew they were leaders in government. But they did not resign—and they did not bow. The American church—and all of American culture—has paid a steep price because we accept preaching that does not square with Scripture. In stark contrast, because Daniel—and, earlier, his three friends (Daniel 3)—courageously and publicly stood against their culture, they changed a pagan culture for the better. Consider the reaction of Nebuchadnezzar after the three Hebrews publicly defied the human king's law in favor of God's law:

> Blessed be the God of Shadrach, Meshach and Abed-nego, who has sent His angel and delivered His servants who put their trust in Him, *violating the king's command,* and yielded up their bodies so as not to serve or worship any god except their own God. Therefore I make a decree that any people, nation or tongue that speaks anything offensive against the God of Shadrach, Meshach and Abed-nego shall be torn limb from limb and their houses reduced to a rubbish heap, inasmuch as there is no other god who is able to deliver in this way. (Daniel 3:28–29 NASB, emphasis added)

Daniel's courageous stand yielded similar results:

> Then Darius the king wrote to all the peoples, nations and men of every language who were living in all the land: "May your peace abound! I make a decree that in all the dominion of my kingdom men are to fear and tremble before the God of Daniel;

For He is the living God and enduring forever, And His kingdom is one which will not be destroyed, And His dominion will be forever. "He delivers and rescues and performs signs and wonders In heaven and on earth, Who has also delivered Daniel from the power of the lions." (6:25–27 NASB)

The courageous stands of these men, who chose the Word of the Lord over the vox populi (and, incidentally, did not resign their positions, choosing simply not to bow), changed the cultures of their nations for the better. God always honors His Word.

The modern church, A. W. Tozer stated, has fallen victim to the desire to be popular and trendy instead of biblically accurate. "We discuss religion on television and in the press as a kind of game, . . . accepting as one of the ground rules of the game that there is no final test of truth. . . . So we have truth by majority vote and thus saith the Lord by common consent."[24]

Jesus never suggested that His Word would be popular. He promised the opposite:

If the world hate you, ye know that it hated me before it hated you.

If ye were of the world, the world would love his own: but because ye are not of the world, but I have chosen you out of the world, therefore the world hateth you.

Remember the word that I said unto you, The servant is not greater than his lord. If they have persecuted me, they will also persecute you; if they have kept my saying, they will keep yours also.

But all these things will they do unto you for my name's sake, because they know not him that sent me. (John 15:18–21)

He even made it clear to us in the next verse *why* the Word is so countercultural: "If I had not come and spoken unto them, they had not had sin: but now they have no cloak for their sin" (v. 22).

THE CHURCH SURRENDERS THE WORD OF THE LORD

More and more, American Christians make compromises, small surrenders to electability and relevance. More and more, we explain away disobedience, rebellion against the God of heaven, as somehow the best we can do in this present culture to be able to speak to that culture. But God never promised to honor our human calculations. God promised to honor His Word. And He promised it over and over again: "For ever, O Lord, thy word is settled in heaven" (Psalm 119:89). "Thy word is true from the beginning: and every one of thy righteous judgments endureth for ever" (Psalm 119:160). "Thou hast magnified thy word above all thy name" (Psalm 138:2). "Verily I say unto you, Till heaven and earth pass, one jot or one tittle shall in no wise pass from the law, till all be fulfilled" (Matthew 5:18).

God has never ceased to glorify His Word. "Heaven and earth shall pass away, but my words shall not pass away" (Matthew 24:35).

But there is another side to the same coin. While God promised to honor His Word, He also made clear that it is the Word of God that is the ultimate judge of human action.

Christ set up the Word of God as the final measure of human action: "If ye continue in my word, then are ye my disciples indeed" (8:31). "He that rejecteth me, and receiveth not my words, hath one that judgeth him: the word that I have spoken, the same shall judge him in the last day" (12:48). "If a man love me, he will keep my words: and my Father will love him, and we will come unto him, and make our abode with him. He that loveth me not keepeth not my sayings: and the word which ye hear is not mine, but the Father's which sent me" (14:23–24).

Why, then, are we so reluctant to tell a dying culture and a decayed church, "Thus saith the Lord . . . "? If wisdom is thinking God's thoughts after Him, why are we so afraid to simply repeat the plain message without sugarcoating it to fit an unfit culture?

Admittedly there are parts of God's Word that are difficult to understand. I'm not sure I can identify "the king of the north" and "the king of the south" in Daniel 11 or the locusts with stingers in Revelation 9. But I can easily read the plain truths of Matthew 19:4–9. Those need no interpretation. I can clearly read of the destruction of Sodom and Gomorrah and hear the New Testament echo in the words of Paul: "The men, leaving the natural use of the woman, burned in their lust one toward another; men with men working that which is unseemly, and receiving in themselves that recompense of their error which was meet. And even as they did not like to retain God in their knowledge, God gave them over to a reprobate mind, to do those things which are not convenient" (Romans 1:27–28). "Be not deceived: neither fornicators, nor idolaters, nor adulterers, nor effeminate, nor abusers of themselves with mankind, nor thieves, nor covetous, nor drunkards, nor revilers, nor extortioners, shall inherit the kingdom of God" (1 Corinthians 6:9–10). The Word of the Lord is not difficult to understand in its explicit condemnation of homosexuality.

Yet more and more, the church is rejecting clear commands, cutting off parts of the Bible that don't fit the culture and twisting the rest into a pretzel to make God's Word conform to the dictates of our sinful hearts. Consider the website of Q Christian Fellowship: "We are a diverse community with varied backgrounds, cultures, theologies and denominations, drawn together through our love of Christ and our belief that every LGBTQ+ person, indeed, *every* person is a beloved child of God."[25]

And the corruption has invaded the heart of the church. Eugene Peterson, best known for his Bible paraphrase, *The Message*, stated in 2017, "I think that kind of debate about lesbians and gays might be over. People who disapprove of it, they'll probably just go to another church. So we're in a transition and I think it's a transition for the best, for the good. I don't think it's something that you can parade, but it's not a right or wrong thing as far as I'm concerned." He added that he would personally officiate a homosexual "wedding,"[26] although he later appeared to retract those statements.[27] In 2013 Rob Bell, the former pastor of Mars Hill Bible Church, stated, "I am for marriage. I am for fidelity. I am for love, whether it's a man and woman, a woman and a woman, a man and a man.

I think the ship has sailed and I think the church needs—I think this is the world we are living in and we need to affirm people wherever they are."[28]

In 2014 Dan Haseltine, lead singer for popular band Jars of Clay, opened fire on Twitter: "I just don't see a negative effect to allowing gay marriage. No societal breakdown, no war on traditional marriage." "Most people read and interpret scripture wrong. I don't think scripture 'clearly' states much of anything regarding morality." "I don't particularly care about Scriptures stance on what is 'wrong.' I care more about how it says we should treat people."[29]

Mark Twain has been quoted as saying, "It ain't those parts of the Bible that I can't understand that bother me, it is the parts that I do understand."[30] The Bible is no more difficult to understand in today's culture than it has been before. It is harder to *obey*.

The modern American church resembles King Saul. God commanded him to utterly destroy the Amalekites, even their animals (1 Samuel 15). And he almost did. He kept their king alive and the best of their sheep and oxen. When Samuel went to see him the next day, what did Saul say? "I have performed the commandment of the Lord" (v. 13). And what did Samuel reply? "What meaneth then this bleating of the sheep in mine ears, and the lowing of the oxen which I hear?" (v. 14). Saul is the mirror of the American church, in rebellion against clear divine commands because they don't seem to make sense to the public yet pridefully daring to tell God that His judgment is flawed. God—and our unbelieving neighbors—keep hearing sheep and oxen, and they know what we dare not admit to ourselves. We are rebels.

And the watering down, the "small" compromises around the edges, have led to a point where even the basic foundations of the gospel are now under attack *within* the "church" itself.

I would argue, even if I believe as historical fact Jesus, the Son of God, came to Earth, died for my sins, rose from the dead three days later, and wants to forgive my sins and take me to Heaven—if I do not believe anything else He said is authoritative to my life—it is impossible to still be a genuinely converted disciple.

On Nov. 26, the *Christian Post* ran a story titled, "SBC Pres. JD Greear says he'll refer to trans individuals by their preferred pronouns."

"Some people on one side are going to say, 'Hey, we got to tell the truth. And the truth is this person is male or female. So I would be lying if I called somebody who is female and identified as male,'" Greear added.[31]

"There are others who would say, 'Look, as a courtesy, you should refer to a transgender person by their preferred pronoun as sort of a 'generosity of spirit' kind of approach. You see evidence in the Bible of that."

"If a transgender person came into our church, came into my life, I think my disposition would be to refer to them by their preferred pronoun when we want to talk about gender," Greear said.[32]

Greear wrote a book entitled, *Above All: The Gospel Is the Source of the Church's Renewal.* My contention is that Greear, and much of American evangelicalism, has determined that as long as we believe the same thing about how to get to heaven, and we get that part right, we can essentially pick and choose what other parts of Scripture are authoritative.

THIS IS IDOLATRY.

Romans 10:9 puts it bluntly. "If you confess with your mouth Jesus as Lord, and believe in your heart that God raised Him from the dead, you will be saved" (NASB).

Here is what I think the church is missing. We believe what we call "the Gospel." We believe in Jesus as Savior. But we refuse to acknowledge Him as LORD. And that little failure is an eternal failure. It is the difference between saving faith, and idolatry. Philippians 2:9-11 tells us, "Wherefore God also hath highly exalted him, and given him a name which is above every name: That at the name of Jesus every knee should bow, of things in heaven, and things in earth, and things under the earth; And that every tongue should confess that Jesus Christ is Lord, to the glory of God the Father." We are playing with fire, literally, when we lead folks to believe that they need not bow the knee now, and they can just do it later.

God's Word leaves absolutely no room for "pronoun hospitality." In Matthew 19:3-6, the Pharisees came to Jesus, hoping to get Him to weaken God's standard of sexual ethics. "The Pharisees also came unto him, tempting him, and saying unto him, Is it lawful for a man to put away his wife for every cause? And he answered and said unto them, Have ye not read, that he which made them at the beginning made them male and female, And said, For this cause shall a man leave father and mother, and shall cleave to his wife: and they twain shall be one flesh? Wherefore they are no more twain, but one flesh. What therefore God hath joined together, let not man put asunder."

Here is the heart of the problem. We have exchanged the eternal Word of God as the moral authority, for the shifting sands of cultural opinion. Sure, the Word says "He made them male and female." In other words, the Creator ordained it this way, and there are no other options. But the culture wants more options, so we agree to go along. Sure, we cloak it in "Christian-speak." We call it "pronoun hospitality." Or "generosity of spirit." Or "loving them to Jesus." Or being "nonjudgmental." But in the end, we have dethroned the Creator God of the universe and substituted "the wisdom of the world." And that is idolatry.

Jesus never sugarcoated sin. When He spoke to the woman at the well, as soon as He hooked her interest with the promise of living water, He went straight to her problem. "Go, call your husband." When she attempted to get Him to show some "generosity of spirit," with the half-truth "I have no husband," He went straight to the point. "Thou hast well said, I have no husband: For thou hast had five husbands; and he whom thou now hast is not thy husband."

She "identified" as a "good moral person." But He pointed out that she wasn't. He pointed out at once she was a five-time adulterer, living in open sin. Sure, He didn't throw out hateful words—"Yeah, you have no husband, you harlot!" But neither did He for a moment "use her preferred pronoun." He went straight back to the Word—"Thou shalt not commit adultery," and identified her for what she was, an adulterer. And she immediately knew He spoke the truth. "Sir, I perceive that thou art a prophet." Because He told the Truth—not because He accepted her false premise and let her accept it, too.

We use the wrong measuring stick. We try to be "Christlike," but we allow the World, not the Word, to determine what that means. We try to show "grace," without pointing out why grace is needed. Grace is utterly meaningless if I am OK as I am.

We like to quote John 3:17. "For God sent not his Son into the world to condemn the world; but that the world through him might be saved." A great truth. But let's read on:

"He that believeth on Him is not condemned: but he that believeth not is condemned already, because he hath not believed in the name of the only begotten Son of God. And this is the condemnation, that light is come into the world, and men loved darkness rather than light, because their deeds were evil. For every one that doeth evil hateth the light, neither cometh to the light, lest his deeds should be reproved." Jesus came to save, because we were condemned already in our sins!

In John 12:47-48, Jesus clarifies: "And if any man hear my words, and believe not, I judge him not: for I came not to judge the world, but to save the world. He that rejecteth me, and receiveth not my words, hath one that judgeth him: the word that I have spoken, the same shall judge him in the last day."

Jesus ends the Sermon on the Mount with words that should painfully arrest the attention of the American church. "Not every one that saith unto me, Lord, Lord, shall enter into the kingdom of heaven; but he that doeth the will of my Father which is in heaven. Many will say to me in that day, Lord, Lord, have we not prophesied in thy name? and in thy name have cast out devils? and in thy name done many wonderful works? And then will I profess unto them, I never knew you: depart from me, ye that work iniquity. Please, Dr. Greear, American evangelical pastors—"This is my beloved Son, in whom I am well pleased; hear ye him!" (Matthew 17:5).

Jesus told us in the same chapter that "wide is the gate, and broad is the way, that leadeth to destruction, and many there be which go in thereat: Because strait is the gate, and narrow is the way, which leadeth unto life, and few there be that find it" (Matthew 7:13-14). John warns us in 1 John 4:1, "Beloved, believe not every spirit, but try the spirits whether they are of God: because many false prophets are gone out into the world." False prophets are only effective if people don't readily perceive their message as false. It has to have enough truth to make us comfortable. And cloaking the message in words like "gospel," as Greear does, is as comforting as it gets.

The American church has followed the damning example of the ancient Greeks. We have made us a god in our own image. The ancient Greek gods were lustful, drunken, and beset with all the sins the people themselves wanted to commit. "Worship" of these gods was perfectly comfortable, because the "gods" demanded no change of life. They were perfectly willing to be "pronoun hospitable." None of the intolerant inflexibility of "He which made them in the beginning made them male and female."

I say again, it is idolatry. God's words in Isaiah 1 should also arrest the attention of the American church. God's people were continuing to "do the Temple thing," offering sacrifices and observing appointed feast days. But they had mixed it with idolatry. And God's wrath burned white-hot against them.

"Hear the word of the Lord, ye rulers of Sodom; give ear unto the law of our God, ye people of Gomorrah. To what purpose is the multitude of your sacrifices unto me? saith the Lord: I am full of the burnt offerings of rams, and the fat of fed beasts; and I delight not in the blood of bullocks, or of lambs, or of he goats. When ye come to appear before me, who hath required this at your hand, to tread my courts? Bring no more vain oblations; incense is an abomination unto me; the new moons and sabbaths, the calling of assemblies, I cannot away with; it is iniquity, even the solemn meeting. Your new moons and your appointed feasts my soul hateth: they are a trouble unto me; I am weary to bear them. And when ye spread forth your hands, I will hide mine eyes from you: yea, when ye make many prayers, I will not hear: your hands are full of blood. Wash you, make you clean; put away the evil of your doings from before mine eyes; cease to do evil; Learn to do well; seek judgment, relieve the oppressed, judge the fatherless, plead for the widow. Come now, and let us reason together, saith the Lord: though your sins be as scarlet, they shall be as white as snow; though they be red like crimson, they shall be as wool. If ye be willing and obedient, ye shall eat the good of the land: But if ye refuse and rebel, ye shall be devoured with the sword: for the mouth of the Lord hath spoken it" (Isaiah 1:10-20).

We had better wake up! God told His people that their worship itself had become iniquity; that He would no longer hear their prayers; that He HATED their worship services.

How dare men who claim to speak for God sit in judgment over His Word? "My people hath been lost sheep: their shepherds have caused them to go astray, they have turned them away on the mountains: they have gone from mountain to hill, they have forgotten their restingplace" (Jeremiah 50:6).

In Ezekiel 34:6-11, God has a message for the compromising pastors of American evangicalism. "My sheep wandered through all the mountains, and upon every high hill: yea, my flock was scattered upon all the face of the earth, and none did search or seek after them. Therefore, ye shepherds, hear the word of the Lord; As I live, saith the Lord God, surely because my flock became a prey, and my flock became meat to every beast of the field, because there was no shepherd, neither did my shepherds search for my flock, but the shepherds fed themselves, and fed not my flock; Therefore, O ye shepherds, hear the word of the Lord; Thus saith the Lord God; Behold, I am against the shepherds; and I will require my flock at their hand, and cause them to cease from feeding the flock; neither shall the shepherds feed themselves any more; for I will deliver my flock from their mouth, that they may not be meat for them. For thus saith the Lord God; Behold, I, even I, will both search my sheep, and seek them out."

We have "changed the truth of God into a lie" (Romans 1:25). We have defied the command of Colossians 3:5, "Mortify therefore your members which are upon the earth; fornication, uncleanness, inordinate affection, evil concupiscence, and covetousness, which is idolatry." Not the culture, but God's own Church!

You believe Christ can handle your eternal destiny after you die! You absolutely believe and proclaim His words "I give unto them eternal life; and they shall never perish, neither shall any man pluck them out of my hand." You trust him to rescue you from Hell. But you don't believe enough to proclaim His words "He which made them at the beginning made them male and female"? Proverbs 30:5 declares, "Every word of God is pure: He is a shield unto them that put their trust in Him." It's a massive eternal gamble you're taking. If you can't trust Christ on things of this life, if every word of God is not trustworthy, how can you gamble that any of them are? And on what basis do you choose which words to believe? The ones that are acceptable to sinners in the culture. This is idolatry!

Pastors for the sake of the souls of condemned sinners, tell them the truth! "The soul that sinneth, it shall die!" (Ezekiel 18:20). You are gathering the blood of eternal souls into your hands. "When I say unto the wicked, Thou shalt surely die; and thou givest him not warning, nor speakest to warn the wicked from his wicked way, to save his life; the same wicked man shall die in his iniquity; but his blood will I require at thine hand" (Ezekiel 3:18).

The culture changes. God does not. In the culture, what is "right" today is "wrong" tomorrow. But "I am the LORD; I change not" (Malachi 3:6). Away with nonsensical internet memes: "No one ever became a Christian because Christians told them they were wrong." NONSENSE! No one ever repented of his sin because the church refused to call it sin, out of a misguided "generosity of spirit."

Every time in Scripture when a man or woman turned to Christ, it was out of a realization of lostness, of inability to please God "as I am." "What must I do to be saved?" "Lord, what wilt thou have me to do?" "What shall we do, that we might work the works of God?"

Acts 2:37-38: "Now when they heard this, they were pricked in their heart, and said unto Peter and to the rest of the apostles, Men and brethren, what shall we do? Then Peter said unto them, Repent, and be baptized every one of you in the name of Jesus Christ for the remission of sins, and ye shall receive the gift of the Holy Ghost."

That is the gospel! We are "dead in our sins," we are "enemies," we are "condemned already," we are "children of wrath, even as others." And that must change, if our eternal destiny is to change. "Therefore if any man be in Christ, he IS a new creature: old things ARE passed away; behold, ALL things ARE become new" (2 Corinthians 5:17).

"The word that I have spoken, the same shall judge him in the last day" (John 12:48). You can't change that. Please, don't fool sinners into thinking they can ignore the authority of His Word over their actions for their entire lives, then suddenly die and live eternally with Him because they accept His death and resurrection as historical facts. "Except ye repent, ye shall all likewise perish!" Luke 13:5. Jesus said it. We can't change it. Pastors, tell them!

Christ came to speak the Truth. And the devil is "a liar and the father of lies" (John 8:44). "To this end was I born, and for this cause came I into the world, that I should bear witness unto the TRUTH" (John 18:37). By contrast, the first words of Satan given in Scripture are these, "Yea, hath God said . . . ?" The first assault of the devil is to question the validity of God's Word, to suggest that it doesn't make cultural sense to "abide in Me, and My words abide in you" (John 15:7). It is not loving to overlook the sin that damns. It is not "Christlike" to reject Christ's words, to refuse to carry Christ's message of Truth, to accept the culture's denial of God's Word instead of bearing witness to the truth.

It is not "humility" to refuse to call sin what God calls it to "avoid giving offense." It is false humility. Worse. It is pride, arrogance, rebellion against the crown rights of King Jesus. Jesus does not call us to always be "inoffensive."

Peter puts it plainly. "Unto you therefore which believe He is precious: but unto them which be disobedient, the stone which the builders disallowed, the same is made the head of the corner, And a stone of stumbling, and a rock of offence, even to them which stumble at the word, being disobedient: whereunto also they were appointed. But ye are a chosen generation, a royal priesthood, an holy nation, a peculiar people; that ye should shew forth the praises of Him who hath called you out of darkness into His marvellous light." There is nothing offensive about a "gospel" that says, "you can have your sin and have salvation too." Christ is offensive to the culture precisely because "I am THE way, THE truth, and THE life, and NO MAN cometh to the Father but by Me" (emphasis added).

The modern Church gets it completely wrong. You can't "love them to Jesus" by tolerating their sin. The culture is not going to love you. They didn't love Christ. They crucified Him. Why? "If I had not come and spoken unto them, they had not had sin: but now they have no cloak for their sin" (John 15:22). They hated the light, because their deeds were evil. And they still do.

Paul nails it in Galatians 1:6-10: "I marvel that ye are so soon removed from him that called you into the grace of Christ unto another gospel: Which is not another; but there be some that trouble you, and would pervert the gospel of Christ. But though we, or an angel from heaven, preach any other gospel unto you than that which we have preached unto you, let him be accursed. As we said before, so say I now again, if any man preach any other gospel unto you than that ye have received, let him be accursed. For do I now persuade men, or God? or do I seek to please men? for if I yet pleased men, I should not be the servant of Christ."

Some of the saddest words in Scripture are these: "because of the Pharisees they did not confess Him, lest they should be put out of the synagogue: For they loved the praise of men more than the praise of God" (John 12:42).

James' words are a stinging rebuke to America's compromised pulpits: "Ye adulterers and adulteresses, know ye not that the friendship of the world is enmity with God? Whosoever therefore will be a friend of the world is the enemy of God" (James 4:4).

Pastors have a God-given duty. "They shall teach my people the difference between the holy and profane, and cause them to discern between the unclean and the clean" (Ezekiel 44:23). It is not "generosity," it is not "grace," it is not "pastoral," to follow the world's pretense instead of the Word's eternal standard. It is a sure sign of God's judgment, and a call for more. "Woe unto them that call evil good, and good evil; that put darkness for light, and light for darkness; that put bitter for sweet, and sweet for bitter!" (Isaiah 5:20). Woe unto them. Woe unto them! WOE UNTO THEM!

I fear too many in evangelical pulpits truly fail to understand the biblical requirements of regeneration. It's time our pulpits begin again to speak "the whole counsel of God!" You want to be Christlike? Give them Christ's message! "From that time Jesus began to preach, and to say, Repent: for the kingdom of heaven is at hand" (Matthew 4:17).

The culture is damning souls. Forget the culture. It's damned. It's dying. Point them to God's Word! "For ever, O Lord, thy word is settled in heaven" (Psalm 119:18). "For thou hast magnified thy word above all thy name" (Psalm 138:2). "Heaven and earth shall pass away, but my words shall not pass away" (Matthew 24:35).

On an interview with Larry King in 2005, megachurch leader Joel Osteen said this about Christ, salvation, and eternity:

> You know, I'm very careful about saying who would and wouldn't go to heaven. I don't know. . . . Well, I don't know if I believe they're wrong. I believe here's what the Bible teaches and from the Christian faith this is what I believe. But I just think that only God [will] judge a person's heart.[33]

When King asked Osteen whether atheists go to heaven, he added,

> I'm going to let God be the judge of who goes to heaven and hell. I just—again, I present the truth, and I say it every week. You know, I believe it's a relationship with Jesus. But you know what?

I'm not going to go around telling everybody else if they don't want to believe that that's going to be their choice. God's got to look at your own heart. God's got to look at your heart, and only God knows that.[34]

Osteen's gospel is no gospel at all. Essentially, in Osteen's view, Christ died for nothing, since all roads lead to the same place anyway. Or at least, if they don't, it's not for him to say.

It is not humility to refuse to be categorical where the Word of God is categorical. It is proud. It is rebellion against the King of Kings. It damns souls. And it destroys nations. "When I say unto the wicked, O wicked man, thou shalt surely die; if thou dost not speak to warn the wicked from his way, that wicked man shall die in his iniquity; but his blood will I require at thine hand" (Ezekiel 33:8). To refuse to judge where God has judged is not humility. God said it makes us accessories to the murder of eternal souls.

Truly the American church is judged by the Word of the Lord, and our land is condemned because we have rejected its plain truth: "Whosoever shall be ashamed of me and of my words, of him shall the Son of man be ashamed, when he shall come in his own glory, and in his Father's, and of the holy angels" (Luke 9:26). It seems beyond question that when Christ views the American church, He must be as ashamed of us as we are of His Word.

It is as simple as this. If the entire Word of God cannot be trusted for what it plainly says, none of it can be trusted. If you don't believe the Genesis account of how God created your mortal body, don't count on Him to recreate it in immortality. The accuracy of Scripture on *all* points is vital to its trustworthiness on *any* point. Paul said as much: "If Christ be not risen, then is our preaching vain, and your faith is also vain" (1 Corinthians 15:14). If God is a liar just once, on the smallest point, your eternal security is one giant game of chance.

Jesus gave us no room to compromise on His Word: "Why call ye me, Lord, Lord, and do not the things which I say?" (Luke 6:46). This is not a rhetorical question. He followed up:

Whosoever cometh to me, and heareth my sayings, and doeth them, I will shew you to whom he is like:

He is like a man which built an house, and digged deep, and laid the foundation on a rock: and when the flood arose, the stream beat vehemently upon that house, and could not shake it: for it was founded upon a rock.

But he that heareth, and doeth not, is like a man that without a foundation built an house upon the earth; against which the stream did beat vehemently, and immediately it fell; and the ruin of that house was great. (vv. 47–49)

And truly the ruin of America—and of the American church—is great.

CHAPTER 4

IS THERE ABSOLUTE TRUTH?
ARE YOU ABSOLUTELY SURE?

My wife and I have been involved with Republican Party politics in Virginia for decades, working tirelessly for its candidates. In Virginia, every two years, each local Republican and Democratic Party holds a mass meeting to choose a new chairman and new members.

One year, a coalition of Democrats and renegade Republicans (many of whom were county employees or married to county employees) hatched a scheme to oust the Republicans from a Virginia county's board of supervisors. The plan involved teaming with local Democrats to invade the Republican meeting and throw the local GOP folks out. Then they could throw the Republicans off the board of supervisors in the next election.

The leader of the cabal announced his campaign for Republican chairman. But then his supporters began to mobilize county employees and their families to attend the Republican meeting to "throw out the extremists." Up to that point, all was fine.

But very quickly his supporters realized that they wouldn't win among Republicans. And that's when their strategy changed. They began overtly urging Democrats to attend the meeting, lie about their party affiliation, and thus vote, as Democrats, for the person to chair the Republican party! Historically, Republicans attended Republican meetings, Democrats attended Democrat meetings, and then each party supported its own candidates in the fall. But a hostile takeover of one party's process by supporters of the other party was something entirely different.

At the Republican mass meeting, hundreds of people jammed the venue. Among them were Democrat donors and numerous folks committed to the defeat of local Republican candidates. The rigged ballot elected the challenger as chairman. His team threw every loyal Republican off the county's Republican committee and elected a handful of the challenger's loyalists to be the new "Republican" committee.

Once the meeting concluded, the local Republicans quickly realized how effective the challenger's deceptive effort had been. They immediately appealed the outcome to the State Central Committee (SCC), the governing body of the Republican Party of Virginia.

Eventually the SCC ruled that the challenger's campaign had cheated by working to get committed Democrats to vote as Republicans at the Republican meeting. They overturned the result.

The challenger's team immediately sued the party. The Republican Party moved to dismiss the lawsuit, and the court threw it out.

Amazingly the challengers refused to recognize the court's ruling. Only after a protracted legal fight and multiple court rulings in the party's favor was the battle finally legally resolved in the party's favor, when the challengers agreed to pay to settle the case.

It was an expensive lesson in the pitfalls of running an entire campaign on openly false premises and trying to declare a lie to be the truth.

* * * * *

I capitalize the word *Truth* frequently throughout this book—and particularly in this chapter—because I believe the word is that important and because I believe Truth is associated with and integral to the credibility of God Himself. Indeed, Jesus plainly stated in John 14:6, "I am the way, the truth, and the life." Just as He is the Word of God, Jesus is—He embodies, He personifies—the Truth. John echoed the thought: "He that hath the Son hath life; and he that hath not the Son of God hath not life" (1 John 5:12).

As Dr. R. C. Sproul put it, "Truth is defined as that which corresponds to reality as perceived by God, because God's perception of reality is never distorted. It's a perfect perception of reality."[35]

THE CHURCH SURRENDERS THE FIGHT FOR TRUTH

Barna Group is probably the leading researcher on religious belief among Americans, and the group tracks religious opinion in many other areas of the world as well.

Since 1995 Barna Group has tracked the prevalence of what it describes as a "biblical worldview" among self-described American Christians. To be honest, Barna's definition of *biblical worldview* in their 2017 study seems quite basic. A biblical worldview seems to me to require more. But certainly it is impossible to have a biblical worldview without *at least* these beliefs:

- Absolute moral truth exists.
- The Bible is totally accurate in all the principles it teaches.
- Satan is a real being or force, not merely symbolic.
- People cannot earn their way into heaven by trying to be good or do good works.
- Jesus Christ lived a sinless life on earth.
- God is the all-knowing, all-powerful creator of the world who still rules the universe today.[36]

Seems simple enough. This doesn't even include basics such as the virgin birth or the bodily resurrection of Jesus Christ. And the study's results are seemingly more predictable given that Barna asked these questions of "practicing Christians" (defined as those "who go to church at least monthly and consider their faith very important in their life").

The percentage of these "practicing Christians" who believe these six basic truths? Seventeen percent![37]

By contrast, fifty-two percent (in another Barna survey) believed that the Bible teaches that "God helps those who helps themselves."[38] The quote actually comes from a work by Algernon Sidney and was popularized by Benjamin Franklin in *Poor Richard's Almanack.*

So exactly what *do* American "Christians" believe? In 2017 Barna also studied what competing worldviews were held by these "practicing Christians." A full twenty-eight percent believe that "all people pray to the same god or spirit, no matter what name they use for that spiritual being."[39] And twenty-seven percent believe that "meaning and purpose come from becoming one with all that is"—a firmly pagan view of Eastern religions and one rejected by the Bible.[40]

Perhaps most troubling in the 2017 study, almost one quarter of practicing Christians (twenty-three percent) strongly agreed that "what is morally right or wrong depends on what an individual believes."[41]

And it's actually worse than that. A Barna study from 2015 details the beliefs of Americans—and American Christians—about the nature of Truth.

Barna asked survey participants to respond to the statement "Whatever is right for your life or works best for you is the only truth you can know." The percentage of Americans who strongly or somewhat agreed with the statement? Fifty-seven percent.[42] Far more troubling, a full forty-one percent of practicing Christians agreed![43]

This basic worldview problem translates into a cultural problem. Sixty-five percent of Americans agree either strongly or somewhat that "every culture must determine what is acceptable morality for its people."[44]

When presented with the statement "The Bible provides us with absolute moral truths which are the same for all people in all situations, without exception," only fifty-six percent of practicing Christians strongly agreed.[45]

Finally, presented with the question "Is moral truth absolute or relative to circumstances?" Forty-four percent of Americans say it is relative, and twenty-one percent "have not given it much thought." Only thirty-five percent of Americans believe moral truth is absolute.[46] Most shocking, only fifty-nine percent of practicing Christians believe moral truth is absolute. (Twenty-eight percent say it is relative; fourteen percent have never thought about it.)[47]

Our beliefs about the nature of Truth invariably, unavoidably determine all our other beliefs. David Kinnaman, president of Barna Group, stated that the "morality of self-fulfillment" has all but replaced Christianity as America's moral norm.[48]

The 2015 Barna study looked at the attitudes that make up this new morality of self-fulfillment. It notes what it calls six "guiding principles" (I'll call them "fundamentals of the faith of me-worship"):

- "The best way to find yourself is by looking within yourself": seventy-six percent of practicing Christians agree.
- "People should not criticize someone else's life choices": seventy-six percent of practicing Christians agree.
- "To be fulfilled in life, you should pursue the things you desire most": seventy-two percent of practicing Christians agree.
- "The highest goal of life is to enjoy it as much as possible": sixty-seven percent of practicing Christians agree.
- "People can believe whatever they want, as long as those beliefs don't affect society": sixty-one percent of practicing Christians agree.
- As an unavoidable corollary to the previous five, "any kind of sexual expression between two consenting adults is acceptable." And yes, a full forty percent of practicing Christians agree.[49]

In a similar Barna study in 2001, only ten percent of African American adults believed that morality is absolute.[50] Given that relativistic morality enabled slavery, this is a shocking statistic.

Let's consider the reality of these figures. If the majority is correct, the bombing of innocent civilians in the World Trade Center on September 11, 2001, was not absolutely wrong. The German concentration camps were not absolutely wrong. Slavery in America was not absolutely wrong. Timothy McVeigh's bombing of the Murrah Federal Building and Dylann Roof's shootings at Emanuel AME Church in Charleston in 2015 were not absolutely wrong. These horrific events were wrong only because the culture says so.

And much of the church has fallen for the lie. "In the name of the most-favored opinions of our modern culture, some evangelicals have even abandoned the clearest, strongest, most unambiguous truths about God himself. . . And many other evangelicals are too confused or too afraid to challenge such a feckless betrayal of faith."[51]

But if there is *no* absolute Truth, none of these events can be categorically said to be wrong. And maybe you are wrong, and the slaveholders or Dylann Roof or Adolf Hitler were actually right, given their time, circumstances, upbringing, or "how their truth applied to them."

Even from a philosophical perspective, divorced from biblical roots, this argument makes no sense. Let's look at it another way. You tell me there's no such thing as absolute Truth. Okay, defend that. *Absolutely* no absolute Truth? Are you categorically telling me that there is *nothing* absolutely true? That cannot be. The statement that nothing is absolutely true is itself an absolute statement. It is the statement that *everything* is acceptable. And it denies my right to believe differently from you—that something somewhere is unacceptable.

Let's try another tack. Is it morally acceptable for me to take my gun, enter your home, and take everything you have at gunpoint? To assault your spouse and children? To injure you? If so, why should the law stop me? If not, you have to abandon your "no absolutes" principle.

At its base what Barna terms the "morality of self-fulfillment"—me-worship, if you will—is not a moral philosophy at all. It is not a principled position. It is not even, as it so loudly proclaims to be, a tolerant position.

At its root, the "new morality" is nothing more than repackaged old selfishness. It is a one-way street. In reality, it proclaims, "I have all the rights, and you can't stop me. I can do as I please, with no concern for the effect on others. I can do what I want, and so can you, unless you get in my way. Then guess who gets to do what they want?" It is no more or less complicated than morally clueless Israel during the period of the judges: "Every man did that which was right in his own eyes" (Judges 21:25). For all its high-sounding claims of inclusion, it is in reality just a harsh, Darwinian code of survival for whoever happens to be the biggest bully on the block.

AMERICA'S NEW MORALITY IS JUST OLD IMMORALITY

And that's just the philosophical, utilitarian, consequentially based argument. Let's weigh the new morality against Scripture and see what we get. How do the six fundamentals of me-worship stack up against Truth? Let's take them one at a time.

1. THE BEST WAY TO FIND YOURSELF IS BY LOOKING WITHIN YOURSELF.

Is this statement true according to the Bible? Is it even morally neutral according to the Bible? (Hint: As we'll discuss later, *nothing* is morally neutral.)

The entire focus of me-worship is wrong. It serves the wrong god—me. The entire Bible is focused on finding God—or rather, on God sending His Son to find me. The whole focus of me-worship is on worshipping me—finding me, fulfilling me, aggrandizing me. Self-esteem, self-actualization, self-worth.

And the American culture has prostrated itself before the new god: "Be all you can be." "You deserve a break today." "Be kind to yourself." "If it feels good, do it." "It's five o'clock somewhere." The walls and marquees of our public schools are alive with the refrain. Cultural stars trumpet it:

- "If you believe in yourself anything is possible." (Singer Miley Cyrus)
- "If you believe in yourself and feel confident in yourself, you can do anything. I really believe that." (Model Karlie Kloss)
- "Whatever you want in your life, other people are going to want too. Believe in yourself enough to accept the idea that you have an equal right to it." (Journalist Diane Sawyer)
- "What I've learned in these 11 years is you just got to stay focused and believe in yourself and trust your own ability and judgment." (Dallas Mavericks owner Mark Cuban)

Jesus actually addressed this principle head on in Matthew 16:25: "Whosoever will save his life shall lose it: and whosoever will lose his life for my sake shall find it."

Matthew 16 is set in the context of Christ beginning to explain to His disciples that He must go to Jerusalem to be tortured and crucified by sinful human beings. Peter berated Christ and argued that this would never happen. Christ turned and rebuked not Peter but the satanic selfishness behind Peter's statement: "Get thee behind me, Satan: thou art an offence unto me: for thou savourest not the things that be of God, but those that be of men" (v. 23).

Peter had fallen hook, line, and sinker for the new morality. Jesus was supposed to remove the hated Romans and set up a kingdom with plenty of loaves and fish and miraculous healings for everyone. Instead, He was taking a course for suffering, humiliation, and death as God's "wonderful plan for His life"! Never!

Worse yet, this was not just for Jesus: "Then said Jesus unto his disciples, If any man will come after me, let him deny himself, and take up his cross, and follow me. For whosoever will save his life shall lose it: and whosoever will lose his life for my sake shall find it" (vv. 24–25).

Jesus was not looking within Himself to find Himself. He was not even looking to find Himself. Instead,

> being found in appearance as a man, He humbled Himself by becoming obedient to the point of death, even death on a cross. For this reason also, God highly exalted Him, and bestowed on Him the name which is above every name, so that at the name of Jesus every knee will bow, of those who are in heaven and on earth and under the earth, and that every tongue will confess that Jesus Christ is Lord, to the glory of God the Father. (Philippians 2:8–11 NASB)

He "endured the cross, despising the shame" (Hebrews 12:2 NASB). Instead of "finding Himself," He emptied Himself. We are to do the same.

The world offers me-worship. God offers a cross. One way is true. One is not. *Both cannot be.* On the first claim of the new morality, God and man are at war. And we each have to choose.

2. PEOPLE SHOULD NOT CRITICIZE SOMEONE ELSE'S LIFE CHOICES.

This is an easy one. And no, I don't mean "Judge not, that ye be not judged" (Matthew 7:1). That's one of two Bible passages that make up the world's entire scriptural knowledge. The other is a vague understanding that Jesus did not stone an adulteress (John 8:1–11), so apparently what isn't stoned is condoned.

Consider Ezekiel 33:8: "When I say unto the wicked, O wicked man, thou shalt surely die; if thou dost not speak to warn the wicked from his way, that wicked man shall die in his iniquity; but his blood will I require at thine hand." Or Jonah 1:2: "Arise, go to Nineveh, that great city, and cry against it; for their wickedness is come up before me." Or Isaiah 58:1: "Cry aloud, spare not, lift up thy voice like a trumpet, and shew my people their transgression, and the house of Jacob their sins." Or Isaiah 5:20: "Woe unto them that call evil good, and good evil; that put darkness for light, and light for darkness; that put bitter for sweet, and sweet for bitter!" Or Psalm 82:2: "How long will ye judge unjustly, and accept the persons of the wicked?"

Or Christ in John 7:24: "Judge not according to the appearance, but judge righteous judgment." Or Christ in Luke 12:56–57: "You hypocrites! You know how to analyze the appearance of the earth and the sky, but why do you not analyze this present time? And why do you not even on your own initiative judge what is right?" (NASB).

Or Titus 1:9–13:

> Holding fast the faithful word as he hath been taught, that he may be able by sound doctrine both to exhort and to convince the gainsayers. For there are many unruly and vain talkers and deceivers, specially they of the circumcision: whose mouths must be stopped, who subvert whole houses, teaching things which they ought not, for filthy lucre's sake. . . . Wherefore rebuke them sharply, that they may be sound in the faith.

Or 2 Timothy 4:2: "Preach the word; be instant in season, out of season; reprove, rebuke, exhort with all long suffering and doctrine." Who are we to "reprove, rebuke, exhort" if we can't criticize lifestyle choices?

The church has made the colossal mistake of allowing the world to define *love*. It's not loving, we're told, to try to "impose our values" on others. But as the great missionary Amy Carmichael put it so well,

> If I am afraid to speak the truth, lest I lose affection,
> or lest the one concerned should say, "You do not understand,"
> or because I fear to lose my reputation for kindness;
> if I put my own good name before the other's highest good,
> then I know nothing of Calvary love.
> If I am content to heal a hurt slightly,
> saying "Peace, peace," where is no peace;
> if I forget the poignant word "Let love be without dissimulation"
> and blunt the edge of truth,
> speaking not right things but smooth things,
> then I know nothing of Calvary love.[52]

3. TO BE FULFILLED IN LIFE, YOU SHOULD PURSUE THE THINGS YOU DESIRE MOST.

See number 1.

4. THE HIGHEST GOAL OF LIFE IS TO ENJOY IT AS MUCH AS POSSIBLE.

See number 1.

5. PEOPLE CAN BELIEVE WHATEVER THEY WANT, AS LONG AS THOSE BELIEFS DON'T AFFECT SOCIETY.

This is impossible. What I believe is not irrelevant to how I live. In fact, what I believe *determines* how I live. Nothing in life is truer than James's statement that "faith without works is dead" (James 2:20). A living faith cannot fail to display itself in how I live. And if large numbers of people are displaying living faith, those beliefs must inevitably affect society.

William Penn's beliefs compelled him to pay the Native Americans a fair price for his colony in Pennsylvania, while the materialism of the Dutch settlers of

New York led to the Native Americans being cheated out of Manhattan Island in exchange for a few tools and trinkets. The materialism of America's slaveholding class led to immense human misery among African Americans, while the Quaker conductors on the Underground Railroad risked loss of their own freedom in jail and loss of their material possessions for the freedom of others.

Modern America prides itself on its ability to separate the secular and the sacred. It is, at least for the moment, tolerant of "Christianity" that limits itself to well-insulated services on Sundays. When that Christianity stands up for the lives of the unborn out in the real world, tolerance goes out the window.

The beliefs of a nation's people will determine that nation's destiny. It has always been—*and will always be*—true that "righteousness exalteth a nation: but sin is a reproach to any people" (Proverbs 14:34). No nation is or can be morally neutral.

The old canard says, "You can't legislate morality." The truth is, you can't avoid legislating morality. Every law says, "It's not okay to do this thing" or "You must do this thing." *Every* law legislates morality. Morality *will* be legislated. The only question is, Whose morality?

6. ANY KIND OF SEXUAL EXPRESSION BETWEEN TWO CONSENTING ADULTS IS ACCEPTABLE.

Paul said this is not true: "Know ye not that the unrighteous shall not inherit the kingdom of God? Be not deceived: neither fornicators, nor idolaters, nor adulterers, nor effeminate, nor abusers of themselves with mankind, nor thieves, nor covetous, nor drunkards, nor revilers, nor extortioners, shall inherit the kingdom of God" (1 Corinthians 6:9–10).

He repeated himself in Galatians 5:19: "The works of the flesh are manifest, which are these; Adultery, fornication, uncleanness, lasciviousness."

Revelation 21 paints a beautiful picture of heaven. And verse 8 paints a frightful picture of those on the outside: "But the fearful, and unbelieving, and the abominable, and murderers, and whoremongers, and sorcerers, and idolaters, and all liars, shall have their part in the lake which burneth with fire and brimstone: which is the second death."

God's people need not even resort to the Old Testament and the lengthy Mosaic proscriptions of all sorts of immoral behavior. The New Testament is clear enough by itself.

WITHOUT ABSOLUTE TRUTH, THERE IS NO ETERNAL SECURITY

Truth necessarily divides. The Scriptures make clear that eternity is divided between those in heaven and those in hell. And they repeat again and again that sexual immorality has no place in heaven's economy.

The Creator does not allow for alternative "truths" depending on the whims of people and cultures. There is One who *is* the Truth. "Let God be true, but every man a liar" (Romans 3:4).

The Bible tells us in Romans 1:20 that God has written eternal Truth on the hearts of men: "The invisible things of him from the creation of the world are clearly seen, being understood by the things that are made, even his eternal power and Godhead; so that they are without excuse."

The book of Judges is perhaps the clearest biblical warning of the dangers of a culture adrift from absolute Truth. The book opens with a united nation, mostly triumphant but making small compromises: "Neither did [the Israelites] drive out the inhabitants . . . but the Canaanites would dwell in that land" (1:27). Before long the nation was plunged into rampant idolatry and oppression by foreign dictators. One of the final scenes in the book is a Levite giving his concubine to a mob to be raped to death so he could escape harm (19:22–28). The book concludes with an epitaph that sounds to us quite all American: "In those days there was no king in Israel. Every man did that which was right in his own eyes" (21:25). Sort of a libertarian paradise. And all concept of self-government and individual rights was destroyed by the me-worshipping mob.

A more recent example is the contrast between the American and French Revolutions. Outwardly they seemed similar. Both were struggles for freedom from oppressive autocrats. We cried, "Life, Liberty, and the pursuit of Happiness." They cried, "Liberty, Equality, Fraternity."

But the American Revolution had a completely different basis. Ours was based on a belief in eternal Truth: "We hold these truths to be self-evident, that all men are created equal, that they are endowed by their Creator with certain unalienable Rights." Our struggle was founded on God and Truth. The result was the freest nation in the history of the world.

The French? Their Revolution was founded on the supremacy of man rather than God, on Enlightenment human wisdom, on an outright rejection of eternal Truth and divine authority. In an effort to stamp out all vestiges of Christian influence, the French revolutionaries went so far as to change their week from seven to ten days to avoid the reminder of God working six days and resting on the seventh.

The result was predictable. The French Revolution went from bad to worse. Mob rule became the order of the day. The guillotine settled political disputes. Before long the mob turned on itself, and Robespierre and others who had ruthlessly wielded the guillotine fell victim to it themselves. And the people exchanged a single dictator for a committee of dictators. During the two hundred years since our Constitution was written, the French have had sixteen constitutions.

A belief in eternal Truth has produced stability and freedom. The French experiment in the "morality of self-fulfillment" has produced misery, instability, cultural rot, and historical insignificance.

The existence of absolute Truth is absolutely necessary to the existence of the God of the Bible. One cannot exist without the other. Throughout Scripture, Christ made claims that are absolute. And to deny those is to accuse God of lying: "He that believeth not God hath made him a liar; because he believeth not the record that God gave of his Son" (1 John 5:10).

Since your eternal security is based on God's promises, absolute Truth is also the measuring stick of your eternal security. In 1 Corinthians 15:12–22, Paul made a compelling argument for the necessity of absolute Truth:

> If Christ be preached that he rose from the dead, how say some among you that there is no resurrection of the dead?

But if there be no resurrection of the dead, then is Christ not risen:

And if Christ be not risen, then is our preaching vain, and your faith is also vain.

Yea, and we are found false witnesses of God; because we have testified of God that he raised up Christ: whom he raised not up, if so be that the dead rise not.

For if the dead rise not, then is not Christ raised:

And if Christ be not raised, your faith is vain; ye are yet in your sins.

Then they also which are fallen asleep in Christ are perished.

If in this life only we have hope in Christ, we are of all men most miserable.

But now is Christ risen from the dead, and become the firstfruits of them that slept.

Since by man came death, by man came also the resurrection of the dead.

For as in Adam all die, even so in Christ shall all be made alive.

If the Truth of the Resurrection is not absolute, "your faith is vain; ye are yet in your sins. Then they also which are fallen asleep in Christ have perished" (vv. 17–18). If the Truth of the Resurrection is not absolute, every human soul without exception is condemned to eternal hell.

That is why the truth of 1 John 5:13 is so blessedly comforting: "These things have I written unto you that believe on the name of the Son of God; that ye may know that ye have eternal life, and that ye may believe on the name of the Son of God." We can know. But only if there is absolute Truth.

That is what is at stake in the battle for absolute Truth. All eternity. Fortunately Truth stands regardless of our recognition of it. Truth is unaffected by whether I believe it or not. Truth judges me; I do not judge Truth.

Eternal Truth is like gravity. You may not like it. But you can't change it. You can pretend it doesn't exist. But it does not change. It will break you, and it will still be here, as much the Truth as ever.

CHAPTER 5

CHRISTIANITY IS NOT "TOLERANT": THERE IS NO GOSPEL WITHOUT CONFRONTATION

Back to the Republican Party story from Chapter 4. As the political and legal battle wore on, numerous well-meaning folks suggested that the party should "reach out" and show "openness" by embracing the folks who had attempted a hostile takeover under blatantly false pretenses.

The challengers demanded that the party simply surrender unconditionally. To fight for its beliefs, they told the watching press, was "extreme" and "exclusive." (Never mind that it was their "inclusive" team that threw the existing members off the local GOP committee.)

The party stood its ground and reminded the press that it was the stated intention of the challengers to throw all the Republicans off the board of supervisors if they took over the GOP committee and that it was the party's job to elect more Republicans.

In fact, soon after the legal battle ended, some of the challengers began running as Independents against the Republican candidates they had promised to defeat if they could attract enough stealth Democrats to the Republican meeting!

That November, the Republicans won, giving the county a conservative Republican majority on its board of supervisors. The victory bought the citizens years of no tax increases.

Inclusion *was defined by the opposition as "unconditional surrender of the principles the party believed in." The loyal volunteers rejected the call, being willing instead to be smeared as "intolerant" in order to ensure their principles prevailed and that they offered the voters candidates who actually believed in the principles the party claimed to espouse.*

The citizens won the battle the party fought.

* * * * *

THE GOSPEL IS NOT "TOLERANT"

America may have once been a Christian nation. She has not been for some time. America's new national "morality of self-fulfillment" is wise enough not to market itself quite so clearly. Instead, our national religion is the religion of "tolerance."

Now, don't be confused. It is commendable to understand and accept some differences of opinion in others. It is commendable not to seek to use the force of government to punish alternative views.

But "tolerance," as practiced in America today, means something else entirely. To tolerate an opposing idea now means I cannot put forth my own competing ideas and argue for their superiority. It essentially means I have no right to make moral judgments about the conduct of others. To be tolerant of an opposing view now means I have to support, endorse, even fund positions I view to be destructive. To fail to do so means I fit in the lowest life form imaginable—the "intolerant."

The church has largely adopted—or at least tacitly accepted—the world's terminology here. We have frantically tried to adapt the Bible to fit the religion of tolerance. We have even created a new "tolerant Jesus" to fit what culture demands. Tolerant Jesus refuses to condemn adultery. He doesn't talk much about hell (the real Jesus did). He doesn't talk much about sin. His signature verse—in fact, largely His only verse—is "Judge not, that ye be not judged" (Matthew 7:1). Tolerant Jesus wouldn't be caught dead hurting someone's feelings. He is mortally afraid He might offend someone. In fact, the worst sin of which modern American Christians can be guilty is to be offensive (to be offensive is to be intolerant).

THE WAR OF THE GODS

According to Scripture, as long as people have worshipped other gods, there has been a battle of those gods against Jehovah God. The battle in Exodus that featured ten plagues was not primarily between Moses and Pharaoh or even between God and Pharaoh. It was between Jehovah God and the gods of the Egyptians.

The Egyptians worshipped a god of the Nile River, so God turned its water to blood. They believed in the sun god Ra, so God sent days of thick darkness, "a darkness that can be felt" (Exodus 10:21 NIV).

The Egyptian sorcerers called upon their gods to mimic the "tricks" Moses and Aaron played, such as turning water into blood and producing snakes out of wooden rods (Exodus 7:10–11, 20–22). But when it came to reproducing lice, their gods failed them. "Then the magicians said unto Pharaoh, This is the finger of God" (Exodus 8:19). They saw what Pharaoh would deny right until the Red Sea swallowed his army—that God was at war with their gods.

Finally on Passover night God dropped the hammer: "I will pass through the land of Egypt this night, and will smite all the firstborn in the land of Egypt, both man and beast; and against all the gods of Egypt I will execute judgment: I am the Lord" (Exodus 12:12). The Egyptians also equated Pharaoh with the gods, so God struck his firstborn and those of all his people.

When God's people turned to the worship of Baal, the battle continued. Baal was considered the god of rain and dew, so God sent Elijah to tell Ahab, "There shall be neither dew nor rain these years, except by my word" (1 Kings 17:1 NASB). And for more than three years, there was none.

When the Philistines captured the ark of God and placed it in the temple of their god, Dagon, they came in the next morning and found that the statue of Dagon had fallen on its face before the ark of God (1 Samuel 5:1–3).

But the very earliest mass idolatry recorded in Scripture occurred at the Tower of Babel. Scripture does not mention the name of any pagan idol involved at the time. However, the context makes clear that the opposing god at Babel was the same god opposing Jehovah today—the god Me. "They said, Go to, let us build us a city and a tower, whose top may reach unto heaven; and let us make us a name, lest we be scattered abroad upon the face of the whole earth" (Genesis 11:4).

God had commanded man to "be fruitful and multiply, and fill the earth" (Genesis 1:28 NASB). The builders wanted to consolidate their power, to build a tower to symbolize that power, and to "make us a name." It was similar to Satan's determination to "be like the most High" (Isaiah 14:14). And as always, God acted decisively against the false religion, the Church of Me.

Somehow the Church of Me sounds to us less heathenish than Baal or Ra or Moloch or an Asherah pole or worshipping the stars. But God treats it seriously.

JESUS IS "INTOLERANT"

The prevailing image of "Tolerant Jesus" is a creation of dumbed-down American Christianity, a pale caricature of the Jesus of the Bible. The real Jesus was not afraid to be offensive. The real Jesus didn't lose a great deal of sleep trying to be inclusive—another buzzword we have adapted from the world.

In fact, a careful review finds that Jesus said some of the most radically exclusive statements—yes, the most "intolerant" statements—in all of human history. Let's consider a few.

"I am *the* way, *the* truth, and *the* life: *no man* cometh unto the Father but by me" (John 14:6, emphasis added). It is fair to call this the most "intolerant" statement in all of history. The statement categorically condemns to eternal hell every human being in history who seeks God any other way than through Jesus Christ. No matter how sincere, no matter how moral, no matter how well intentioned.

Throughout this book, I use the imagery of a clash of gods. God versus Caesar. God versus idols. God versus man. Since Adam and Eve, humankind has faced a choice. Who will be god—God or man? Here in one verse Christ has destroyed the modern American idea that self-fulfillment is the highest value. He destroyed the idea that I can do as I please as long as I don't hurt someone else and that that is somehow good enough. He destroyed our libertarian, almost anarchist insistence on individual freedom of choice. Certainly I can choose any road I please. But God just as certainly controls the consequence of that choice. Man who would be God is left doomed.

Christ destroyed the idea that no one can judge another's idea of how to achieve salvation. He set Himself up as rightly possessing that right to judge. Consider the grave warning in His prophecy of the sheep and the goats:

> When the Son of man shall come in his glory, and all the holy angels with him, then shall he sit upon the throne of his glory:
>
> And before him shall be gathered all nations: and he shall separate them one from another, as a shepherd divideth his sheep from the goats:
>
> And he shall set the sheep on his right hand, but the goats on the left.
>
> Then shall the King say unto them on his right hand, Come, ye blessed of my Father, inherit the kingdom prepared for you from the foundation of the world:
>
> For I was an hungred, and ye gave me meat: I was thirsty, and ye gave me drink: I was a stranger, and ye took me in:
>
> Naked, and ye clothed me: I was sick, and ye visited me: I was in prison, and ye came unto me. . . .
>
> And the King shall answer and say unto them, Verily I say unto you, Inasmuch as ye have done it unto one of the least of these my brethren, ye have done it unto me.
>
> Then shall he say also unto them on the left hand, Depart from me, ye cursed, into everlasting fire, prepared for the devil and his angels. . . .
>
> And these shall go away into everlasting punishment: but the righteous into life eternal. (Matthew 25:31–46)

Consider a similar warning from Jesus in Matthew 7: "Not every one that saith unto me, Lord, Lord, shall enter into the kingdom of heaven; but he that doeth the will of my Father which is in heaven. Many will say to me in that day, Lord, Lord, have we not prophesied in thy name? and in thy name have cast out devils? and in thy name done many wonderful works? And then will I profess unto them, I never knew you: depart from me, ye that work iniquity" (vv. 21–23).

You heard that right. Jesus, the meek and mild, the One Who blessed the children, the One Who prayed, "Father, forgive them; for they know not what they do" (Luke 23:34), pronouncing eternal doom on many who, apparently, sincerely thought they had been acting in His name. It's hard to be less "tolerant" than that. The great white throne judgment, it appears, is not a democratic process.

The modern church has an artist's conception of Jesus as soft, quiet, pale, weak, almost simpering. He is a Boy Scout leader leading a chorus of "Kum Ba Yah" around a campfire. Then we read His condemnation of the Pharisees in Matthew 23, and we are slapped in the face by His language. We almost get angry at Him for being so unlike the artist's conception. His attack is worth quoting extensively here. He went on for almost a whole chapter! By the time He's about four verses in, we are very uncomfortable. He was being so "mean." He was being so "intolerant." He was being so "un-Christlike." Except this is Christ!

> Woe unto you, scribes and Pharisees, hypocrites! for ye shut up the kingdom of heaven against men: for ye neither go in yourselves, neither suffer ye them that are entering to go in.

> Woe unto you, scribes and Pharisees, hypocrites! for ye devour widows' houses, and for a pretence make long prayer: therefore ye shall receive the greater damnation.

> Woe unto you, scribes and Pharisees, hypocrites! for ye compass sea and land to make one proselyte, and when he is made, ye make him twofold more the child of hell than yourselves.

> Woe unto you, ye blind guides, which say, Whosoever shall swear by the temple, it is nothing; but whosoever shall swear by the gold of the temple, he is a debtor!

> Ye fools and blind: for whether is greater, the gold, or the temple that sanctifieth the gold?

And, Whosoever shall swear by the altar, it is nothing; but whosoever sweareth by the gift that is upon it, he is guilty.

Ye fools and blind: for whether is greater, the gift, or the altar that sanctifieth the gift? . . .

Woe unto you, scribes and Pharisees, hypocrites! for ye pay tithe of mint and anise and cummin, and have omitted the weightier matters of the law, judgment, mercy, and faith: these ought ye to have done, and not to leave the other undone.

Ye blind guides, which strain at a gnat, and swallow a camel.

Woe unto you, scribes and Pharisees, hypocrites! for ye make clean the outside of the cup and of the platter, but within they are full of extortion and excess.

Thou blind Pharisee, cleanse first that which is within the cup and platter, that the outside of them may be clean also.

Woe unto you, scribes and Pharisees, hypocrites! for ye are like unto whited sepulchres, which indeed appear beautiful outward, but are within full of dead men's bones, and of all uncleanness.

Even so ye also outwardly appear righteous unto men, but within ye are full of hypocrisy and iniquity.

Woe unto you, scribes and Pharisees, hypocrites! because ye build the tombs of the prophets, and garnish the sepulchres of the righteous,

And say, If we had been in the days of our fathers, we would not have been partakers with them in the blood of the prophets.

Wherefore ye be witnesses unto yourselves, that ye are the children of them which killed the prophets.

Fill ye up then the measure of your fathers.

Ye serpents, ye generation of vipers, how can ye escape the damnation of hell?

Wherefore, behold, I send unto you prophets, and wise men, and scribes: and some of them ye shall kill and crucify; and some of them shall ye scourge in your synagogues, and persecute them from city to city:

That upon you may come all the righteous blood shed upon the earth, from the blood of righteous Abel unto the blood of Zacharias son of Barachias, whom ye slew between the temple and the altar. (vv. 13–35)

Wow!

"Fools and blind." "Hypocrites." Generation of vipers." "The damnation of hell." "Whited sepulchres." "Twofold more the child of hell than yourselves." Wow! Where is the inclusiveness? Where is the tolerance? Where is the meek and mild Jesus? Where is the seeker sensitivity?

As A. W. Tozer wrote, "The Bible has no compromise whatsoever with the world. . . . The Bible . . . sends us out into the world, but never to compromise with the world; and never to walk in the way of the world."[53] Blogger Matt Walsh is a favorite of mine. He has a knack for unvarnished truth. Sometimes unvarnished truth is shocking because we're so used to sugarcoating everything. Walsh wrote a column titled "Jesus Didn't Care about Being Nice or Tolerant."

> We've turned the Son of God into a purple dinosaur puppet . . . In Matthew 18, [He says] it would be better to drown in the sea with a stone around your neck than to harm a child. Had our modern politicians been around two thousand years ago, I'm sure they'd go on the cable news shows and . . . insist that there's "no place for that kind of language." No place for the language of God.[54]

HAVE WE BECOME ENEMIES OF GOD?

The Bible makes clear that before salvation we are not neutral toward God; we are enemies: "If, when we were enemies, we were reconciled to God by the death of his Son, much more, being reconciled, we shall be saved by his life" (Romans 5:10). As Jesus Himself put it, "He that is not with me is against me; and he that gathereth not with me scattereth abroad" (Matthew 12:30).

James also put it rather starkly: "Ye adulterers and adulteresses, know ye not that the friendship of the world is enmity with God? whosoever therefore will be a friend of the world is the enemy of God" (James 4:4). Modern American Christians are quite comfortable with both feet in the world and a couple of toes in God's camp for eternal security's sake. James warned us our calculation is wrong. By desiring to coexist comfortably with the world and its "do it yourself" religion, we put ourselves in the dangerous position of enemies of God.

Paul warned, "Know ye not, that to whom ye yield yourselves servants to obey, his servants ye are to whom ye obey; whether of sin unto death, or of obedience unto righteousness? But God be thanked, that ye were the servants of sin, but ye have obeyed from the heart that form of doctrine which was delivered you. Being then made free from sin, ye became the servants of righteousness" (Romans 6:16–18).

Paul wasn't leaving a lot of shades of gray here. The Bible is clear—salvation is a radical transformation. It is a whole new nature, a change of masters, a defection from one army to another, with eternal war declared against the old: "I see another law in my members, warring against the law of my mind, and bringing me into captivity to the law of sin which is in my members. O wretched man that I am! who shall deliver me from the body of this death? I thank God through Jesus Christ our Lord" (Romans 7:23–25).

The church today is spending countless hours and dollars trying to become more "seeker friendly." We are desperate to make church a place where sinners are made comfortable instead of called to repentance. We offer an easy prayer for fire insurance, without requiring that people change their gods. Tolerance is now the highest virtue, not obedience. Inclusion, not repentance.

But our approach is doomed to failure. In her book *Total Truth*, Nancy Pearcey compared early evangelical churches with the churches that were legally established by the government.

> It is a common assumption that, in order to survive, churches must accommodate to the age. But in fact, the opposite is true: In every historical period, the religious groups that grow most rapidly are those that set believers at odds with the surrounding culture. As

a general principle, the higher a group's tension with mainstream society, the higher its growth rate.[55]

The principle is all too applicable today, in light of the withering of mainline denominations, even as they reject "controversial" biblical truths. Regardless of what the numbers say, Christ requires that we dethrone Satan and self and submit to a new Master.

Paul's voice cries out to the American church for a total paradigm shift, a total course correction: "What? Shall we continue in sin, that grace may abound? *God forbid*" (Romans 6:1–2, emphasis added). "If any man be in Christ, he is a new creature: old things are passed away; behold, *all* things are become new" (2 Corinthians 5:17, emphasis added).

> What fellowship hath righteousness with unrighteousness? and what communion hath light with darkness?
>
> And what concord hath Christ with Belial? or what part hath he that believeth with an infidel?
>
> And what agreement hath the temple of God with idols? for ye are the temple of the living God; as God hath said, I will dwell in them, and walk in them; and I will be their God, and they shall be my people.
>
> Wherefore come out from among them, and be ye separate, saith the Lord, and touch not the unclean thing; and I will receive you. (2 Corinthians 6:14–17)

Simon Greenleaf (1783–1853) was the Royall Professor of Law at Harvard, one of the foremost legal scholars in Western history, and was considered by a chief justice of the United States Supreme Court to be "the highest authority in our courts."[56] In his *Testimony of the Four Evangelists*, Greenleaf wrote,

> The religion of Jesus Christ aims at nothing less than the utter overthrow of all other systems of religion in the world; denouncing them as inadequate to the wants of man, false in their foundations, and dangerous in their tendency. . . . These are no ordinary claims; and it seems hardly possible for a rational being to regard them

with even a subdued interest; much less to treat them with mere indifference and contempt. If not true, they are little else than the pretensions of a bold imposture. . . . But if they are well founded and just, they can be no less than the high requirements of heaven, addressed by the voice of God to the reason and understanding of man, concerning things deeply affecting his relations to his sovereign, and essential to the formation of his character and of course to his destiny, both for this life and for the life to come.[57]

The British writer Dorothy Sayers put it quite succinctly: "In the world [acedia or sloth] calls itself tolerance; but in hell it is called despair. . . . It is the sin that believes in nothing, cares for nothing, seeks to know nothing, interferes with nothing, enjoys nothing, loves nothing, hates nothing, finds purpose in nothing, lives for nothing, and remains alive only because there is nothing it would die for."[58] That's the consequence of the modern definition of tolerance; without the ability to make moral judgments, there's no measuring stick for human behavior and no purpose for human existence.

Paul didn't have a foot in both camps. James didn't call for inclusion. The Truth of God's Word leaves no room for the error of American humanism. Christianity cannot coexist with idolatry. And Jesus is *not* tolerant.

CHRISTIANITY DEMANDS CONFRONTATION

One of the greatest challenges to Christian effectiveness in the culture is the church's reluctance to confront evil. We are deeply influenced in this regard by many norms of our own church culture. We have been weakened by weak preaching. We have been influenced by artists' portrayals of the meek and mild Jesus, looking almost girlish in His spotless white robe and smile that's gentle to the point of being simpering. We gravitate to verses such as "Whosoever shall smite thee on thy right cheek, turn to him the other also" (Matthew 5:39) and "The servant of the Lord must not strive" (2 Timothy 2:24), and like in so many of our theological turns, we have taken one aspect of God's nature and blocked out its opposite entirely.

As G. K. Chesterton wrote, "The popular imagery carries a great deal to excess the sentiment of 'Gentle Jesus, meek and mild.'"[59] He went on to say,

> There is nothing meek and mild, there is nothing even in the ordinary sense mystical, about the tone of the voice that says "Hold thy peace and come out of him." It is much more like the tone of a very business-like lion-tamer or a strong-minded doctor dealing with a homicidal maniac.[60]

Jesus was not a pacifist with a limp handshake. Nor are we called to be. We hear preaching about how Jesus rejected the suggestion of James and John, "the sons of thunder" (Mark 3:17), to call down fire from heaven on a Samaritan city that rejected Him (Luke 9:52–56). We entirely miss that His words of rebuke carried such authority that the furious James and John never questioned His decision. When Jesus called James and John to follow Him, they "immediately left the ship and their father, and followed him" (Matthew 4:22). When He called Matthew, the tax collector with the full faith and credit of the Roman government behind him, Matthew immediately left his collection booth and followed Him (Matthew 9:9).

Jesus fasted forty days and forty nights and still had the strength to resist the devil's temptations (Luke 4:1–13). He survived a Roman beating of a degree that had killed many men, carried His cross part of the way from Jerusalem to Calvary, and survived an additional six anguished hours thereafter (Mark 15:15–37; John 19:17). He walked by some estimates ten thousand to twenty thousand miles in three years of ministry.[61] He was a carpenter by trade.

He called out the Pharisees in the harshest terms, as we have seen. He premeditated His attack on the temple money changers, crafted a whip, overthrew their tables, drove out the animals, and physically flogged the money changers out of the temple (John 2:13–16). The scene was one of a riot, not one of turning the other cheek.

The church mistakes Christ's command to forgive our personal enemies for a command of complete pacifism, nonviolence, and a total aversion to conflict. As Matt Walsh wrote, "I've studied the New Testament and found not a single instance of Christ calling for a "dialogue" with evil or seeking the middle ground on an issue."[62]

In another article, Walsh wrote,

> Christians *ought* to be outraged, incensed, and infuriated by heinous attacks against *God, faith, and virtue*. Jesus tells us to turn the other cheek when someone slaps us, but He makes no such recommendation when someone slaps God or His commandments.
>
> Jesus flipped tables and physically accosted people who made a mockery of the temple (John 2:13). . . . [Now] Christ is the Temple. He is the Lord. He is our Master in Heaven, and His servants ought to be flipping tables to defend His Name. . . .
>
> We are hypocrites, you and I. We lack the courage of our convictions. . . .
>
> Tolerance. Horrible, shameful tolerance . . .
>
> I think it's about time for some determined, decisive, glorious intolerance.[63]

And don't tell me, "Well, Jesus was God. He could get angry and challenge Pharisees and read their hearts, but we can't." While Christ's reason for coming to earth was not a political one, Scripture is replete with examples of other heroes who challenged the culture even more directly than Christ, at least in a political sense. John the Baptist publicly told King Herod, "It is not lawful for you to have your brother's wife" (Mark 6:18 NASB). And John was citing the law of God (Leviticus 20:21). There was nothing whatever in Roman civil law that forbade Herod's incest. John was specifically demanding that the heathen civil king subject himself to the moral law of God. And he lost his head for doing so (Matthew 14:1–11). In 2 Samuel 12, Nathan the prophet called King David a murderer (he was). Elijah told King Ahab that God would take his life as punishment for the "legal" murder of Naboth (1 Kings 21:17–19). In each case, telling the truth required directly challenging the most powerful man in the land.

A FEARFUL CHURCH EXCHANGES BIBLICAL
FAITHFULNESS FOR "NICENESS"

We completely misunderstand and pervert forgiveness. Forgiveness is something I extend to someone who has wronged me. I cannot forgive people for sins they have committed against someone else. I can no more forgive the abortion doctor than I can forgive Adolf Hitler. They have not wronged me. My responsibility is to shout from the housetops against their injustice and to defend the helpless.

Yet some Christian leaders have imbibed the "nice doctrine" of complete pacifism to an extent that shocks the conscience. In a 2015 article John Piper suggested that he would not use deadly force to protect his wife or daughter from a home invader! He wrote, "I think I can say with complete confidence that the identification of Christian security with concealed weapons will cause no one to ask a reason for the hope that is in us. They will know perfectly well where our hope is. It's in our pocket."[64]

Piper presented a long strand of verses warning of coming persecution and commanding Christians to be willing to suffer for their faith. He then conflated this into a biblical mandate to allow home invaders to harm our families, which has exactly nothing to do with being willing to suffer persecution for our faith. This misreading of Scripture leads to a false conclusion.

In an essay called "Some Things Are Not Negotiable," Tozer gave a modern echo of the New Testament warnings: "To seek to be friends with those who will not be the friends of Christ is to be a traitor to our Lord. Darkness and light can never be brought together by talk."[65] He wrote with a hint of sarcasm,

> Tolerance, charity, understanding, good will, patience and other such words and ideas are lifted from the Bible, misunderstood and applied indiscriminately to every situation. The kidnaper will not steal your baby if you only try to understand him; the burglar caught sneaking into your house with a gun is not really bad; he is just hungry for fellowship and togetherness; the gang killer taking his victim for a one-way ride can be dissuaded from committing

murder if someone will only have faith in his basic goodness and have a talk with him. And this is supposed to be the teaching of Jesus, which it most certainly is not.[66]

Unfortunately, similar preaching of absolute nonconfrontationalism has deeply infected the modern church, with devilish consequences to the church and the culture at large. A brief survey of history reveals what a poor choice too many in the modern church are making.

In the 1850s it was a crime under federal and many state laws to assist runaway slaves. Penalties could include fines, jail sentences, and, for both black and white Underground Railroad conductors, death, often in the most horrible fashions imaginable.[67] But the Quakers and other Christians, confident in their biblical responsibility, defied Caesar, challenged the culture, and risked everything to honor the second great commandment—"Thou shalt love thy neighbour as thyself" (Matthew 22:39). Of course, it was "divisive." The Southern Baptists and many other Christians were perfectly fine with slavery and even managed to pervert Scripture into a defense of their sin.

So we have Christian conductors, unafraid to be "intolerant" of evil, unafraid to defy the civil authorities (even though their freedom to preach Christ was not at stake), unafraid of being accused as "too political," and unafraid to be bitterly "divisive," even within the church. They were unafraid because Truth spurred them on; "the love of Christ constrain[ed them]" (2 Corinthians 5:14). They shunned all the disgusting spiritualized excuses we use today as fig leaves for our silence and complicity.

But today, with the murderous tally from abortion at more than sixty million, pastors won't address—and church members won't stand in any meaningful way against—our own holocaust. I submit that if we lived in the 1850s, the vast majority of us in the American church today would do exactly as much about slavery as we are currently doing about the abortion holocaust. Which is to say, nothing at all.

Most of the church today is in open rebellion against Proverbs 24:11–12:

Deliver those who are being taken away to death,
And those who are staggering to slaughter, Oh hold them back.
If you say, "See, we did not know this,"
Does He not consider it who weighs the hearts?
And does He not know it who keeps your soul?
And will He not render to man according to his work? (NASB)

The fact is, when I am wronged, I am to forgive. But when an innocent person is wronged, I am to stand in that person's defense. When my God is blasphemed, I am to stand for His name. And when the truth of His Word is denied, I am to proclaim Truth from the housetops.

And Matthew 18's command about personal reconciliation (go to the offender personally, then to the offender with one or two witnesses, then to the church) is just that—a prescription for personal reconciliation after personal offenses. It is utterly inapplicable to the Christian's role in challenging the culture.

IF WE CARRY GOD'S MESSAGE, WE MUST DEFEND IT AGAINST FALSEHOOD

The more fundamental the truth that is challenged, the more vocal should be my voice in its defense. The more public the lie, the bigger pulpit I should seek to proclaim the truth. Paul did not whisper in Peter's ear in a back corner. He "withstood him to the face" (Galatians 2:11), in front of God and everybody, because of the public nature of Peter's compromise on the gospel of salvation by faith and the fundamental nature of the truth he had compromised.

Consider Elijah in his challenge to the prophets of Baal (1 Kings 18). The very lordship of God was being challenged. And Elijah wasn't very nice. He wasn't concerned that he might be divisive within "God's people." He wasn't concerned that he had to go reason with each Baal worshipper privately before he could call out public sin publicly, as many modern Christians believe, misunderstanding Matthew 18. And unlike the modern mis-interpreters of Romans 13, he never tempered his preaching of truth out of a misguided understanding that Ahab was "ordained of God" and therefore entitled to unlimited obedience. (Elijah was made of sterner stuff—and more biblical stuff.)

He ordered King Ahab to "gather to me all Israel unto mount Carmel" (v. 19). He flung down a daring challenge in front of the civil ruler and all the people. This would seem strange at best to the Christian pacifist understanding of Romans 13. And if he lost, it would likely mean his life. Ahab had been looking for him for three years to kill him.

Then "Elijah came unto all the people, and said, How long halt ye between two opinions? If the Lord be God, follow him: but if Baal, then follow him. And the people answered him not a word" (v. 21).

Elijah laid out an elaborate object lesson for the people. The prophets of Baal started their bizarre dancing and chanting. And Elijah got even less nice: "It came to pass at noon, that Elijah mocked them, and said, Cry aloud: for he is a god; either he is talking, or he is pursuing, or he is in a journey, or peradventure he sleepeth, and must be awaked" (v. 27).

At this point Elijah would have been driven out of most modern churches for being so "unChristlike." He would be drummed out with a lecture on "speaking the truth in love" (Ephesians 4:15).

But the stakes were too high for niceties or concern about being offensive. When his turn came, Elijah's prayer laid out the stakes and revealed the reason he had flung down the gauntlet in front of the culture: "Hear me, O Lord, hear me, that this people may know that thou art the Lord God, and that thou hast turned their heart back again" (v. 37). In answer to his prayer, "the fire of the Lord fell, and consumed the burnt sacrifice, and the wood, and the stones, and the dust, and licked up the water that was in the trench. And when all the people saw it, they fell on their faces: and they said, The Lord, he is the God; the Lord, he is the God" (vv. 38–39).

Tozer wrote, "When men believe God they speak boldly. When they doubt they confer. Much current religious talk is but uncertainty rationalizing itself

. . . It is impossible to imagine Moses or Elijah so occupied."[68] He then made this declaration:

> All great Christian leaders have been dogmatic. To such men two plus two made four. Anyone who insisted upon denying it or suspending judgment upon it was summarily dismissed as frivolous. They were only interested in a meeting of minds if the minds agreed to meet on holy ground. We could use some gentle dogmatists these days.[69]

Wilberforce also eschewed the fear that he would be "too political" in exercising his faith as a member of Parliament to end slavery in England. And one voice that encouraged him to do so? It was that of John Wesley, the great preacher of the Great Awakening. In the last letter written before he died, Wesley wrote to Wilberforce:

> If God be for you, who can be against you? Are all of them together stronger than God? O be not weary of well doing. Go on, in the name of God and in the power of his might, till even American slavery (the vilest that ever saw the sun) shall vanish away before it. . . .
>
> That he who has guided you from your youth up may continue to strengthen you in this and all things is the prayer of, dear sir,
>
> Your affectionate servant,
>
> John Wesley[70]

Wesley serves as a shining example of a faithful preacher, encouraging and supporting biblical principles in the culture, fearless of being accused of being political or divisive.

Even until recent days, American pulpits have flamed with courageous preachers unafraid to apply God's Word to all of human existence, even when "controversial" or "confrontational."

Listen to A. W. Tozer:

> There are times when it is a sin to be at peace. There are circumstances when there is nothing to do but to stand up and

vigorously oppose. To wink at iniquity for the sake of peace is not a proof of superior spirituality; it is rather a sign of a reprehensible timidity which dare not oppose sin for fear of the consequences. For it will cost us heavily to stand for the right when the wrong is in the majority, which is 100 percent of the time.[71]

He continued:

We have developed in recent times a peace-loving, soft-spoken, tame and harmless brand of Christian of whom the world has no fear and for whom it has little respect. . . . We fear to talk against the destructive sins of modern civilization for fear someone will brand us as bigoted and narrow. Little by little we have been forced off the hard earth into a religious cloud-land where we are permitted to wing our harmless way around . . . saying nothing that might stir the ire of the sons of this world.[72]

And again:

A new Decalogue has been adopted by the neo-Christians of our day, the first word of which reads "Thou shalt not disagree"; and a new set of Beatitudes too, which begins "Blessed are they that tolerate everything, for they shall not be made accountable for anything." It is now the accepted thing to talk over religious differences in public with the understanding that no one will try to convert another or point out errors in his belief. The purpose of these talks is not to confront truth, but to discover how the followers of other religions think and thus benefit from their views as we hope they will from ours.[73]

Tozer derided the idea that unity, compromise, and tolerance are good things when fundamental truth is at stake:

It is a truism that people agree to disagree only about matters they consider unimportant. No man is tolerant when it concerns his life or the life of his child, and no one will agree to negotiate over any religious matter he considers vital to his eternal welfare.

Imagine Moses agreeing to take part in a panel discussion with Israel over the golden calf; or Elijah engaging in a gentlemanly dialogue with the prophets of Baal. Or try to picture our Lord Jesus Christ seeking a meeting of minds with the Pharisees to iron out differences . . . or Luther crawling into the presence of the pope in the name of a broader Christian fellowship.[74]

Yet what Tozer considered unimaginable and laughable is not only accepted but also more or less demanded by the modern American church. Unity in and of itself is the goal to which the church is shackled; exactly what we are united behind is considered unimportant. But it is not.

Consider the words of the great J. Gresham Machen on the necessity of a biblical worldview that applies the whole Word to the whole world:

The field of Christianity is the world. The Christian cannot be satisfied so long as any human activity is either opposed to Christianity or out of all connection with Christianity. Christianity must pervade not merely all nations, but also all of human thought. The Christian, therefore, cannot be indifferent to any branch of earnest human endeavor. It must all be brought into *some* relation to the gospel. It must be studied either in order to be demonstrated as false, or else in order to be made useful in advancing the Kingdom of God. The Kingdom must be advanced not merely extensively, but also intensively. The Church must seek to conquer not merely every man for Christ, but also the whole of man. We are accustomed to encourage ourselves in our discouragements by the thought of the time when every knee shall bow and every tongue confess that Jesus is Lord. No less inspiring is the other aspect of that same great consummation. That will also be a time when doubts have disappeared, when every contradiction has been removed, when all of science converges to one great conviction, when all of art is devoted to one great end, when all of human thinking is permeated by the refining, ennobling influence of Jesus, when every thought has been brought into subjection to the obedience of Christ.[75]

By abandoning the battle for truth in society, we have destroyed our credibility. Society no longer takes us seriously. And the gospel has been the casualty.

> We may preach with all the fervor of a reformer and yet succeed only in winning a straggler here and there, if we permit the whole collective thought of the nation or of the world to be controlled by ideas which, by the resistless force of logic, prevent Christianity from being regarded as anything more than a harmless delusion. Under such circumstances, what God desires us to do is to destroy the obstacle at its root.[76]

It is difficult to follow the command to "contend for the faith" (Jude 1:3) if we are unwilling to be contentious. Machen called on the church to train pastors with the biblical and apologetics training to defend faith against secular philosophies.

> Instead of making our theological seminaries merely centres of religious emotion, we shall make them battle-grounds of the faith, where, helped a little by the experience of Christian teachers, men are taught to fight their own battle, where they come to appreciate the real strength of the adversary and in the hard school of intellectual struggle learn to substitute for the unthinking faith of childhood the profound convictions of full-grown men. Let us not fear in this a loss of spiritual power. The Church is perishing to-day through the lack of thinking, not through an excess of it.[77]

But today, "sadly, Christians have often wimped out and grown silent instead of being bolder for the Gospel. Christians get subdued into thinking they're not supposed to rise up."[78]

David Hankins, the executive director of the Louisiana Baptist Convention, gave a sermon to students at the New Orleans Baptist Theological Seminary in 2010. It was entitled "The Confession of the Lost," based on Jeremiah 8:20: "The harvest is passed, the summer is ended, and we are not saved." Hankins nailed the problem of a church that has failed to confront a radically decaying culture. He said that Jeremiah 8:20 "speaks of lost opportunity. It speaks of ignored warning. It speaks of a certain, impending judgment that's coming on the people of God."

Hankins noted that Jeremiah's warnings are not merely history from thousands of years ago but timely, dire warnings pulled directly from today's American news headlines.

He urged,

> My challenge to you today is to become Jeremiahs for your generation, so that . . . you will boldly, unashamedly, unapologetically call them to turn before it's everlastingly too late, before there is nothing else to say but, "The harvest has passed and the summer is ended, and we are not saved." . . .
>
> It's not breaking news for you to realize that this culture is awash in sin. . . . There's no heart for repentance. The problem is that our culture has a diametrically opposed view of sin than God does.

"Let me tell you what the challenge is for you Jeremiahs in this culture," Hankins then said. "It is for you to stand up and call sin, sin. . . . Baptist preachers, we ought to put on the prophet's garb and call them to repentance."[79]

Speaking of abortion, the late, great Southern Baptist preacher Dr. Adrian Rogers said,

> Those who know the Lord dare not be silent . . .
>
> Who are the conspirators in the crime? Those Supreme Court justices who found a right to abortion in the Constitution; physicians, responsible for prolonging life, who now take life for money; abortion providers like Planned Parenthood, who are reaping a windfall in this harvest of death; willing mothers and fathers who are having their offspring put to death. All these are perpetrators in this crime, but there are others—the silent ones who will not speak up. Are you one of those? We dare not, we must not, be silent.[80]

The silence of the American church in the face of the evils of our day is the silence of death. Christ gave a chilling warning to the silent American church: "Then shall he answer them, saying, Verily I say unto you, Inasmuch as ye did it not to one of the least of these, ye did it not to me. And these shall go away into everlasting punishment: but the righteous into life eternal" (Matthew 25:45–46).

Jesus said, "I will build my church; and the gates of hell shall not prevail against it" (Matthew 16:18). Gates are defensive. Jesus implied that His church will be on the offense. How utterly we have let Him down.

Abraham Kuyper captured it nicely: "When principles that run against your deepest convictions begin to win the day, then battle is your calling, and peace has become sin; you must, at the price of dearest peace, lay your convictions bare before friend and enemy, with all the fire of your faith."[81]

CHAPTER 6

"NO OTHER GODS BEFORE ME": FROM THE TEMPLE OF GOD TO A TEMPLE OF IDOLS

In Campbell County, where I live, 2017 was a discouraging year for conservatives. The Republican board of supervisors held the line against tax increases. But the liberal-dominated school board refused to raise teacher pay, and their supporters blamed the liberal school board's failure on the "extremist" Republicans on the board of supervisors. If the board of supervisors would only raise taxes, our opponents claimed, the school board could raise teacher pay. The conservative board of supervisors, however, cut unnecessary spending, so all county employees except school employees actually received raises in 2017. But Virginia law leaves pay raises for school employees in the hands of the school board, so the board of supervisors was helpless to raise teacher pay.

But our opponents' plan worked with too many voters. They ran a liberal school board member and a liberal principal against the two conservative Republicans seeking reelection for supervisor. Amazingly enough, the school board member had voted for the budget that failed to raise teacher pay, yet she blamed it on the Republican supervisor! They also ran candidates against the two Republicans running for school board, repeatedly accusing the board of supervisors of slashing school spending (in reality, there was not a dime of school cuts under the Republican majority on the board of supervisors). Eventually the liberal candidates narrowly won the two supervisor races and both school board races.

Losing on issues of taxes alone wouldn't have been so bad. But the Timberlake school board race, with John Kinchen as our candidate, encapsulated for me the depth of the Christian community's struggle to choose its God (or god?).

Kinchen advocated keeping taxes low while cutting unnecessary spending in order to raise teacher pay. But the central theme of his campaign was a call for returning values to the classroom.

As exhibit A, as I explained in Chapter 1, Kinchen campaigned against the 2016 Obama administration order to take federal funding from any school district that refused to allow transgender students to use the bathroom of their choice.

The week before the election, his campaign found a two-page spread in the local high school yearbook, lionizing the "bravery" of a student whose hobby was cross-dressing for class. Kinchen ran a Facebook ad arguing that taxpayer dollars ought not to be used to promote sinful lifestyles in the schools.

Although he redacted the student's name and picture, it blew up in our faces. Social media went crazy. The media happily trumpeted that Kinchen had "victimized a child." As the pressure increased, Kinchen signs started to disappear from the yards of even conservative Christians, who either couldn't stand the heat or switched sides in the closing days.

Professing Christian voters began to attack Kinchen as he knocked on their doors, telling him he needed to repent. Even at his own church, folks told him, "I agree with you, but you shouldn't have made a political issue out of it."

More so than any of the other local elections in 2017, Kinchen's race was a clear clash between a campaign for biblical values and a campaign focused on promising more money.

I spent Election Day making voter phone calls and organizing volunteers, right up until the polls closed. On election night we lost by a heartbreaking seventy-three votes.

As I tried to process what had happened, the full significance took a while to sink in. The race had been a clear choice between "It is written" and "All these things will I give thee, if thou wilt fall down and worship me" (Matthew 4:9). I had watched a community change gods in front of my eyes. This wasn't New York City or Las Vegas. In the shadow of Liberty University, in the shadow of a city known as the city of churches, the buckle of the Bible Belt, my community had rejected a direct appeal to *conscience in exchange for a direct appeal to dollars. I wouldn't have believed it if I hadn't seen it unfold all day long.*

* * * * *

Our America is a land full of idolatry. We talked in Chapter 5 about the clash between Jehovah and other gods. And it's easy to look back at Old Testament Israel and marvel at their unbelief and the ease with which they turned from God to a dumb golden calf. But what's more difficult is how to apply these lessons to modern America. No one here worships idols of wood or stone, right?

In reality, the lessons of Scripture are deeply relevant to today's America.

Idolatry is not an Old Testament problem. Christ repeatedly hammered at idolatry in His day, not only in Matthew 6, as discussed below, but in Matthew 10:37–38: "He that loveth father or mother more than me is not worthy of me: and he that loveth son or daughter more than me is not worthy of me. And he that taketh not his cross, and followeth after me, is not worthy of me."

Again we are warned in the last verse of 1 John: "Little children, keep yourselves from idols" (5:21). The Bible doesn't waste words. If the warning is there, it is because God knew we needed it. An idol is simply defined as anything that is more important in my life than God Himself. Anything that soaks up the allegiance I owe to God, anything that consumes resources that should go toward doing my duty to God, is an idol. And America has plenty of them.

FINANCIAL PROSPERITY

An obvious idol is financial prosperity. Ancient Israel fell prey to it with the golden calf: "These be thy gods, O Israel, which brought thee up out of the land of Egypt" (Exodus 32:4). We saw an obvious appeal to it from the Bill Clinton campaign theme. In an effort to distract from attacks on his moral character, the campaign coined the slogan "The economy, stupid."

I hear echoes of this in the reaction of the American church to Donald Trump. In response to Trump's crude jokes about nonconsensual assaults of women (and at least Clinton's Lewinsky affair was consensual), far too many simply argued that economic issues like a border wall with Mexico, fair trade with China, and bringing jobs home to America were more important. And after Trump was elected and had meaningful accomplishments such as the selection of Justice Neil Gorsuch for the Supreme Court, I continued to hear far more comments about "what Trump is doing for my 401(k)" than expressions of gratefulness for victories in the culture war.

Christ leveled a frontal attack on the idol of financial success:

> Lay not up for yourselves treasures upon earth, where moth and rust doth corrupt, and where thieves break through and steal:
>
> But lay up for yourselves treasures in heaven, where neither moth nor rust doth corrupt, and where thieves do not break through nor steal:
>
> For where your treasure is, there will your heart be also . . .
>
> No man can serve two masters: for either he will hate the one, and love the other; or else he will hold to the one, and despise the other. Ye cannot serve God and mammon. (Matthew 6:19-24)

Christ not only warned of the existence of the golden idol but also gave us a clear test to gauge our own hearts—the amount we invest: "Where your treasure is, there will your heart be also" (v. 21). In other words, I am to examine where I invest my money, where I invest my time, where I invest my emotional energy. Perhaps how I spend my time tells even more than where I put my money. Both time and money are finite resources. However, with time, I can make more money. No amount of money will buy me any more time. Time is the greatest resource and the one which, once expended, is gone forever.

Christ differentiated between the way the world looks at money and the way a Christ follower is supposed to: "Take no thought, saying, What shall we eat? or, What shall we drink? or, Wherewithal shall we be clothed? (For after all these things do the Gentiles seek:) for your heavenly Father knoweth that ye have need of all these things. But seek ye first the kingdom of God, and his righteousness; and all these things shall be added unto you" (vv. 31-33).

For unbelievers, the "Gentiles," life revolves around Monday through Friday. Theirs is the struggle to create wealth, to live the American dream, to buy the bass boat for weekends and the beach house for retirement. Any obligation to God is a subordinate thought.

For the Christ follower, we are to "seek . . . *first* the kingdom of God" and to count on Him to add "all these things" (v. 33, emphasis added).

Additionally, Jesus offered many parables, such as the parable of the talents in Matthew 25, characterizing His people as stewards of resources belonging to God, with an obligation to use what is given in service to God.

PUBLIC OPINION

Popular opinion can be an idol. "Among the chief rulers also many believed on him; but because of the Pharisees they did not confess him, lest they should be put out of the synagogue. For they loved the praise of men more than the praise of God" (John 12:42–43).

Jesus warned us that such "belief" does not qualify as saving faith: "Whosoever therefore shall confess me before men, him will I confess also before my Father which is in heaven. But whosoever shall deny me before men, him will I also deny before my Father which is in heaven" (Matthew 10:32–33).

Just as with money, we must also choose between the approval of men and the applause of heaven. Neither Christ nor the world allows neutrality: "If the world hate you, ye know that it hated me before it hated you. If ye were of the world, the world would love his own: but because ye are not of the world, but I have chosen you out of the world, therefore the world hateth you" (John 15:18–19).

In Galatians 2 Paul related a story of a dispute he had with Peter in Antioch. Peter, a committed Jew, failed to stand against those who demanded that Gentile Christians add the rituals of the Jewish ceremonial laws to the work of Christ on Calvary. "When Peter was come to Antioch, I withstood him to the face, because he was to be blamed. For before that certain came from James, he did eat with the Gentiles: but when they were come, he withdrew and separated himself, fearing them which were of the circumcision" (vv. 11–12).

Paul fearlessly—and publicly—called out Peter for his failure to stand for the principle of salvation by faith alone:

> When I saw that they walked not uprightly according to the truth of the gospel, I said unto Peter before them all, If thou, being a Jew, livest after the manner of Gentiles, and not as do the Jews, why compellest thou the Gentiles to live as do the Jews?
>
> We who are Jews by nature, and not sinners of the Gentiles,
>
> Knowing that a man is not justified by the works of the law, but by the faith of Jesus Christ, even we have believed in Jesus Christ, that we might be justified by the faith of Christ, and not by the works of the law: for by the works of the law shall no flesh be justified. (vv. 14–16)

Peter's failure, like the chief rulers' "belief" in Christ, stemmed from desire to win a popularity contest. In our modern culture, where people will put the most private information on social media, just hoping for fifteen seconds of fame, we are particularly susceptible to making decisions under peer pressure. Public opinion can become our idol. "Instead of looking for approval to . . . the Audience of One, we look for it in the shifting sands of public opinion."[82]

In his work *Prophetic Untimeliness*, the great contemporary British theologian Os Guinness spoke of the "idol of relevance." "How on earth," he asked, "have we Christians become so irrelevant when we have tried so hard to be relevant?"[83]

He did not leave his own question unanswered:

> By our breathless chase after relevance without a matching commitment to faithfulness, we have become not only unfaithful but irrelevant; by our determined efforts to redefine ourselves in ways that are more compelling to the modern world than are faithful to Christ, we have lost not only our identity but our authority and our relevance. Our crying need is to be faithful as well as relevant . . .
>
> Thus for followers of Jesus Christ . . . it is time to challenge the idol of relevance.[84]

He added,

> The faith-world of John Wesley, Jonathan Edwards, John Jay, William Wilberforce, . . . Hudson Taylor, D. L. Moody, Charles Spurgeon, Oswald Chambers . . . and John Stott is disappearing. In its place a new evangelicalism is arriving in which therapeutic self-concern overshadows knowing God, spirituality displaces theology, end-times escapism crowds out day-to-day discipleship, marketing triumphs over mission, references to opinion polls outweigh reliance on biblical exposition, concerns for power and relevance are more obvious than concern for piety and faithfulness, talk of reinventing the church has replaced prayer for revival.[85]

Guinness agreed with the contention that the church has adapted to the world's language and paradigm. He outlined the four-step process by which modernism wins and the gospel loses:

1. Assumption. The church assumes that "some aspect of modern thought or life is . . . significant, and therefore worth acknowledging, or superior to what Christians know or do, and therefore worth adopting."[86]

2. Abandonment. The church then abandons any of the old theology that doesn't fit the modern ideal, without questioning whether the old doctrine was true. "The modification or removal of offending assumptions is permanent."[87]

3. Adaptation. "What remains of traditional beliefs and practices is altered to fit with the new assumption."[88]

4. Assimilation. "The result is worldliness, or Christian capitulation to some aspect of the culture of its day."[89]

At this point in the history of the American church, we have almost totally assimilated to modern culture. At one time what offended God offended us. Now we are instead offended by what offends the world.

Guinness issued a dire warning, which we would do well to heed: "For all the lofty recent statements on biblical authority, a great part of the evangelical community has made a historic shift. It has transferred authority from *Sola Scriptura* (by Scripture alone) to *Sola Cultura* (by culture alone)."[90] That statement freezes the blood—all the more so because it is true.

He further noted,

> As the reinterpretations deepen, the losses steadily mount:
>
> First, there is a loss of courage. The reinterpretations are always in one direction only.
>
> Second, there is a loss of continuity. The diluted faith is no longer the faith of our fathers and mothers . . . It is a different faith.
>
> Third, there is a loss of credibility. There is too little of believable substance that any thoughtful person is asked to believe.
>
> And finally, there is a loss if identity. . . ."At that point the creed becomes a way of saying what the infidel next door believes too."[91]

It is no wonder the world looks at us and laughs. Our shallow worship is surpassed only by our utter irrelevance outside the walls of the church: "Evangelicals were once known as 'the serious people.' It is sad to note that today many evangelicals are the most superficial of religious believers—lightweight in thinking, gossamer-thin in theology, and avid proponents of spirituality-lite in terms of preaching and responses to life."[92]

As Guinness wrote, "When society is increasingly godless and the church increasingly corrupt, faithfulness carries a price: The man or woman who lives by faith does not fit in."[93]

Popular opinion, the "idol of relevance," cannot be our end in itself. Truth, as dictated by God's Word, must be the end. As French philosopher Simone Weil put it, "To be always relevant, you have to say things which are eternal."[94] It's time the church got back to that.

ENTERTAINMENT AND LEISURE TIME

Perhaps one of the greatest idols in today's America is leisure time. I have noticed that we all think we are terribly busy. We all think we are working much more than we actually are. We all think we have little time for leisure. The statistics say we are dead wrong.

According to the Bureau of Labor Statistics, the average American banks a full five hours of leisure time each day![95] That's thirty-five hours a week, almost as much as a forty-hour work week! And that may be a conservative estimate. Nielsen, the television ratings company, reported that the average American watches over five hours of television daily![96]

According to a LifeWay Research study, only nineteen percent of churchgoers read their Bibles daily.[97] According to the *Washington Post*, the average American spends seven minutes or less on religious activities each day (Monday through Saturday)—though on Sundays that figure "balloons" to almost thirty-five minutes.[98] According to Gallup, only thirty-eight percent of Americans attend even one church service weekly![99] "Not surprisingly, religious practices spike on Sunday. But even on Sundays, Americans spend more time grooming themselves than they do praying or going to church."[100]

Meanwhile, we spend five hours a day watching television. It's a good bet most of that time is not watching Dr. Charles Stanley or the Christian Broadcasting Network.

According to the Bureau of Labor Statistics, the average American consumer spends over $2,900 per year on entertainment.[101] According to Barna Group, twelve percent of "born again Christians" tithed in 2012.[102] While seventy-nine percent of evangelicals reported making charitable contributions, the numbers show this isn't tithing.[103] Eighty-seven percent of Americans reported making $2,500 or less in charitable contributions in 2012; seventy-five percent gave $1,000 or less in total charitable contributions (including religious ones).[104] Meanwhile, the *average* American spent $2,900 on entertainment!

Whether it's our time or our money, our choices make it clear—leisure time is an idol in modern America. It has displaced God from our priority list almost entirely.

The ancient Roman empire managed to blind the eyes of its people to the corruption of the government with the simple expedient of "bread and races." The Roman satirical poet Juvenal wrote, "Long ago, the people cast off its worries, when we stopped selling our votes. A body that used to confer commands, legions, rods, and everything else, has now narrowed its scope, and is eager and anxious for two things only: bread and races."[105]

Michael Snyder, an author and 2018 Republican congressional candidate from Idaho, put it well: "We are simply not the same country that we used to be. Americans are proud, selfish, greedy, arrogant, ungrateful, treacherous and completely addicted to entertainment and pleasure. Our country is literally falling apart all around us, but most Americans are so plugged into entertainment that they can't even be bothered to notice what is happening."[106]

Jesus said, "Where your treasure is, there will your heart be also" (Matthew 6:21). American Christianity has a serious heart problem.

It is interesting to consider what an impartial observer from a foreign land would conclude that American Christians worship. I'm not sure what the answer would be. But it is a certainty that such an observer could not conclude that the object of our worship is the God of the Bible.

EDUCATION

This is perhaps the most sacred of sacred cows. Even raising the topic is essentially taboo, almost "un-American." But honesty demands that it be raised nonetheless.

In early America the purpose of education was to allow the individual to gain knowledge of God. Our founders were not far removed from the era when the common people were told they must approach God through priests and popes. They were kept intentionally illiterate in order that they might approach God only through their religious leaders, thus arrogating vast power to those leaders.

Our early founders reacted to this just as viscerally as later generations reacted to taxation without representation. In 1647 the Massachusetts legislature passed the first public school law in American history. The act became known as the Old Deluder Satan Act. It reads in part,

It being one chief project of the old deluder, Satan, to keep men from the knowledge of the Scriptures, as in former times by keeping them in an unknown tongue . . . that so at least the true sense and meaning of the original might be clouded by false glosses of saint-seeming deceivers; that learning may not be buried in the grave of our fathers in church and commonwealth, the Lord assisting our endeavors—

It is therefore *ordered*, that every township in this jurisdiction, after the Lord hath increased them to the number of fifty householders, shall then forthwith appoint one within their town to teach all such children as shall resort to him, to write and read; whose wages shall be paid, either by the parents or masters of such children, or by the inhabitants in general.[107]

But as we will discuss at length later, education in America has morphed from being a means to aid men and women in their understanding of God to being a means to the creation and perfection of a good democratic citizen and thus a good democratic state. Education has also morphed from being a means of improving the mind to being primarily a means of improving one's financial position. This confluence of emphases has produced an ideal of education that is held up as an end in itself, a goal in itself, the ultimate realization of the American dream.

Education certainly has a unique heritage in American history. Booker T. Washington saw education as the way "up from slavery" (as he titled his autobiography) for African Americans following the War between the States. His Tuskegee Institute did much to make his dream a reality.

Generations of American parents have seen education as the way to "give our children more opportunities than we had ourselves." And education certainly has its place. I am the beneficiary of seven years of higher education, culminating in a law degree.

But like with so many other good things, Americans have tended to worship "the creature more than the Creator" (Romans 1:25)—to worship the blessings of God rather than the God who gives blessings.

Consider the dollar figures. During the 2016 campaign Donald Trump noted that our federal and state governments lavish $620 billion on K–12 education alone, over $12,000 per student.[108] Yet, at every level, we are constantly told that we are shortchanging our children. We are constantly told that education is underfunded. Never mind that the United States ranks third in the entire world in per-pupil spending.[109]

That figure doesn't even count student fund-raisers or parental expenditures on books, school supplies, or uniforms. It figures only government spending.

According to the College Board, it costs an average of $20,090 for an in-state student to attend a public university for one year. For out-of-state students the cost increases to $34,220. More than forty-four million people in the US hold a combined $1.4 trillion in student debt.[110] And according to the US Department of Education's National Center for Education Statistics, in 2015 America spent more per student on postsecondary education than any other of twenty-five countries surveyed.[111]

"Where your treasure is, there will your heart be also" (Matthew 6:21). America continues to pile its treasure into the promise of education as the remedy for what ails us.

A quick Google search reveals the talking points:

- "Higher education stimulates a person's innate quest for information and creates strong, empowered decision-makers who contribute positively to our community, country and global society." (Anne Rondeau, president of the College of DuPage)[112]
- "Education is our passport to the future, for tomorrow belongs only to the people who prepare for it today." (Malcolm X)[113]
- "Early childhood education is the key to the betterment of society." (Maria Montessori, founder of the Montessori education system)
- "Establishing lasting peace is the work of education; all politics can do is keep us out of war." (Maria Montessori)

- "Until we get equality in education, we won't have an equal society." (Supreme Court Justice Sonia Sotomayor)[114]
- "Democracy cannot succeed unless those who express their choice are prepared to choose wisely. The real safeguard of democracy, therefore, is education." (Franklin D. Roosevelt)
- "Public education is our greatest pathway to opportunity in America. So we need to invest in and strengthen our public universities today, and for generations to come." (Michelle Obama)[115]
- "A quality education grants us the ability to fight the war on ignorance and poverty. . . . Encouragement of higher education for our youth is critical to the success of our collective future." (Former Representative Charles Rangel)[116]
- "From kindergarten to graduation, I went to public schools, and I know that they are a key to being sure that every child has a chance to succeed and to rise in the world." (Dick Cheney)[117]
- "Education is the silver bullet to improve this Nation's standing worldwide . . . and our teachers know that." (Former Representative Solomon Ortiz)
- "When the students are occupied, they're not juvenile delinquents. I believe education is a capital investment." (Former Senator Arlen Specter)
- "A liberal education is at the heart of a civil society, and at the heart of a liberal education is the act of teaching." (Former Major League Baseball Commissioner Bart Giamatti)
- "Our progress as a nation can be no swifter than our progress in education." (John F. Kennedy)
- "Education then, beyond all other devices of human origin, is the great equalizer of the conditions of men,—the balance-wheel of the social machinery." (Horace Mann)[118]
- "Education is our only political safety. Outside of this ark, all is deluge." (Horace Mann)[119]

The American education complex, whether K–12 or higher education, has become a vast industry, utilizing marketing techniques as well as any private corporation. It also utilizes built-in advantages such as compulsory taxpayer support and massive government subsidies, which most private businesses simply do not have.

The National Education Association, the leading American teacher's union, markets the theme that education is the solution to humanity's problems. On its website it offers teachers a number of quotes to help them "prepare remarks or materials for American Education Week."[120]

- "There is a place in America to take a stand: it is public education. It is the underpinning of our cultural and political system. It is the great common ground. Public education after all is the engine that moves us as a society toward a common destiny . . . It is in public education that the American dream begins to take shape." (Tom Brokaw)
- "Education is the vaccine for violence." (Edward James Olmos)
- "A teacher affects eternity." (Henry Adams)

None of this chapter is intended to denigrate the value of financial success, influence, relaxation, or learning. The point is to ask us to consider— have any of these things grown so all encompassing, so indispensable to us, that they have begun to consume resources that should have been devoted to God's work? Have any of these even begun to tempt us to place our trust in the temporal instead of the eternal? Have we bought the line that public education (or education generally) is the underpinning of our cultural and political system or that teaching academic facts affects eternity? If we have, I submit we have made ourselves an idol.

Isaiah spoke of ancient Judah. But his words are just as applicable to modern, virtual-reality America: "Their land also is full of idols; they worship the work of their own hands, that which their own fingers have made" (2:8).

Ezekiel's description of ancient Israel is likewise straight out of our own headlines:

> The word of the LORD came unto me, saying,
>
> Son of man, these men have set up their idols in their heart, and put the stumblingblock of their iniquity before their face: should I be enquired of at all by them?
>
> Therefore speak unto them, and say unto them, Thus saith the Lord God; Every man of the house of Israel that setteth up his idols in his heart, and putteth the stumblingblock of his iniquity before his face, and cometh to the prophet; I the Lord will answer him that cometh according to the multitude of his idols;
>
> That I may take the house of Israel in their own heart, because they are all estranged from me through their idols.
>
> Therefore say unto the house of Israel, Thus saith the Lord God; Repent, and turn yourselves from your idols; and turn away your faces from all your abominations.
>
> For every one of the house of Israel, or of the stranger that sojourneth in Israel, which separateth himself from me, and setteth up his idols in his heart, and putteth the stumblingblock of his iniquity before his face, and cometh to a prophet to enquire of him concerning me; I the Lord will answer him by myself:
>
> And I will set my face against that man, and will make him a sign and a proverb, and I will cut him off from the midst of my people; and ye shall know that I am the Lord. (14:2–8)

America—and the American church—have done the same. We have broken the Great Commandment: "Thou shalt have no other gods before me" (Exodus 20:3). Now, "should [God] be enquired of at all by [us]" (Ezekiel 14:3)? We wonder why the glory of God has departed. It hasn't; we have departed from Him and served other gods.

Joshua's call rings with a warning tone today, just as much as when he gave it: "If it seem evil unto you to serve the Lord, choose you this day whom ye will serve; whether the gods which your fathers served that were on the other side of the flood, or the gods of the Amorites, in whose land ye dwell: but as for me and my house, we will serve the Lord" (Joshua 24:15).

By and large, the American church has demonstrated by our actions (regardless of our words) that we are content to worship "the gods of the Amorites, in whose land [we] dwell." We would do well to heed Joshua's command in verse 23: "Now therefore put away . . . the strange gods which are among you, and incline your heart unto the Lord God of Israel."

CHAPTER 7

"REDEEMING" ROMANS 13

My three years' time studying at Liberty University School of Law was one of the most challenging experiences of my life. I was going to school full-time, and trying at the same time to work more or less full-time to feed a wife and two small children.

But it was an incredibly rewarding and memorable time too. It was rewarding to find myself forced to stretch beyond what I had done before, mentally and theologically.

One class was taught by Liberty's law school dean, Mat Staver, and his assistant dean, Rena Lindevaldsen. It was called "Foundations of Law." It emphasized the Juedo-Christian foundations of the Anglo-American legal system, going back to and beyond Blackstone.

But one day in particular shook me up, and forced me to reconsider thoughts I had considered settled.

The professor asked us a tough question. To what extent is civil disobedience justified in resisting the murder of unborn children? At first, I gave the easy, stock answer I had developed over time. "Well, maybe civil disobedience would be OK, but it's not going to be effective in changing hearts and minds. We should work through the political system for change instead."

But then the professor went for the jugular. WHY did I hold that position? Did I really believe an unborn child was fully human? And if so, would I not be civilly disobedient if the child slated for death had already been born?

It shook me to my toes. I absolutely believed the biblical and scientific facts that an unborn child is created in God's image (biblical), with her own independent DNA (scientific). Then WHY was I inconsistent?

Suppose the abortion clinic were instead a day care center? Suppose at the end of each work day, if a parent called in to say that he did not wish to pick his infant up anymore, that the baby was just too inconvenient, the workers took the unwanted baby to the back door and threw the baby over a cliff to his death? And suppose the Supreme Court had declared these "very-late-term abortions" legal? Would I REALLY sit by and do nothing? Would I not use physical force, in violation of the law, and try to snatch that baby to a place of safety?

Why, then, was my position different for an unborn child? Where had I gotten my "logic?" It certainly wasn't from Scripture, which clearly teaches, "My substance was not hid from thee, when I was made in secret, and curiously wrought in the lowest parts of the earth. Thine eyes did see my substance, yet being unperfect; and in thy book all my members were written, which in continuance were fashioned, when as yet there was none of them" (Psalm 139:15-16). The Bible clearly teaches that an unborn child is as human at conception as she is at six years old.

I had to come to grips with the sobering, shocking reality instead of drawing my conclusions from the Word of God, I had allowed Caesar to determine for me what was "right," based on what was "legal." And it was in no small part due to hearing preaching on Romans 13:1-7, and the "sinfulness" of opposing the civil government.

It was a life-altering moment. Never again have I been content to believe that Romans 13 is an excuse to sit silently by while injustice occurs all around, with government sanction. Unfortunately, the same false preaching that had distorted my view of truth continues to be preached in pulpits across America, with devastating effects—especially for those voiceless babies.

This chapter is written in their memory—and with a prayer that Christian America would reject the false teaching, and take a biblical stand against state injustice once again.

* * * * *

In all of Scripture, perhaps no passage has been subjected to greater exegetical malpractice than this passage. And perhaps there is no passage in

Scripture where this malpractice has had more devastating consequences to America. I speak of Romans 13:1-7.

Many preachers like to preach against "proof-texting"—that is, picking one verse or passage in isolation and building an entire theology around it. Yet, when it comes to the proper response of the Christian to the State—the civil government—these same preachers are often all too happy to violate their own rule. They twist Romans 13 into something it is not, in the process doing violence to the vast array of advice and warning the rest of Scripture gives in relation to government.

Perhaps the key passage used to argue against Christian involvement in civil government is Romans 13:1-7:

> Let every soul be subject unto the higher powers. For there is no power but of God: the powers that be are ordained of God.
>
> Whosoever therefore resisteth the power, resisteth the ordinance of God: and they that resist shall receive to themselves damnation.
>
> For rulers are not a terror to good works, but to the evil. Wilt thou then not be afraid of the power? do that which is good, and thou shalt have praise of the same:
>
> For he is the minister of God to thee for good. But if thou do that which is evil, be afraid; for he beareth not the sword in vain: for he is the minister of God, a revenger to execute wrath upon him that doeth evil.
>
> Wherefore ye must needs be subject, not only for wrath, but also for conscience sake.
>
> For for this cause pay ye tribute also: for they are God's ministers, attending continually upon this very thing.
>
> Render therefore to all their dues: tribute to whom tribute is due; custom to whom custom; fear to whom fear; honour to whom honour.

Yet to get from Paul's inspired words to an "ethic" of Christian noninvolvement, theologians I will call "Christian Pacifist" ("CP") or "Radical Two Kingdoms" ("R2K") theologians (much more on them in Chapter 11) have to argue, either implicitly or explicitly, for two propositions—neither of which can survive careful biblical exegesis.

First, they must argue that Romans 13 is a blanket order of absolute (or almost-absolute) Christian submission to any edict from a government official. This is the easier proposition to hang a theory upon, but it is not scripturally supportable.

Second, they have to argue that Romans 13, as a blanket order of submission to government, is the ONLY biblical command to Christians regarding their relationship to government. He must find a way to dismiss without addressing the avalanche of biblical commands regarding government outside of Romans 13. This is even more impossible to do honestly.

Sometimes Mark 12:17 is used in conjunction with Romans 13. Here, Jesus tells the Pharisees, "Render to Caesar the things that are Caesar's, and to God the things that are God's." Far too many Christian leaders do a cursory reading of these two passages, without any consideration of the wealth of other scriptural passages on God's expectations for His people with regard to government, and from these two passages alone construct a "Christian ethic" of government. It can be stated in one sentence: "The Christian is bound to absolute obedience to all instructions of any government official unless commanded to personally and directly take any action explicitly forbidden in the text of Scripture."

Regardless of the array of other biblical passages, this cursory reading of Romans 13 and Mark 12:17 falls far short of "rightly dividing the Word of truth" in these passages alone. A little careful review of the text and context shows why.

The shallow justification most often offered goes like this: "If Christ and Paul, living under a brutal Roman dictatorship with no rights to self-government at all, commanded obedience to government, then the Christian's responsibility to government is only to obey, not to seek change. Paul and Christ never urged people to work to change government."

But the R2K theorists' reasoning, when the text and history are viewed carefully, actually undercuts their own argument. Both Mark 12 and Romans 13, read carefully and in the context of the times, are fairly revolutionary statements.

The Roman Empire was rather unique among ancient world empires, in that Rome did not generally wipe out conquered nations and take the inhabitants away as captives. Instead, Roman policy generally was to allow conquered nations to generally continue their customary religious and social practices, as long as they paid the required tribute to Rome, and acknowledged Caesar, the Roman emperor, as the supreme power. Rome generally allowed conquered nations to continue worshipping their god(s) of choice, as long as Caesar was acknowledged as supreme. In fact, many Romans themselves were polytheistic.

The one non-negotiable was submission to Caesar—considered to be both a divine religious figure and the political head of state—as the supreme power.

The problem for the Jews, which the Pharisees sought to exploit against Jesus, was that the Old Testament taught them that Jehovah was supreme, and that "thou shalt have no other gods before Me" (Exodus 20:3). The Pharisees themselves had reached a cozy compromise with Caesar, in which they could serve as religious leaders for the Jewish people, preserving an outward appearance of the worship of Jehovah, but only by the consent and with the imprimatur of Caesar.

In an effort to trap Jesus, they demanded of Him, "Is it lawful to give tribute to Caesar, or not?" (Mark 12:14). They hoped to either get Jesus to forbid tribute to Caesar, which would get Him killed by the Romans, or to declare Jehovah subservient to Caesar, which would violate the First Commandment.

What they got was, contrary to a lazy reading of the text, a truly revolutionary statement given the political reality of the day. Jesus did command proper submission to Caesar, the State. But the truly revolutionary statement is the rest of the verse "[Render] to God the things that are God's."

In so doing, Jesus issued a direct challenge to both the state religion and the political government of Rome. He expressly upheld the First Commandment, that Jehovah IS the supreme authority over man, not Caesar. In the end, His proclamation of God's authority over Caesar was a charge brought against Him before Pilate. "If thou let this man go, thou art not Caesar's friend: whosoever maketh himself a king speaketh against Caesar" (John 19:12).

But the real import of Christ's words was not felt until after His ascension. The brutal Roman persecution of the Church under Nero, Diocletian and other Caesars was not because the early Christians proclaimed Jesus. As R.C. Sproul, Jr. points out in his blog,

> The Christians' problem was more political than narrowly theological. You see the very first creed of the church was just three words long, but managed to confront Rome at its heart. Christians were those who confessed Christ is Lord. They died by the thousands because they would not confess that Caesar is Lord.[121]

Today, the World's demand is the same. They aren't too concerned if the Church preaches Jesus, just as long as we keep it within the church and interpersonal contacts. As long as the Church does not assert God's authority over nations, and man's universal accountability to Him as the ultimate Source of all law, we don't present a problem. To quote Sproul again,

> We're like the Pharisees. We have our worship services, our private convictions, and that's where our faith ends. The rest of our lives are committed to the authority of the state, and to the diversions and distractions the broader culture provides. We are in no danger because we are no danger. When the world calls our convictions "hate" we simply change them, insisting that our response to the wholesale turning over of God's created order is more love, more appeasement, more assurance that we are not a danger . . .

> We worship a Jesus who will save us from our sins, but whose reign we're willing to negotiate. We worship a state that simply requires of us that we be nice and keep our convictions to ourselves. We worship distraction, so that we won't have to face our idolatry. We worship the acceptance of the broader culture, and sacrifice all else to get it.[122]

But that is emphatically not the response of Christ in Mark 12. Instead, He proclaimed anew the old truth of the First Commandment, that man is accountable first to Jehovah, and only secondarily to the State.

This brings us to Romans 13. And again, a lazy reading of the passage is debunked by a more careful one. It is important to consider that Paul's words are more than just "religious" pronouncements. His discourse in Romans 13 certainly carries divine authority, but it is more than a purely theological treatise. His argument is also intensely logical; it is divine truth applied with careful, God-centered reasoning.

Paul's careful exposition instructs Christians to submit to earthly authority. But he begins his argument in verse one with a foundational appeal - not to Caesar's authority, but to Jehovah's. "For there is no power but of God: the powers that be are ordained of God."

Paul's argument for Christian submission is expressly based in the reality that human government exercises only delegated authority. Again, in the context of his day this is revolutionary. Paul is only sharpening and making more explicit Christ's earlier statement in Mark 12. Christians are to submit, NOT because Caesar is sovereign, but because he is NOT.

The crux of Paul's argument is a classic logical if/then syllogism. If human government exercises power delegated from God, then Christians are to obey it. Not because government is omnipotent, but expressly because it is not. He repeats the syllogism in verse six: "For for this cause pay ye tribute also: for they are God's ministers, attending continually upon this very thing."

Why are Christians to pay taxes? Not because Caesar says so, but because government officials are "ministers of God." Their divinely appointed job is stated in verses three and four: "attending continually" to praising good works, and "execut[ing] wrath upon him that doeth evil."

It is critical to grasp the significance of Paul's words, inspired by the Holy Spirit. Paul never commands Christians to submit or to pay taxes because of the State's authority. " . . . God is the foundation of all authority, He exercises that foundation because He is the author and the owner of His creation. He is the foundation upon which all other authority stands or falls."[123]

We are to obey "for this cause"—because human government was ordained by God—as far back as Noah and now reaffirmed by Paul—to exercise delegated authority from God, to reward good and punish evil.

Think very carefully. If Christians are to submit "for this cause," that is, because the State exercises delegated authority to reward good and punish evil, then if the "cause" disappears, so does the effect. Government officials, no less than "ordinary citizens," are accountable to God for their actions. God's commands as to how we are to treat others are no less applicable to those in civil government than those outside. Thus, when a government official acts in violation of God's commands to him, and ceases to "reward the good and punish the evil"—assuming we take God's Word at face value, the "cause" for Christian submission vanishes!

Here the R2K theologian will counter with the example of Peter in Acts 5:29, who, when told to stop preaching in the name of Jesus, replied, "We ought to obey God rather than men." The R2K theologian cannot argue that civil disobedience is never permissible, but will limit it to one of two categories. Christian civil disobedience is permissible either where a Christian is forbidden from pursuing a purely evangelistic action—preaching Jesus—or perhaps more broadly where a Christian is expressly ordered to personally participate in doing—or omitting to do—something directly forbidden or ordered in the Word of God.

But there is simply no support for this in the text of Acts 5:29. Peter never said, "We must obey God rather than men where preaching Jesus is concerned." No such limitation appears in the text. Nor is it a necessary implication that "we must obey God" only when commanded to personally participate in a sin ourselves. Instead, the CP theorist must impose his own extra-biblical beliefs upon the text; he cannot reach his conclusion from the words themselves.

Does not the same God who commands us to be saved also command us to tell other men? And did not the same Jesus who tells us "If ye love Me, keep

My commandments," also tell us to "Go ye therefore and teach all nations . . . teaching them to observe all things whatsoever I have commanded you"? Can enforced silence in the face of another's injustice be a Christian ethic? Not on the basis of Acts 5:29 or Romans 13.

Nor has this been a position the Church has historically taken, as we cover in detail in another chapter. Would the R2K theologian truly argue Corrie ten Boom violated Romans 13 by hiding Dutch Jews from the Nazis? No law ordered her to personally kill any Jews. No law prevented her from praying for protection for the Jews. She was never commanded to personally, actively participate in the State's unjust actions. But she was not content with an "ethic of silence," in an effort to be "her brother's keeper" and "love her neighbor as herself."

Would the R2K theologian argue that the largely Christian population that ran the Underground Railroad in violation of the Fugitive Slave Act in pre-Civil War America was in violation of Romans 13? No law commanded the Quaker "stationmasters" on the Railroad to own slaves themselves. No law commanded them not to pray for the slaves to reach safety. But they were not satisfied with an "ethic of silence." Their obedience to God's higher law moved them to disobey—beyond evangelism only, and beyond the level of a direct command to participate in slavery themselves.

In 1750, Dr. Jonathan Mayhew preached an historic sermon entitled "A Discourse Concerning Unlimited Submission and Non-Resistance to the Higher Powers." John Adams called Mayhew "the morning gun of the Revolution." Mayhew also pointed to Paul's if/then syllogism:

> [D]oes this argument conclude for the duty of paying tribute, custom, reverence, honor and obedience, to such persons as (although they bear the title of rulers) use all their power to hurt and injure the public? such as are not God's ministers, but Satan's? such as do not take care of, and attend upon, the public interest, but their own, to the ruin of the public? that is, in short, to such as have no natural and just claim at all to tribute, custom, reverence, honor and obedience?[124] . . . For what can be more absurd than

an argument thus framed? "Rulers are, by their office, bound to consult the public welfare and the good of society: therefore you are bound to pay them tribute, to honor, and to submit to them, even when they destroy the public welfare, and are a common pest to society, by acting in direct contradiction to the nature and end of their office . . .

We may very safely assert these two things in general, without undermining government: One is, That no civil rulers are to be obeyed when they enjoin things that are inconsistent with the commands of God: All such disobedience is lawful and glorious[125] . . . . disobedience to them is a duty, not a crime.[126]

Mayhew goes on to reason that the biblical command to children to submit to parents is similar to the command to Christian citizens to submit to government. Yet the command to children is also qualified in scripture. Let us examine Ephesians 6:1-4 from a CP vantage point.

Children, obey your parents in the Lord: for this is right. Honour thy father and mother; which is the first commandment with promise; That it may be well with thee, and thou mayest live long on the earth. And, ye fathers, provoke not your children to wrath: but bring them up in the nurture and admonition of the Lord.

Certainly children are to submit to parents. Under a CP line of reasoning, this command is absolute unless the child is ordered to personally participate in an action expressly forbidden by Scripture. Yet, as Mayhew notes, even in the parent/child context the biblical command to submit is not absolute. The instruction is qualified, in the text itself. Children are to obey "in the Lord." And fathers, in the same passage and context, are instructed to bring up children in the admonition "of the Lord." As long as the father fulfills his responsibility, the child is bound to obey. But, as Mayhew argues,

Suppose this parent at length runs distracted, and attempts, in his mad fit, to cut all his children's throats: Now, in this case, is not the reason before assigned, why these children should obey their parent while he continued of a sound mind, namely, their common good, a reason equally conclusive for disobeying and resisting him, since he is become delirious, and attempts their ruin?[127]

Under these circumstances—that is, a father seeking the destruction of the life of a child and his siblings, the child is no longer bound to blindly submit (even though he himself is not being required to wield the knife). Rather, he must obey "in the Lord," but is justified in resisting in defense of his life and those of his siblings, when the father ceases to govern in the "admonition of the Lord," and attempts the destruction of those over whom he is charged with exercising authority delegated from God.

Mayhew concludes:

> To conclude: Let us all learn to be free, and to be loyal. Let us not profess ourselves vassals to the lawless pleasure of any man on earth. But let us remember, at the same time, government is sacred, and not to be trifled with. . . . Let us prize our freedom; but not use our liberty for a cloak of maliciousness. . . . For which reason I would exhort you to pay all due Regard to the government over us; to the KING and all in authority; and to lead a quiet and peaceable life.— And while I am speaking of loyalty to our earthly Prince, suffer me just to put you in mind to be loyal also to the supreme RULER of the universe, by whom kings reign, and princes decree justice. To which king eternal immortal, invisible, even to the ONLY WISE GOD, be all honor and praise, DOMINION and thanksgiving, through JESUS CHRIST our LORD. AMEN.[128]

The great Scottish theologian Samuel Rutherford interpreted Romans 13 in this way.

> It is no more lawful for me to resign to another my power of natural self-defence than I can resign my power to defend the innocent drawn to death, and the wives, children, and posterity that God had tyed me unto. (2.) The people can no more resign power of self-defence, which nature hath given them, than they can be guilty of

self-murder, and be wanting in the lawful defence of kingdom and religion, (3.) Though you make one their king with absoluteness of power, yet when he use that transcendent power, not for the safety but for the destruction of the state, it is known they could not resign to another that power which neither God nor nature gave them, to wit, a power to destroy themselves.[129]

In such a nation as ours, a "government of the people," where standing for the laws of God may be as simple as casting a vote on an informed, biblical basis, civil disobedience is certainly not always necessary. In no way does this book argue a Christian should be anything other than a law-abiding citizen in every way possible. But the cheap and lazy claim that Romans 13 forbids resistance to State injustice, even carefully considered in the light of the text alone and without responsible cross-referencing, is insupportable. Certainly, then, if the claim Romans 13 is a blanket command of unquestioning submission is unscriptural, certainly the claim the Christian's ONLY responsibility with regard to the State is submission, is straying even farther afield from the text.

Aside from the evidence of the text of Romans 13 and Mark 12 themselves, careful biblical exegesis requires that these verses be considered in light of the mass of other scriptures pertaining to government, and to the role of God's people in it.

In Proverbs 31, a mother instructs her son, a king, in his duty to God as a government official. "It . . . is not for kings to drink wine; nor for princes strong drink: Lest they drink, and forget the law, and pervert the judgment of any of the afflicted" (Proverbs 31:4-5).

"Open thy mouth for the dumb in the cause of all such as are appointed to destruction. Open thy mouth, judge righteously, and plead the cause of the poor and needy" (Proverbs 31:8-9).

Exodus 23:6-8: "Thou shalt not wrest the judgment of thy poor in his cause. Keep thee far from a false matter; and the innocent and righteous slay thou not: for I will not justify the wicked. And thou shalt take no gift: for the gift blindeth the wise, and perverteth the words of the righteous."

Amos 5:12: "For I know your manifold transgressions and your mighty sins: they afflict the just, they take a bribe, and they turn aside the poor in the gate from their right."

Psalm 82:3-4: "Defend the poor and fatherless: do justice to the afflicted and needy. Deliver the poor and needy: rid them out of the hand of the wicked.

Perhaps the most disturbing passage to a Church committed to an "ethic of silence" is Proverbs 24:11-12:

> "If thou forbear to deliver them that are drawn unto death, and those that are ready to be slain; If thou sayest, Behold, we knew it not; doth not he that pondereth the heart consider it? and he that keepeth thy soul, doth not he know it? and shall not he render to every man according to his works?"

Pro-life activist Penny Lea tells of an old man who related his haunting testimony to her after she spoke one night.

> I lived in Germany during the Nazi holocaust. I considered myself a Christian. I attended church since I was a small boy. We had heard the stories of what was happening to the Jews, but like most people today in this country, we tried to distance ourselves from the reality of what was really taking place. What could anyone do to stop it?
>
> A railroad track ran behind our small church, and each Sunday morning we would hear the whistle from a distance and then the clacking of the wheels moving over the track. We became disturbed when one Sunday we noticed cries coming from the train as it passed by. We grimly realized that the train was carrying Jews. They were like cattle in those cars!
>
> Week after week that train whistle would blow. We would dread to hear the sound of those old wheels because we knew that the Jews would begin to cry out to us as they passed our church. It was so terribly disturbing! We could do nothing to help these poor miserable people, yet their screams tormented us. We knew exactly at what time that whistle would blow, and we decided the only way to keep from being so disturbed by the cries was to start singing our hymns.

By the time that train came rumbling past the church yard, we were singing at the top of our voices. If some of the screams reached our ears, we'd just sing a little louder until we could hear them no more. Years have passed and no one talks about it much anymore, but I still hear that train whistle in my sleep. I can still hear them crying out for help. God forgive all of us who called ourselves Christians, yet did nothing to intervene.[130]

Yet in the sad and unscriptural logic of the CP theorists, this man followed Romans 13, and Corrie ten Boom lived in violation of it.

I close this chapter by going back to the words of Jesus. When asked what was the greatest commandment, He replied, "Thou shalt love the Lord thy God with all thy heart, and with all thy soul, and with all thy mind. This is the first and great commandment. And the second is like unto it, Thou shalt love thy neighbour as thyself" (Matthew 22:37-39).

Loving God and loving our neighbor. Serving Caesar doesn't make the list. And loving our neighbors as ourselves cannot be squared with the CP "ethic of silence."

In the midst of a nation where the unborn are legally dismembered and sold for spare parts, silence not only is not biblically commanded; it is biblically forbidden.

If we consider "the whole counsel of God," and actually take the words as divinely inspired, the "ethic of silence" becomes, as Dr. Joel McDurmon puts it, "a doctrine made up by lazy theologians for lazy Christians."[131] Or, to put it simply, just plain disobedience.

May we as His people reject the "ethic of silence." Let us not embrace the rejection Jesus promises in Matthew 25:45-46: "Then shall he answer them, saying, Verily I say unto you, Inasmuch as ye did it not to one of the least of these, ye did it not to me. And these shall go away into everlasting punishment: but the righteous into life eternal."

That is the "ethic of silence." It is NOT Romans 13.

CHAPTER 8

GOD AND CAESAR: "I AM GOD, AND THERE IS NONE OTHER"

You have heard the story of the fishermen Peter and John, told by their rulers to cease preaching Jesus Christ. You've heard that two ordinary people had the courage to stand and say, "We must obey God rather than men" (Acts 5:29 NASB).

I've seen that courage with my own eyes.

My parents, Rick and Marilyn Boyer, were committed to a Christian education for their kids. When I was in kindergarten, our church's school was really too far away for Mom to carry two babies and kindergarten and first-grade boys there every day.

So she convinced my dad to let her try homeschooling us. He wasn't sure what to think of her crazy idea. But he let her try.

Now, this was in the 1970s. No one had heard of homeschooling. My parents had never heard of it. We didn't know another soul who was doing it. But she tried it. And she liked it. She persuaded Dad to let her do it again for my first-grade year.

My mom had left teacher's college to get married. My dad was a veteran of the US Air Force and the Campbell County Sheriff's Office. They had never been in trouble a day in their lives. Until then.

What began as a convenience quickly morphed into a conviction, a ministry. Based on the commands in Deuteronomy 6 to teach God's Word to your children "when thou sittest in thine house, and when thou walkest by the way, and when thou liest down, and when thou risest up" (v. 7), they began to believe it was God's will for their family that they homeschool all their (what turned out to be fourteen) children.

The county school superintendent disagreed. We heard, though I can't confirm, that he was the son of a Baptist preacher but had rejected his dad's faith. Whatever the case, he charged my folks with truancy.

The first stop was the school board. They found my parents truant, on a six-to-one vote. Only the late Hiram Payne, the lone African American person on the board, voted in our favor. I attended the meeting, a scared-to-death six-year-old, knowing only that these strangers wanted to take me away from my family.

My parents followed the example of Peter and John: "We must obey God rather than men" (Acts 5:29 NASB). They were hauled before the juvenile court judge, who also served a term as a state legislator.

My younger brothers and I waited at a friend's house, hopeful and scared. I will never forget my parents' faces when they walked in that night. I knew the news was bad.

My parents' response was unchanged: "We must obey God." But now they were dealing with reality. My parents told me that if the worst happened and they went to jail for a while, we would go to Kansas to live with my paternal grandmother. If that happened, I was to make sure my little brothers said their prayers before bed every night.

I will never forget that charge. The load on my six-year-old shoulders has left a mark to this day. Little children should be able to trust that their parents have the world under control. I knew that mine did not. I knew only that some powerful people wanted to take us out of the home and maybe put Mom and Dad in jail. I just wished we'd be left alone.

We went into hiding. It was actually a nosy neighbor who had initially complained to the schools that we were "truant." So until after the school bus ran every day, we couldn't go outside. We did truant officer drills. If even the mailman knocked on the door, we four boys would scamper off and slide under the bed until he left.

It was a futile exercise; the schools knew where we lived, and if they wanted to push it . . .

Eventually the school board realized that they had to either put this couple in jail or back down themselves. They finally agreed to a compromise. Our church's school *agreed to let Mom have an empty classroom. She could "homeschool" us there on the church grounds, just as if she were at home. For some reason, that made the school board feel better, and they agreed to the compromise. A year or two later, as other courageous parents joined the movement, the state legislature liberalized the homeschooling statute.*

At last we could go outside during school hours. We were "out from under the bed."

The courage my mom and dad showed indelibly influenced me. I knew they were scared. But they wouldn't back down. And the aggressive, all-consuming drive of human government for power over individuals impressed me as well. The past quarter century, I've spent my free time (and some time I couldn't afford) in trying at every level, in every way I could, to reduce and limit that power.

I don't want my kids to ever feel that load on their shoulders. But I'm glad I did. It made me who I am.

* * * * *

Chesterton said, "It is only by believing in God that we can ever criticise the Government. Once abolish . . . God, and the Government becomes the God. That fact is written all across human history. . . . Wherever the people do not believe in something beyond the world, they will worship the world. But, above all, they will worship the strongest thing in the world."[32]

GOD VERSUS THE WORLD: THE BATTLE FOR THE HUMAN SOUL

America's Christian theologians have spent decades arguing about the proper relationship of church and state, all the while entirely missing the biblical heart of the matter. A truncated reading of Romans 13—and the fact that, for too many, Romans 13 is the only passage on government they read—have left far too much of the church believing that our only biblical response to government is absolute submission. The result has been, in essence, the surrender of biblical inerrancy to the world and the practical dethroning of Jesus Christ by His own church.

This is strong language. It is also historically accurate.

What the bulk of the modern church fails to realize—even those committed to challenging sin in the culture—is that *culture war* is a misnomer. This war is not primarily about the culture. It is about the eternal human soul. It is true that no earthly endeavor gains eternal life. It is equally true that truth accepted or denied on earth results in eternal life either gained or lost.

The church has tragically accepted the world's foundational premises and adopted the world's vocabulary, its terminology. *Love* now means the approval of evil. *Hatred* means denying that others have absolute rights to behave however they please. *Tolerance* means the surrender of the concept of absolute truth— which inevitably means surrendering the authority of God and the inerrancy of Scripture. *Rights* are now defined as absolute freedom to do anything I may desire, without eternal consequences or even moral disapproval in this life.

The reality is stark and demands strong language. The so-called culture war is a titanic clash of religions. Even more to the point, it is a war of God versus god. There are two deities competing for supreme power and total control of the minds and actions of humanity. One is Jehovah; the other is Caesar, the secular state. It is impossible to serve both. And the stark truth is that, whether we like it or not, to serve one is to be at war with the other.

James made this brilliantly clear: "Ye adulterers and adulteresses, know ye not that the friendship of the world is enmity with God? whosoever therefore will be a friend of the world is the enemy of God" (James 4:4). The cursory Christian view of this passage is naively simplistic: "Okay, before I accepted Jesus, I was of the world; now I am a Christian and a friend of God." The reality is much deeper.

James used strong language, too. He declared anyone claiming Christianity but in league with the world is the equivalent of a faithless spouse. The word *enemy* is pretty strong, too. Choosing to be an enemy of God is a stark choice.

John echoed James's message in 1 John 2:15–16: "Love not the world, neither the things that are in the world. If any man love the world, the love of the Father is not in him. For all that is in the world, the lust of the flesh, and the lust of the eyes, and the pride of life, is not of the Father, but is of the world." John's language is strong, too. Lust and pride are not insignificant sins.

Jesus warned us plainly that "no man can serve two masters: for either he will hate the one, and love the other; or else he will hold to the one, and despise the other" (Matthew 6:24). Yet the realization that the culture war is a war of God versus god somehow still stuns us.

That is the inescapable truth. The entire history of Christianity—indeed the entire history of humanity—has been a bitter war, a life-and-death struggle for the salvation or destruction of the human soul. And the culture war is a central focus, just as surely as the battle for biblical inerrancy. The two are inseparably welded together.

IT'S NOT REALLY A CULTURE WAR— IT'S A CLASH OF GODS

The culture war began before Adam and Eve even entered the scene:

> How art thou fallen from heaven, O Lucifer, son of the morning! how art thou cut down to the ground, which didst weaken the nations!
>
> For thou hast said in thine heart, I will ascend into heaven, I will exalt my throne above the stars of God: I will sit also upon the mount of the congregation, in the sides of the north:
>
> I will ascend above the heights of the clouds; I will be like the most High.
>
> Yet thou shalt be brought down to hell, to the sides of the pit. (Isaiah 14:12–15)

The original sin was Satan's prideful determination to be exalted "above the stars of God"—indeed, to be "like the Most High." In the garden he used the same temptation that had felled him: "The serpent said unto the woman, Ye shall not surely die: for God doth know that in the day ye eat thereof, then your eyes shall be opened, and ye shall be as gods, knowing good and evil" (Genesis 3:4–5). Basically Satan was denying eternal judgment, promising perfection and satisfaction in this life alone, free of the constraints of God's law on human action. This rebellion against God would allow people to be "as gods" themselves. Like Satan, humanity could not resist the temptation. And the battle for supremacy over the human soul has raged ever since.

But though we are "freed" to be gods ourselves, we cannot escape the image of God carved into our creation. We are, inescapably, worshippers. God created us to worship Him. When we rebel against Him, we do not cease to worship; we simply change the object. And the most natural object of worship is ourselves.

When this happens, the individual naturally moves from worshipping himself or herself to worshipping the achievements, power, and wealth of humanity's collective efforts. This quickly turns to worship of government: "Human beings worship their own actions and efforts as divine. And since the political state is the most powerful expression of collective human action, the state itself becomes the greatest manifestation of the divine."[33][1]

The Tower of Babel is perhaps the earliest biblical example of the struggle between God and Caesar:

> They said, Go to, let us build us a city and a tower, whose top may reach unto heaven; and let us make us a name, lest we be scattered abroad upon the face of the whole earth.
>
> And the LORD came down to see the city and the tower, which the children of men builded.
>
> And the Lord said, Behold, the people is one, and they have all one language; and this they begin to do: and now nothing will be restrained from them, which they have imagined to do. (Genesis 11:4–6)

The builders of Babel were looking to build a secular state. They wanted to make a name for themselves and avoid "being scattered abroad upon the face of the whole earth." The entire effort was to build an economic and political

---

1 From the book *Worshipping the State: How Liberalism Became Our State Religion* by Benjamin Wiker. Copyright © 2013. Published by Regnery Publishing. All rights reserved. Reprinted by special permission of Regnery Publishing, Washington, D.C.

structure that would dominate the world and render almighty God unnecessary. It would replace God with the almighty state as the supplier of human needs.

Of course, this was not just a political and economic operation. The state of Babel explicitly rejected God's command to "multiply, and replenish the earth" (Genesis 1:28). History tells us "the plain in the land of Shinar" where they built (11:2) became the site of the Sumerian civilization, and the tower became the prototype for Sumerian ziggurats, towers built with temples at the top to worship the sun and the moon—the "creature more than the Creator" (Romans 1:25), as Paul put it. The state of Babel was, at its deepest level, a religious rebellion, the exaltation of man and the state over God.

GOD VERSUS CAESAR: THE STRUGGLE FOR SUPREMACY

If the Garden of Eden marked the beginning of the struggle between God and Caesar, the climax of the struggle was Jesus's appearance on the human scene, and it only exacerbated the battle. Jean-Jacques Rousseau claimed that "Jesus [coming] to establish a spiritual kingdom on earth . . . brought about the end of the unity of the State, and caused the internal divisions that have never ceased to stir up Christian people."[134] In other words, the claim that Caesar was inferior to God unleashed a war.

As we consider the proper Christian response to the state today, we are forced to consider Christ's forceful confrontation with Caesar, which provides the basis for our response today. Let's briefly take a look at the condition of things under Caesar as god when Christ came, then examine just how radical Christ's confrontation with Caesar really was.

Catholic professor Dr. Benjamin Wiker wrote a book entitled *Worshipping the State: How Liberalism Became Our State Religion*. Though I do not agree with all Dr. Wiker's theology nor precisely with his view on the separation of church and state, his work is an incredible history of the battle between Christianity and the state, between God and Caesar. You do yourself a disservice not to read it.

Wiker examined the moral and cultural condition of Rome in Christ's day:

There were few brakes on sexuality in the Roman Empire at the time of Christ—a fact that is directly related to pagan religion. . . .

With sexuality free from religious restraint, the results were predictable. . . . Prostitution was morally and legally sanctioned. . . . Marriage was in bad shape. Divorce was easy, adultery common, and concubinage licit.

By the time of Christ, homosexuality was just as widespread among the Romans as it was among the Greeks. . . . The Romans had adopted the pederasty of the Greeks (aimed, generally, at boys between the ages of twelve and eighteen).[135]

By Nero's time, things had reached rock bottom: "He not only had a passion for . . . boys . . . but he also 'married' other men and even a boy, sometimes playing the part of the woman in the union and sometimes the man." (These facts are confirmed by the Roman writer Tacitus.)[136]

Nor was unrestrained perversion the only parallel with today. Abortion was common, and "the killing of deformed infants was mandated by Roman law."[137] Into this toxic brew came Jesus Christ, and with His coming, the ancient struggle between God and the state reached a new level.

Many Christian theologians combine Christ's instructions about paying taxes to Caesar (Matthew 22:15–22; Mark 12:13–17) with Romans 13 to reach the conclusion that Christ commanded silent submission to the Caesar who presided over such debauchery. In fact, the opposite is true, and the radical nature of Christ's challenge to Caesar was borne out by the effect His gospel had on pagan Rome in the next couple of centuries.

By the time of Christ's earthly ministry, the Jewish leaders had reached an uneasy accord with Caesar. Rome allowed the Jews to continue the old sacrificial system, with some "minor" adjustments. The Jewish leaders could continue to conduct temple sacrifices, preserving—at least in the eyes of the public—the outward appearance that Jehovah was sovereign over the Jewish people. In exchange, the Jewish leaders would bow to the recognition that Caesar was in fact sovereign, serving under a high priest selected by Caesar's government.[138] In effect, while still proclaiming God "in church," the Jewish leaders accepted Caesar as lord over their earthly lives.

In an attempt to trip up Christ, the Pharisees asked Him, "Is it lawful to pay taxes to Caesar, or not?" (Mark 12:14 ESV). Answering one way could mean denying God as God, destroying Christ's own claim to be God and thus (rightfully) His credibility with the people, and answering another way would hopefully get Him killed by the Romans. Christ asked for a coin, and one of the questioners presented a Roman denarius coin.

It is crucial to understand how Caesar viewed himself. The very coin used by the Pharisees bore the inscription "Tiberias Caesar Augustus, Son of the Deified Augustus." On the reverse was the phrase "Pontif Maxim," short for "Pontifex Maximus" or "high priest"![139] The Roman emperor was considered the religious leader, and in fact, after death many emperors were considered gods.

The tension must have been electric. "Jesus answering said unto them, Render to Caesar the things that are Caesar's, and to God the things that are God's" (Mark 12:17). Tragically many today read this as a command of blind submission. It is, in fact, the opposite.

Jesus stared into the face of the Roman god and declared him dethroned. He first declared that Caesar was *not* God, then, in a declaration of war, ordered God's people *not* to render to Caesar what was God's! This was open civil disobedience. Caesar demanded worship as God. Jesus forbade it.

Over the next couple of centuries, Christians challenged the pagan practices of Rome in the first "culture war." The first-century *Didache* (meaning "teaching" in Greek and bearing the full title *The Teaching of the Lord Given to the Gentiles by the Twelve Apostles*)—along with voluminous quotations from Jesus and Paul—contains direct commands against the pagan Roman practices.

Didache 1:2 states, "The way of life is this: first, you shall love God who created you; second, your neighbor as yourself; all those things which you do not want to be done to you, you should not do to others."[140] And *Didache* 2:2 says, "You shall not murder. You shall not commit adultery. You shall not corrupt boys. You shall not be promiscuous. You shall not steal. You shall not practise divination. You shall not practise with magic potions. You shall not kill a child in the womb nor expose infants. You shall not try to take your neighbours' goods."[141]

"The original pagan embrace of this world was broken by Christians preaching a kingdom not of this world—and a more severe morality to go with it. . . . The empire no longer commanded one's total allegiance, and the embrace of this fallen world was loosened as converts reached beyond this life toward the next."[142] But the Christians' focus on the next life—their replacement of Caesar with Jesus— forced them to challenge the cruelty and barbarity of Caesar in this life as well.

"Of course, there would not have been any antagonism against the church if the church had kept to itself. But it did not, because of the command of Jesus Christ himself, 'Go, therefore, make disciples of all the nations . . . and teach them to observe all the commands I gave you.'"[143]

Had the early Christians said only "Accept Jesus to obtain eternal life," Caesar would have had no objection. The Romans already had a massive pantheon of gods. One more or less wouldn't have offended them at all. And had the Christians been content to limit their message to the life to come, which is essentially the limit of the message of the emasculated modern American church, the Romans still would have had no major concern. But what provoked vicious persecution was their steadfast refusal to proclaim "Caesar is Lord" in the here and now.

Caesar as god wasn't concerned about the hereafter. He was concerned with total power here on earth. The Roman god-man demanded worship—demanded absolute submission—here on earth; the heavenly God-Man did also. And that brought out the lions.

> Why were the Christians in the Roman Empire thrown to the lions? From the Christian's viewpoint it was for a religious reason. But from the viewpoint of the Roman State, they were in civil disobedience. . . . The Roman State did not care what anybody believed religiously;

you could believe anything, or you could be an atheist. But you had to worship Caesar as a sign of your loyalty to the state.[144]

Many modern American Christians would have gotten along just fine under Nero; we are no threat to Caesar's kingdom on earth.

At the time of Christ and Paul, just as today, there was no middle ground. It was—and it is today—God *or* Caesar.

GOD VERSUS CAESAR'S PHILOSOPHY: THE STRUGGLE CONTINUES

From Machiavelli (1469–1527) to the *Humanist Manifesto*, the open warfare between Caesar and God has continued.

Machiavelli [argued] that to reverse the ill effects of Christianity, religion must be re-paganized and the control of education must be wrested from the hands of the church and put into the hands of the state . . .

This has a direct effect on the church. The established secular church must appear to be Christian, but in reality it must be rebuilt on the pagan model of religion that was so marvelously effective in ancient Rome, when religion directly and completely supported the state's earthly security and glory. The state must educate and form its citizens to esteem and hence desire this-worldly glory and the good of the state as the supreme good.

But since the Christian church is so powerful, the return to pagan religion cannot be direct and immediate. It must be accomplished by an entire reconstruction of Christianity from within, by removing or transforming precisely those elements of the church that set it at odds with the kingdoms of this world.[145]

A more "enlightened" modern Machiavellianism prevails today, but the strategy has been devilishly effective. Tragically the church has passively accepted the world's definitions and what the world considers the proper role for the church.

"The current belief that the church must be separated from the state and walled off in private impotence—leaving, by its subtraction from the public square, the liberal secular state—all that is Machiavelli's intention. The playing out of this principle in our courts today is . . . creating a state liberated from the Christian worldview."[146]

Thomas Hobbes (1588–1679) fine-tuned Machiavelli's arguments, positing that "there was *no sin and no right and wrong* until the sovereign declared them to be so, that is, until the king declared something to be illegal. . . . And no one—certainly not the church—can declare something to be a sin that the king allows."[147] "The 'Right to declare what is Sin' had therefore to be taken from the church, and given to the political sovereign."[148]

Hobbes's philosophy has the same pernicious effects today. "The exclusion of religious belief from the public square with the erection of a wall of separation between church and state thereby creates a fully secular state, a state that, in equally excluding all beliefs, orders the public realm according to *un*belief."[149]

To see the connection between society's return to affirming abortion and Hobbes's assertion that we each have the right to define good and evil for ourselves, witness the following statement from our own Supreme Court in *Planned Parenthood v. Casey*: "At the heart of liberty is the right to define one's own concept of existence, of meaning, of the universe, and of the mystery of human life. Beliefs about these matters could not define the attributes of personhood were they formed under the compulsion of the State."[150]

Materialism—the view that there is no supernatural, no eternal, no objective truth—has even flooded into the church. As Ken Ham noted in his book *Already Gone*, large numbers of supposedly Christian young people are rejecting the church because of its "unscientific" belief that God created the world.[151]

Faced with relentless assaults from "science" and with political elites demanding separation of church and state, the church has by and large surrendered virtually all the ground it once claimed for Christ in the arts, literature, education, culture, and government.

"Even Christians generally confine Jesus Christ and His law to private, family, and church circles. As a result, . . . ethical and legal standards are becoming more and more openly pagan."[152] "The materialistic mindset has increasingly taken hold, and the church has become correspondingly anemic."[153] The central question is not about politics but about God. The philosophical attack on Christianity has been, at its heart, an attack on God and His revealed Word. From the perspective of the world, "if [people] think they possess supernaturally revealed doctrinal or moral truths that stand above and judge the state, they're actually dangerous. That's why the Bible has to be reduced to the role of moral cheerleader."[154] "Thus the Bible is reduced to a bunch of old stories from which we may, very carefully, extract moral lessons, or to be more accurate, build up an entire secularized version of morality."[155]

Far too many theologians in the modern church have made the same mistake. We will talk about the gospel but dismiss the entire Old Testament as mere Bible stories. Our justification is that Christ discarded the old covenant. The practical outcome is our surrender of the Bible's authority, and the result "is a church that poses no challenge whatsoever to the secular state. In fact, it serves the cause of secularization at every turn."[156] Caesar—with the active participation of too many Christian leaders—is restored to the throne and Jesus is dethroned in the culture.

By accepting materialistic science and by ignoring Scripture that challenges the secular state, the church has been reduced to moral irrelevance. The same gospel that conquered and ended the vile pagan practices of the Roman Empire is no longer a bold trumpet but a compliant whisper in the face of the new paganism.

Instead of boldly proclaiming doctrinal and moral truths that might appear divisive (even within the church at times), the church resorts to a watered-down religion of politeness. We adopt the world's definition of *love*. We must "love them to Jesus," which is to say we must not lay guilt on them for their sins.

"Declaring that Christianity is *entirely* defined by love of neighbor allows [the liberal state] to wipe out all sources of doctrinal conflict. Everything else is entirely inconsequential, including all the intricate doctrinal differences that Christians over the centuries have thought were so momentous because the salvation of souls might depend on them. All that counts is being good. Or more accurately . . . being nice."[157]

Wiker put it plainly: "To sum up [this] kind of Christianity: *You don't need the Nicene Creed if you're nice.* People who fight over inconsequential dogmas are not nice. They're *intolerant.*"[158]

> [This] love is not the kind of self-sacrificing charity that drove the saints and martyrs such as Paul to lose everything, even to suffer death, in order to bring the truth about salvation to their fellow man. Quite the contrary. [Love means] minding one's own business, not bothering others but just getting along—in a word, tolerance. Faith is, therefore, recast . . . as an affirmation of complete freedom of thought, rather than of specific theological truths. The reason . . . is that faith is fundamentally irrational, concerned only with "nothing but obedience and piety."[159]

This is the "gospel" of the church of Caesar. You can have your beliefs; you can even discuss them with others privately. Just recognize that they believe differently and their beliefs are just as legitimate. And whatever you do, *never* challenge sin in public, outside the walls of the church. Stay inside, keep Jesus personal, so Caesar's reign in the public square is never threatened.

"By pushing the notion that doctrine doesn't matter, and that anyone should be able to believe anything as long as he obeys the civil laws, the state ultimately undermines the church as an authoritative body and puts the authority to define doctrine entirely into the hands of individuals. Instead of a duality between church and state, we now have only a duality between the individual and the state. . . . *Now the individual must face the state alone.*"[160] With ideas like these, Caesar's claim to absolute power has gained more ground.

Jean-Jacques Rousseau (1712–88) offered the next piece in the puzzle of the state church. He replaced the biblical account of Creation with an alternative Eden much like Hobbes's "state of nature." In Rousseau's Eden, the man roamed aimlessly, needing nothing but food, idleness, and procreation. Rousseau replaced the Genesis account of marriage and family with mere animalistic procreation, where the man had no ongoing ties to a female or offspring, no responsibility, nothing but the mindless pursuit of pleasure and comfort. It is a purely utilitarian concept of human government. Thus,

> the liberal state does not define law in terms of the promotion of virtue and the prohibition of vice, but in terms of the protection and promotion of individuals' private pleasures, which—since all such pleasures are natural—are declared to be *rights*. Any limitation of these "rights" is considered unjust; that is, justice is redefined to mean everyone getting as much of whatever he or she wants as long as he or she doesn't infringe on anyone else's pursuit of pleasure.[161]

The modern outworkings of Rousseau's ideals are all too obvious. Government takes on the role of provider to ensure the man does not have to. All restrictions on sex are unjust. Work is discouraged. Wealth must be distributed to maximize pleasure and minimize pain. Private property is a vice, not a virtue.

As the distributor of good, "Rousseau's state requires complete devotion. That's why he cannot allow the existence of any other church."[162] "For Rousseau there can be only one body—the body politic—and Christ cannot be its head."[163] And because all of life is defined by earthly pleasure and pain, Rousseau's state, like Hobbes's, counts on the support of science that limits all reality to the material.

Also because all of life is defined by this earth, the state—Caesar—replaces God as the source of power. "The materialist evolutionary view ... [is] good news for liberalism. It means that we are free to manipulate, to re-create, ourselves. ... The liberal improvement project replaces the church as a vehicle for *regenerating* human beings."[164] There is no need for divine regeneration; the state assumes the role of imposing perfection on earth.

> We must be clear about why socialism became a religion, and more particularly why it wrapped itself in Christian language and ritual and the Christian scheme of salvation, even while it more and more came to attack Christianity explicitly. Secularist socialism was in

great part an outgrowth of de-supernaturalized Christianity. And its adherents believed that it could completely replace Christianity, filling every nook and cranny occupied by the church and Christian culture with an entirely this-worldly religion.[165]

Satan has no raw materials; he must work with counterfeits. Or as he tried with Christ in the desert, he works with some biblical truth taken out of context to destroy its greater message. "From Machiavelli forward, liberalism tried every means to draw this world out of the shadow of the next. And that meant the Bible had to be dealt with—tamed, declawed, rendered submissive."[166] Jesus had to be dethroned from divinity and recast as a good moral teacher: "Jesus the merely moral man was no threat to political power. . . . The church, bereft of the belief in Christ's divinity, collapsed in a heap."[167]

GOD VERSUS CAESAR'S EDUCATION SYSTEM: THE STRUGGLE TODAY

That brings us to the church of Caesar in today's America. The weakening of scriptural principles, the replacement of faith with materialistic science, and the resulting dethroning of Jesus paved the way for the establishment of the modern socialist church of secularism to fill the void. "Christianity was often quite fervent in America, but it was subtly reconstructed to be compatible with passionately this-worldly material pursuits. It was not a Christianity that could produce martyrs or even severe judges of the fallen secular order."[168]

> This revolution occurred first in the universities [between the 1880s and 1930s], from which it spread to the other areas of our culture, using every available means from the media to literature, but especially public education and the federal courts to impose the new liberal morality. This moral revolution could not have succeeded without excluding the churches—or should we say "separating" them?—from the public square and ushering them into the realm of harmless private institutions.[169]

Certainly there is a great tradition of Christian philosophers since Roman times, who have stood for God's government against Caesar. Augustine, Calvin, and Rutherford are just a few who come to mind. "[Augustine] did not subscribe to any sort of 'divine right' of rulers. Nor did he believe that legislation or decrees should pass unquestioned. 'An unjust law is no law at all,' he maintained."[170] Calvin directly counseled resistance to rulers who enforce idolatry by civil power: "Earthly princes lay aside all their power when they rise up against God, and are unworthy of being reckoned in the number of mankind. We ought rather utterly to defy than to obey them."[171]

But Caesar has so completely dominated the university system—and education in general—that the arena of the human mind has been left almost exclusively to the neopagan philosophers. The church has forgotten its history and has lost the intellectual and spiritual edge it needs to do battle with Caesar. The result has been predictable.

> Religious confusion has produced moral confusion. Not only can millions of Americans no longer tell right from wrong, they cannot even think in moral terms. . . . In today's popular mind [and, I would add, much of the evangelical mind] the United States is a secular country where religion is tolerated but must keep its place.[172]

In the name of separation of church and state, the pagan secular church of Caesar has succeeded in being established as the state church in America. The Hobbesian vision of a purely material world with no Creator has been enshrined in the public schools by the Supreme Court, and any alternative view is flatly forbidden.[173] The Rousseauian vision of sexual license divorced from any moral strictures exploded across America in June 2015 with the court's ruling in *Obergefell v. Hodges.* The decision proved the state's "power to impose on us the belief, through the power of the Courts, that we each have the right to define our own concept of existence. . . . The state is not neutral . . . And [this] view acts as an acid dissolving the central Christian doctrines—that our existence is defined by God, that meaning is defined by reality and not by our subjective inclinations, that the universe was created by God, and that the mystery of life has already been determined by the author of life."[174]

Kennedy's words in *Obergefell* are sadly clear: "The Constitution promises liberty to all within its reach, a liberty that includes certain specific rights that allow persons . . . to define and express their identity."[175] Morality, our Supreme Court now asserts, is something individuals can "define and express" for themselves. We have enshrined as a constitutional right the moral anarchy described in Judges 21:25: "Every man did that which was right in his own eyes."

Kennedy tried to cover up the establishment of the church of Caesar with a renewed promise that Christian beliefs are fine, as long as they are privately held and have no authority in society:

> Many who deem same-sex marriage to be wrong reach that conclusion based on decent and honorable religious or philosophical premises, and neither they nor their beliefs are disparaged here. But when that sincere, personal opposition becomes enacted law and public policy, the necessary consequence is to put the imprimatur of the State itself on an exclusion that soon demeans or stigmatizes those whose own liberty is then denied.[176]

But the unavoidable fact is the Christian view of marriage is disestablished and the secular view is imposed on everyone. The vision of the pagan philosophers to return to state-supported Roman hedonism has been accomplished.

CAESAR VERSUS THE CHURCH: IT IS A RELIGIOUS WAR FOR THE HUMAN SOUL

In conclusion, lest there be any doubt the state church is in fact a religion, and the battle between God and Caesar is a battle not primarily of politics but for the human soul, I include here Wiker's contrast between the irreconcilable belief systems of the church of Jehovah God and the church of Caesar:

> Christians affirm that there is only one God, and he created heaven and earth. Secular liberals assert that there is no God, and that nature is the result of blind laws and chance interactions.
>
> Christians believe that the world is full of meaning because it was created by a wise and loving God. Liberals believe that the universe and life itself are ultimately meaningless . . .

Christians believe that human beings are made in the image of God and are the very pinnacle of creation. . . . Liberals believe that a human being is just one more animal, an accidental artifact of blind evolution . . .

Christians believe that the world is fallen, and that sin infects and distorts every human behavior. Liberals believe that human beings are naturally good, and that "evil" is only the result of a bad environment. . . .

Christians believe that the grace of God is necessary to heal human wickedness. Liberals believe that human beings may manipulate their material surroundings, and even human nature itself, to effect their own salvation by their own works.

Christians believe that God became incarnate in Jesus Christ, who is fully divine and fully human, the only God-man in history. Liberals deny the divinity of Christ. . . .They believe that human beings can become their own gods.

Christians believe that political life in this world is tainted and hindered by the presence of sin, so that we cannot place our ultimate hopes in a kingdom of this world. Liberals believe this world is all we have, and that we can bring about an earthly paradise. . . .

For Christians the fundamental institution is the church, the Body of Christ, with Christ as its head. The kingdoms of this world—the nations, the states aimed at sustaining bodily existence and social order in this life—are secondary. Church and state are complementary, but truly distinct in institutional form and function. Liberals, denying the reality of the next world, make this-worldly kingdoms, nations, and states the primary and exclusive powers. If they allow the church to exist, they make it subordinate to the political power or render it an impotent private glee club.

A sign that the secular state is now elevated to the dominant institution is that it has displaced the Gospel of the church with its own gospel, taking over the task of defining human nature, fundamental human institutions, and the human good . . .

Christian sexual morality is defined by the goal of exclusive heterosexual marriage. . . . Liberalism, in rejecting Christianity and

redefining marriage, has redefined all of human sexuality, declaring
liberation from Christian morality . . . to be the sexual good.

Christianity affirms that human life is made in the image of God.
. . . Liberalism denies the soul, and therefore takes upon itself the
authority to define what kind of human life is (and is not) worthy
of the protection of the law . . .

In defining itself from top to bottom directly against Christianity,
secular liberalism is a kind of inverse image, like a photo negative,
of the religion it has so energetically worked to displace for the past
several centuries. It is a kind of anti-Christian religion as extensive in
its claims as the Christianity it denies, with its own set of passionately
held beliefs and dogmas. It doesn't just look like a religion. It doesn't
just function like a religion. It *is* a religion.[177]

All these beliefs, on both sides, form the essence of religion. It is simply untrue
the world is concerned with the secular and the church with the religious. Radical
secularism *is* religious, and if it is left unchallenged, the end will be not only a
return to the massive persecution of Rome but also a massive loss of eternal souls.

THE CHURCH SURRENDERS TO CAESAR: THE PULPITS FLEE FROM THE BATTLE

The influence of the Pietistic political beliefs of theologian John MacArthur
have had a powerful effect on modern evangelicalism and a correspondingly
powerful destructive effect on our culture. His claim that "the moral, social,
and political state of a people is irrelevant to the advance of the gospel"[178] is the
very belief of the church that has led to where we are today. He also said, "Using
temporal methods to promote legislative and judicial change, and resorting to
external efforts of lobbying and intimidation to achieve some sort of 'Christian
morality' in society is not our calling—and has no eternal value,"[179] and this quite
simply misstates the case. To his credit, MacArthur has recently taken a more
biblically correct position on challenging unbiblical trends in the culture. In
2020, MacArthur courageously refused to close the doors of his church when

commanded to do so by California in the face of the Covid-19 virus.[180] But the damage has been done already through thousands of preachers who have gone through his Masters Seminary and absorbed years of preaching about a false dichotomy between the gospel and "temporal methods" of advocating for biblical truth in law and culture. It is very encouraging that MacArthur appears to have drawn a line in the sand, at the point at which the state attempts to shut down the church—other Christian leaders should follow. But the crying need is for leaders like John the Baptist to challenge the state on its own ground, to confront sin in national leaders, and to declare the Law of God is binding on all nations, all leaders, at all times—not just when the state attempts to close the church doors. The attack of the state on his church is the natural and probable consequence of the church refusing to challenge the state long ago. The church is weakened, and the state is emboldened.

Proclaiming God's truth on matters of biblical clarity is not a "temporal method." And it emphatically *is* our calling to proclaim from the housetops that Caesar is *not* God, that the temporal state cannot save, that God's eternal law and not man's changing, repressive standard should be the basis for government.

The harsh truth is that:

> the forced exclusion of the church through secularization has nowhere resulted in the establishing of a neutral, non-religious political state, but rather always in a state with a quite different, hostile political religion—the Religion of Reason, the Religion of Humanity, the worship of the nation as incarnate Spirit, the worship of nature, the worship of race, the worship of human self-deification through human technical progress, the worship of sexuality, . . . the worship of equality, the revival of neo-pagan cults, and who knows what shall be next. Since all of these new worships funnel their aspirations through the state, the state itself becomes the object of worship, a great mirror in whose reflective and magnifying power we can worship ourselves.[181]

It is the abdication of the fervor shown by the early church in Roman times that has led to the reestablishment of the pagan church of Caesar in today's

America. "The de-Christianized secular public square is by no means morally or theologically neutral."[182] In *Abington v. Schempp*, the case that banned Bible reading in public schools, Justice Potter Stewart explained this in his dissent: "A refusal to permit religious exercises [in public schools] thus is . . . not . . . the realization of state neutrality, but rather . . . the establishment of a religion of secularism, or, at the least, . . . government support of the beliefs of those who think that religious exercises should be conducted only in private."[183]

"Secular liberalism has no problem with welcoming a weak and obedient liberal Christianity into the public square."[184] A Christianity willing to be relegated to private interactions or caged within the walls of a church and confined to church activities is easy prey for being dismissed as unscientific or merely religious. MacArthur is wrong. In reality, as the church attempts to ignore the culture, instead of the culture being irrelevant to the spread of the gospel, the church becomes irrelevant to the culture.

> With the triumph of rights-based liberalism over Christianity and natural law morality, we have the effective re-paganization of morality. Abortion, infanticide, contraception, euthanasia, easy divorce, sexual promiscuity, pornography, homosexuality, and pedophilia, all of which were part of pagan Rome's accepted way of life, reappear and are affirmed by the liberal state.[185]

America's history in the past century, accelerating over the past decade, has been full of the bloodshed of the unborn and the rejection of biblical truth in the area of sex and marriage, and the nation is rapidly heading back toward the persecution of the faithful few who refuse to acknowledge that Caesar is Lord.

In truth, the "wall of separation" that has done the most damage to America has not been erected by courts or humanistic education. It is the one evangelical pulpits set up by presenting a false choice between politics and evangelism, declaring the former off limits to Christians and a distraction from our call to the latter.

I use the word *false* here intentionally. Much of the preaching on Christ and the culture in modern evangelicalism is not only terribly wrong in light of history but also blatantly unbiblical.

Perhaps the most egregious example is the reaction by Russell Moore, president of the Southern Baptist Convention's Ethics and Religious Liberty Commission, to the decision by Alabama Supreme Court Chief Justice Roy Moore (no relation to Russell) to defy a lone federal judge who had purported to strike down Alabama's constitutional amendment defining marriage as between one man and one woman. We dealt with that controversy in Chapter 3.

Russell Moore was wrong, both historically and biblically. In addition to the fact that it is legally proper for the chief justice of a state supreme court to defend his state constitution against a lone federal judge purporting to overturn it, Moore's advice to Christian judges in the face of the ruling was biblically wrong:

> In the case of judges and state Supreme Court justices, though, civil disobedience, even when necessary, cannot happen in their roles as agents of the state. Religious freedom and conscience objections must be balanced with a state's obligation to discharge the law. We shouldn't have officials breaking the law, but civil servants don't surrender their conscience simply by serving in government. While these details are being worked out, in the absence of any conscience protections, a government employee faced with a decision of violating his conscience or upholding the law, would need to resign and protest against it as a citizen if he could not discharge the duties of his office required by law in good conscience.
>
> Given the high bar required for civil disobedience, the way to address same-sex marriage in this circumstance is not by defying the rule of law, but by making our case before the legitimate authorities. If we lose, our responsibility is to advocate as citizens for our views.[186]

Moore advised Christian civil magistrates to go quietly away and "protest . . . as a citizen" when the state instructs them to defy the law of God. Perhaps this advice is based on an erroneous interpretation of God's sovereignty, which is often used today to avoid Christian responsibility. However, people in scriptural examples took just the opposite course of the one Moore urged.

When the Israelites rejected God as King—as represented by the religious and political judge Samuel—and demanded a human king, God granted their request. But Samuel didn't simply accept a private, purely religious role and withdraw from the culture.

When God selected a new king, David, it was Samuel who anointed God's choice (1 Sam. 16). In effect, God's spokesman continued to have the leading role in the selection of civil leaders.

We talked about Daniel and his three friends earlier. When Caesar commands otherwise, Christians are emphatically *not* to resign, close their windows, and defuse the contest. As with the three Hebrews, a respectful appeal is in order and, failing that, a bold public stand for King Jesus against Caesar (Dan. 3).

As the great Francis Schaeffer put it,

> It is not:
> GOD and CAESAR
> It was, is, and it always will be:
> GOD
> and
> CAESAR
> The civil government, as all of life, stands under the Law of God.[187]

This is what Jesus taught, and it was revolutionary, even seditious.

THE BIBLE REFUTES CHRISTIAN PACIFISM

Here we should consider Samuel again. In 1 Samuel 13, when King Saul was preparing for battle against the Philistines, Samuel was late for the sacrifice that was to be offered to the Lord before the battle. Making the sacrifice was strictly the office of Samuel, the religious leader ("the church," so to speak), whereas the battle itself was the task of the state.

When Samuel was late, Saul panicked and offered the sacrifice himself. God would not tolerate the civil authority's intrusion into the realm of the sacred. Samuel's judgment was sure and swift. Certainly Saul was God's anointed. But Samuel, as the spokesman for God, pronounced judgment on Saul for his sin and announced that God would choose a replacement (vv. 13–14). Interestingly, Samuel himself, the religious spokesman, anointed David as God's choice for the new civil magistrate. The biblical model of separation of church and state is to preserve the church from the state, not vice versa. God never removed His people from the process of civil government.

Even more interesting is the fact that Samuel's selection of the new king was an act of civil disobedience to Saul: "The Lord said unto Samuel, How long wilt thou mourn for Saul, seeing I have rejected him from reigning over Israel? fill thine horn with oil, and go, I will send thee to Jesse the Bethlehemite: for I have provided me a king among his sons. And Samuel said, How can I go? if Saul hear it, he will kill me" (1 Samuel 16:1–2).

Saul had not commanded Samuel to participate in his disobedience, either in his illegitimate sacrifice or two chapters later when he failed to destroy the Amalekites. But Samuel was still under God's orders to be involved in selecting the next civil ruler, even to the point of civil disobedience to his "Caesar."

Another biblical example is Queen Esther. It was a violation of Persian law—a capital crime—for her to go before the king without being summoned. According to Esther 4:11, the Persian law was as follows: "Whosoever, whether man or women, shall come unto the king into the inner court, who is not called, there is one law of his to put him to death." And unlike Chief Justice Moore, Esther had *not* been ordered by the king to take any wrong actions herself.

But one may object that Esther was not living under the Romans 13 command to obey civil rulers. She was, however, living under the Ecclesiastes 8 command to obey civil rulers:

> I counsel thee to keep the king's commandment, and that in regard of the oath of God.

Be not hasty to go out of his sight: stand not in an evil thing; for he doeth whatsoever pleaseth him.

Where the word of a king is, there is power: and who may say unto him, What doest thou?

Whoso keepeth the commandment shall feel no evil thing: and a wise man's heart discerneth both time and judgment. (vv. 2–5)

If we apply Russell Moore's reasoning, Esther should have submitted to the Persian law (which was not in itself a command to disobey God in any way) and trusted God's sovereignty to deliver His people. What she did instead: "So will I go in unto the king, *which is not according to the law*: and if I perish, I perish" (Esther 4:16, emphasis added). The law itself demanded nothing immoral of Esther—except silence in the face of terrible evil.

If we apply Russell Moore's reasoning, Corrie ten Boom's defiance of the Nazis by hiding Jews was defiance of Romans 13. After all, she was not being forbidden from telling the Jews about Jesus. If we apply Russell Moore's reasoning, the conductors on the Underground Railroad should have returned the slaves to their captors after sharing the gospel with them. Although Moore and MacArthur do not state that these historical figures should have acted as I described, had their interpretation of Romans 13 been preached and accepted in those times, these actions would have been consistent with that preaching. This highlights the tragic real-life effect of biblical misinterpretation.

Daniel and his friends did not resign; they simply refused to bow. Esther not only did not resign but in fact *used her position of authority* to help her gain an audience with the king *in violation of the law*.

This is not a minor point. The church can no longer avoid addressing it. I hear all too often variations on the same theme: "Well, as long as Preacher X believes in the gospel, he can disagree on other things. You can believe in orthodox Christian theology and have differing viewpoints on Christian involvement in politics."

That simply avoids the question. Here is the real question the church must answer: Do we serve only one God, or can we serve two gods? I submit that while believing Jesus is the only way to heaven, many modern evangelical preachers have effectively dethroned Him on earth.

God alone is omnipotent and sovereign. "Thus saith the Lord the King of Israel, and his redeemer the Lord of hosts; I am the first, and I am the last; and beside me there is no God" (Isaiah 44:6). "I am the Lord, and there is none else, there is no God beside me" (Isaiah 45:5).

Russell Moore's view turns Romans 13 on its head. Biblical teaching that Caesar exercises power delegated by God has been turned into a conflation of the voice of Caesar with the voice of God. To equate Caesar with God is to remove God. God makes clear this is impermissible. It is, plain and simple, idolatry. Those preachers who effectively equate Caesar with God would not describe it as idolatry. They might believe it is not. But false preaching is not dangerous because it is obviously false. It is dangerous because it sounds Christian. And—if the basic question of the sovereignty of God, His place as the only God, is left open to question—it doesn't matter if ninety percent of what a preacher says is biblically correct.

The Judaizers in Paul's day were regulars in the Christian church. They too preached Christ. But they added just a little bit to Christ. They preached that you also had to keep the Jewish law. And Paul was adamant that if Christ was not everything, He was not enough. He confronted the false preaching. And whom did he confront? The apostle Peter himself.

> When I saw that they walked not uprightly according to the truth of the gospel, I said unto Peter before them all, If thou, being a Jew, livest after the manner of Gentiles, and not as do the Jews, why compellest thou the Gentiles to live as do the Jews?
>
> We who are Jews by nature, and not sinners of the Gentiles,
>
> knowing that a man is not justified by the works of the law, but by the faith of Jesus Christ, even we have believed in Jesus Christ. (Galatians 2:14–16)

Peter was one of Christ's original eleven apostles. But his compromise on one "small" detail threatened the entire gospel. Paul refused to let it slide. The consequences were too great. And God's people in America can no longer afford to let preachers threaten the gospel because they may be right ninety percent of the time. Just as the "small" compromise of Peter threatened the entire gospel, so does the practical equating of Caesar with God by too many modern evangelical preachers. We'd better get this straight. If God is not God alone, He's not God at all.

It doesn't matter whether you look at the Old Testament or the New. The Old Testament gives no wiggle room: "Hear, O Israel: The Lord our God is one Lord: And thou shalt love the Lord thy God with all thine heart, and with all thy soul, and with all thy might" (Deuteronomy 6:4–5). Nor does the New Testament. Christ was clear: "No man can serve two masters: for either he will hate the one, and love the other; or else he will hold to the one, and despise the other" (Matthew 6:24).

As Wiker put it, "Since the political state is the most powerful expression of collective human action, the state itself becomes the greatest manifestation of the divine."[188] No longer is the state alone demanding worship; now evangelical leaders are, in effect, joining the demand.

The ancient Israelites tried to worship both Baal and Jehovah. That didn't satisfy Jehovah. Read God's cutting words to His people in Isaiah 1:

> Hear the word of the Lord, ye rulers of Sodom; give ear unto the law of our God, ye people of Gomorrah.
>
> To what purpose is the multitude of your sacrifices unto me? saith the Lord: I am full of the burnt offerings of rams, and the fat of fed beasts; and I delight not in the blood of bullocks, or of lambs, or of he goats.
>
> When ye come to appear before me, who hath required this at your hand, to tread my courts?
>
> Bring no more vain oblations; incense is an abomination unto me; the new moons and sabbaths, the calling of assemblies, I cannot away with; it is iniquity, even the solemn meeting.
>
> Your new moons and your appointed feasts my soul hateth: they are a trouble unto me; I am weary to bear them.

And when ye spread forth your hands, I will hide mine eyes from you: yea, when ye make many prayers, I will not hear: your hands are full of blood.

Wash you, make you clean; put away the evil of your doings from before mine eyes; cease to do evil;

Learn to do well; seek judgment, relieve the oppressed, judge the fatherless, plead for the widow. (vv. 10–17)

The people were still doing their temple sacrifices. They were still making "many prayers." They were still observing the Mosaic feast days. But they insisted on adding other gods, and their Sabbath worship had ceased to affect their culture on the other six days. And God was not satisfied. In fact, He was furious—to the point that He promised *not* to answer their prayers. He demanded to be God *alone*. And He still does. He demanded that His people translate their weekend worship into changed lives in the greater culture. And He still does.

It is time the church confronted its leaders when they fail to preach the whole counsel of God. The consequences have been too devastating. In 1 Kings 18:21, Elijah asked Israel a penetrating question: "How long halt ye between two opinions? if the Lord be God, follow him: but if Baal, then follow him." Today's question: "If the Lord be God, follow Him: but if Caesar, then follow him." It's time the American church demanded our preachers give an answer—the right answer.

BACK TO THE BATTLE: A BIBLICAL CALL TO CONTEND FOR THE FAITH AGAINST CAESAR

God will not share His throne: "I am the Lord: that is my name: and my glory will I not give to another" (Isaiah 42:8). Contrary to MacArthur's statement, "the moral, social, and political state of a people" is *not* "irrelevant" to God. His commands to His people all through Scripture to "do justice and judgment" (Proverbs 21:3), "deliver them that are drawn unto death" (Proverbs 24:11), and "judge righteous judgment" (John 7:24) cannot be honored by simply telling Caesar's victims there is a way to go to heaven someday. As Os Guinness wrote, "The Christian faith, unlike the secular varieties of humanism, is also world-denying. Whatever law or practice contradicts God's law or principles must be confronted."[189]

Again, "secular liberalism has no problem with welcoming a weak and obedient liberal Christianity into the public square."[190] Caesar has no problem with religious ceremonies, as long as Caesar is Lord. It is time for leaders with the spirit of Nathan the prophet and Elijah to confront the murderous Caesar with the truth of his sin and pronounce God's just judgment. Anything less is not the gospel; to do less is, in effect, a defection from King Jesus to Caesar.

But there is an alternative—an unabashed return to the bold evangelistic fervor of the early church, which challenged Caesar's pagan philosophies and ended his brutal pagan practices.

> American Christians have been so affected by defeatist theologies . . . that they unthinkingly reject the possibility or desirability of a Christian nation. The truth is, however, that Christ is calling the nations to be His. Nations in the past have professed the Christian faith, and nations in the future will do the same.

> Isaiah prophesied:

> It shall come to pass in the latter days that . . . many peoples shall come, and say, "Come, let us go up to the mountain of the Lord . . . that he may teach us his ways and that we may walk in his paths" (Isaiah 2:2–3).[191]

"The biblical command of obedience still holds under democratic governments, but, as citizens [of democratic nations like America], Christians are now rulers as well as subjects. All the biblical commands to rulers to do justice apply to them as citizens; political activism, rather than quietism, is demanded."[192]

Only a willingness to examine the history of the secular philosophies that have led us to this point—and to reexamine the church's policy of surrender in the "irrelevant" battle between God and Caesar—can stem the tide that is replacing almighty God with the almighty nanny state. And we have a recent example, in the fervor of the pulpits that birthed our American liberty.

Consider the inspiring call to civil rulers from the Reverend Peter Powers as he preached to the newly elected Vermont General Assembly in the midst of our War of Independence in 1778. Why may we not expect the same passion in our pulpits today?

> It is a very plain case that many people in the present day, have very absurd notions of Liberty, as if it consisted in a right for every one to believe, do, or act as he pleases in all things civil, and religious. This is a *Libertine* principle. No man has any right, before God, to believe or practice contrary to scripture. And Liberty consists in a freedom to do that which is right. The great law of nature, the moral law, is the rule of right action. This is the rule of moral and civil Liberty. Man's fall has taken away his freedom of right action; for *whosoever committeth sin is the servant of sin.* In the kingdom of providence Christ gives a civil freedom: in the kingdom of grace he gives a spiritual freedom. The Gospel is *the perfect Law of Liberty*; and this lays the foundation for a perfect moral freedom. It is the spiritual freedom we are especially concerned to seek among the people. And for this we should labor with the greatest painfulness."[193]

Hebrews 11 ought to serve as a wake-up call to a surrendering church. Known as the "Hall of Faith," it is a memorial to God's people across the centuries who demonstrated faith. In verses 32–24, the author wrote,

> What shall I more say? for the time would fail me to tell of Gedeon, and of Barak, and of Samson, and of Jephthae; of David also, and Samuel, and of the prophets:
>
> Who through faith subdued kingdoms, wrought righteousness, obtained promises, stopped the mouths of lions.
>
> Quenched the violence of fire, escaped the edge of the sword, out of weakness were made strong, waxed valiant in fight, turned to flight the armies of the aliens.

The Hall of Faith, from beginning to end, is an action chapter. And most of the characters mentioned were on the front lines of national culture!

Abraham, Isaac, Joseph, Moses, Rahab, and more are mentioned. These were leaders of armies, builders of nations, kings, prophets, warriors. None practiced the artificial bifurcation of the secular and the sacred that has been the most devastating weapon Caesar has employed against the church. None suggested that God's truth applied only to individuals and was irrelevant to nations.

As the British writer Dorothy Sayers put it, "In nothing has the Church so lost Her hold on reality as in Her failure to understand and respect the secular vocation. She has allowed work and religion to become separate departments.... She has forgotten that the secular vocation is sacred."[194]

"Without preaching national submission to Jesus our evangelism can never be more than proclaiming a private Jesus, and our claim that He has all authority lacks public meaning."[195]

But if the church again preaches "the whole counsel of God" (Acts 20:27 ESV) to a dying culture, we regain the credibility that we have lost by surrendering so much of what the world can clearly see the Bible teaches. "If the church broadens its message to address the American people as the kings of this land, calling them in their capacity as rulers to repent and trust in Christ, then its evangelism will take on a fresh clarity and urgency."[196]

May God grant that His church will rise to the challenge once more.

CHAPTER 9

"EVERY HIGH THING THAT EXALTETH ITSELF AGAINST THE KNOWLEDGE OF GOD": THE SCHOOLHOUSE AGAINST THE CHURCH

My home state, Virginia, requires public schools to be accredited based mainly on their Standards of Learning (SOL) scores.

A few years back, our local Lynchburg newspaper ran a story about school accreditation rates. One school in Lynchburg had failed to make the grade. The story quoted the mother of one student. She said, in as many words, "No, I'm not going to take my daughter out of that school. She gets good grades! That school needs students like my daughter to pull its numbers up!"

My wife and I were dumbfounded. Years later, I still am. Here was a mom whose child's school is demonstrably failing its students, but her student was surviving the overall bad trend. And instead of thinking, I need to find a way to do better for my child, *her thought was* I will let my child stay in a failing school, because it will fail even worse if I give her a better chance. *This is still incredible to me.*

How warped can a parent's priorities be? Is it just an intellectual problem, or is it perhaps a spiritual problem?

* * * * *

If I had a healthy aversion to risk, I would never have started writing this chapter. And I already know it will be the hardest one to accept for most readers. But I so firmly believe it is true that we will walk through it. If it is true, it needs to be said. If not, it is a good-faith effort nonetheless, based on how I understand the Scriptures.

As I began to write this chapter, I thought I was the only one who had ever considered these possibilities. But the more I studied, the more I saw that the warnings have been sounded for years. Authors such as Marlin Maddoux, David Barton, Samuel Blumenfeld, former New York State teacher of the year John Taylor Gatto, and Reagan education secretary William Bennett have sounded many similar warnings. This chapter may reinvent the wheel to some degree. But somehow the story needs to be told, so let's begin.

The battle for the human mind and soul is as old as the Garden of Eden. And what is at stake is nothing less than the authority of God's Word and thus the credibility of almighty God Himself.

What we believe—what we think—does more than affect who we are. What we think *is* who we are. Proverbs tells us as much: "As [a man] thinketh in his heart, so is he" (23:7). That's why Proverbs warns that we are to "keep [our] heart with all diligence; for out of it are the issues of life" (4:23).

We touched briefly in Chapter 6 on America's trust in education as the great panacea for human ills. We believe if we could just make humanity more intelligent, we could make us better. We blame everything from poverty to robbery to sexual assault to Islamic terror on a lack of education. We worry endlessly that tight budgets are shortchanging our children's education. The entire focus of our worry is that we are not doing enough. We devote almost no worry to what our children are learning. Yet if Scripture is to be believed, what we learn is more important than how much we learn.

As we noted, the battle for the mind and heart is as old as the Garden of Eden. Remember the first temptation? What attack did the tempter make? "Yea, hath God said . . . " (Genesis 3:1). His first attack was to question the credibility of God and His Word. Once Eve responded with a repetition of God's warning, "Ye shall not eat of it . . . lest ye die" (v. 3), the tempter simply denied God's warning outright: "Thou shalt not surely die" (v. 4).

The decision of Adam and Eve to succumb to the temptation to challenge God's Word opened up thousands of years of human misery. And the tempter has never changed his strategy. And somehow we keep falling for it.

We talked in Chapter 5 about the impossibility of moral neutrality; neither the world nor Christ permits it. Yet somehow Christian America has bought the notion that our public school and higher education systems are morally neutral. We have bought into a damnable dichotomy between the "sacred" (Sunday religious stuff) and the "secular" (Monday through Saturday decisions, mostly economic and morally neutral). We aim for moral neutrality in the secular world and are content to limit our sacred stuff mostly to church and home.

Accordingly, we have bought into the lie that education is—or at least can and should be—morally neutral and just about getting a good education in the three Rs. We keep religion out of the schools and limit it to the church.

Except that we don't.

We humans are incurably religious beings. God has designed us to worship. In His original design we would worship Him. In our fallen state we are no less designed to—driven to—worship. We just worship other gods.

In this chapter I posit the idea that America's public education system—and its higher education system as an extension of the public education system—are in fact ardent practitioners of their religion, for which they proselytize endlessly. The public schools preach the religion of secular humanism. This religion has its strict doctrines, dogmas that cannot be challenged. Secular humanism is not neutral toward Christ; it is His mortal enemy. Like so many other religions, secular humanism is out to subjugate competing worldviews, competing religions. This has had undeniable and unavoidable negative effects on our culture. Finally, I posit the idea that none of this is accidental. We are not in an era of failing schools. The schools are succeeding spectacularly at what they were designed to do by the nineteenth-century thinkers who fathered the American public school movement—to de-Christianize a culture by de-Christianizing its next generation. (I told you this wouldn't be easy to accept—please read on a bit further before you write this off.)

1. AMERICAN PUBLIC SCHOOLS DEMONSTRATE HOSTILITY TO CHRISTIANITY

First let's look at some basic biblical statements. Then let's consider how the public school system responds to those statements.

The Bible opens with a foundational presupposition in Genesis 1:1: "In the beginning God created the heaven and the earth." The creation account goes on to say God created man on the sixth day from the dust of the ground and He created a woman from the man. "But that's so Old Testament," you say. Is it really?

"He answered and said unto them, Have ye not read, that he which made them at the beginning made them male and female?" (Matthew 19:4). See also Mark 10:6: "From the beginning of the creation God made them male and female." Jesus likewise confirmed the historical reality of Noah's ark (Luke 17:27) and Jonah and the great fish (Matthew 12:40).

On the historical reality of God's creation of humanity, Christ based His commands in favor of marriage and against adultery. Christ allowed for no other theory of origins than God's creation.

What does the public school system do with the clear biblical statement that God created? Does it simply veer from Christ's path and allow other possible theories? No. Does it just posit the evolutionary theory as a default position while allowing debate? No.

In fact, the public school system adamantly refuses to consider not just Creation by the God of the Bible but any theory of intelligent design whatsoever. Secular humanism cannot concede a creator. If there is a creator, He has authority to command His creation. The very hypothesis of a creator must be ridiculed, discarded, and even banned from consideration.

This is not an exaggeration. In 1987 the United States Supreme Court considered a case called *Edwards v. Aguillard*.[197] The case challenged a Louisiana statute that required public schools to present the evidence for both sides of the creation/evolution debate. Quite the novel idea for education, right? Present evidence for both sides and let intelligent students consider the evidence for themselves? Inclusion? Diversity? Tolerance?

The statute did not favor creation over evolution in any way. In fact, the schools could choose simply not to teach on the question of origins. But if they taught one side, they had to give evidence for the other side. Seems fair enough.

The Supreme Court shot down the Louisiana statute. And guess who filed friend-of-the-court briefs urging the court to strike it down? If you said "Americans United for Separation of Church and State," you guessed right. Did you also guess the American Federation of Teachers and the American Association of University Professors? You guessed right there too.

The public schools (and our university professors) are not neutrals on God's claim to rights as creator. They are hostiles in the debate.

God tells us, "The fool hath said in his heart, 'There is no God'" (Psalm 14:1). But it is the official position of America's public schools that there is no God, that we came about by mere chance. God tells us, "This book of the law shall not depart out of thy mouth; but thou shalt meditate therein day and night" (Joshua 1:8). What do the schools say?

In 1963 the Supreme Court decided the case of *School District of Abington Township v. Schempp*.[198] In an eight-to-one ruling, the court invalidated a Pennsylvania statute requiring the reading of ten Scripture verses without comment each school day. Somehow the court found the reading of ten verses, with no editorial commentary, was the equivalent of establishing a state religion.

When it comes to your children, during the predominant part of their waking hours, government schools have declared that they will not allow obedience to the command of Joshua 1:8. The Bible is persona non grata in the schools. Caesar wins; God loses. There is no compromise.

The Bible commands us to "pray without ceasing" (1 Thessalonians 5:17). What do the schools say about that?

In 1992 the Supreme Court in its *Lee v. Weisman* decision similarly banned clergy-led prayer as part of high school graduations.[199] Apparently even allowing someone not affiliated with the school to pray as part of a celebration was again the equivalent of establishing a state religion.

When it comes to your children, during the predominant part of their waking hours, government schools have declared that they will not allow obedience to the command of 1 Thessalonians 5:17. Caesar wins; God loses. There is no compromise.

Right in my own part of the country, in 2003 the US Court of Appeals for the Fourth Circuit considered the case of *Child Evangelism Fellowship v. Montgomery County Public Schools.*[200] The schools had a policy of letting nonprofit groups send flyers home with students, along with school-sponsored flyers. Several religious groups were included. But when CEF tried to send flyers inviting students to its meetings, the school objected on the grounds that CEF's meetings were religious.

Just as with the *Edwards v. Aguillard* case out of Louisiana, the usual school suspects showed up with amicus briefs to oppose the idea of treating Christianity the same as other religions. Those filing amicus briefs included (again) Americans United for Separation of Church and State as well as the National School Boards Association, the National Parent Teacher Association, the American Association of School Administrators, and the National Education Association.

When they tell you they want inclusion, diversity, a healthy contest of ideas, they lie. When they tell you they want to "keep religion out of schools," they lie. The reality is nothing less than a concerted war on Christianity, which is recognized as the enemy.

As Charles Colson put it in his work *Kingdoms in Conflict*, "Traditional religious influences have been excluded from public debates." Accordingly, "government is free to make its own ultimate judgments. Hence government ideology acquires the force of religion."[201] And nowhere is this more obvious than in the realm of education. The modern American public school and higher education complex is not irreligious. It is every bit as religious as Christianity. Try running for school board and proposing any sort of objective measure of whether the schools are succeeding, and see how quickly you're subjected to the "Education Inquisition" and accused of hating teachers and not caring about children.

2. THE RELIGION OF THE PUBLIC SCHOOL AND HIGHER EDUCATION COMPLEX: SECULAR HUMANISM

At the most basic level, the ultimate religious question of the ages is this—God's law or man's law? Who is sovereign—God or man? The question actually predates humankind.

In Isaiah 14 the prophet tells a story that is truly prehistoric, before Creation.

> How art thou fallen from heaven, O Lucifer, son of the morning! how art thou cut down to the ground, which didst weaken the nations!

> For thou hast said in thine heart, I will ascend into heaven, I will exalt my throne above the stars of God: I will sit also upon the mount of the congregation, in the sides of the north:

> I will ascend above the heights of the clouds; I will be like the most High.

> Yet thou shalt be brought down to hell, to the sides of the pit. (vv. 12–15)

The first sin was not committed by Adam or Eve. The real original sin was Satan's determination that he would not play second fiddle to almighty God. The intoxication of absolute power was too much for him. And he suspected it would prove too much for humans as well.

In Genesis 3:5, at the Tree of Knowledge of Good and Evil, he gave his theory a test run: "God knows that in the day you eat from it your eyes will be opened, and you will be like God, knowing good and evil" (NASB). And as it had been for Satan, the allure of being God was too much for Adam and Eve.

And for thousands of years since, we have shaken our fists in the face of God, declaring over and over, "I will exalt my throne above the stars of God" (Isaiah 14:13).

Secular humanism is just the aptly named modern incarnation of the oldest false religion going. In fact, in the famous footnote 11 of its 1961 case *Torcaso v.*

Watkins, the US Supreme Court stated, "Among religions in this country which do not teach what would generally be considered a belief in the existence of God are Buddhism, Taoism, Ethical Culture, Secular Humanism and others."[202]

The original *Humanist Manifesto* was drafted in 1933 (there have been two redrafts since—*Humanist Manifesto II* in 1973 and *Humanist Manifesto III* in 2003). Consider its words, and then try to make a reasoned argument it is not a religion.

Today man's larger understanding of the universe, his scientific achievements, and deeper appreciation of brotherhood, have created a situation which requires a new statement of the means and purposes of religion. . . . It is . . . obvious that any religion that can hope to be a synthesizing and dynamic force for today must be shaped for the needs of this age. To establish such a religion is a major necessity of the present. It is a responsibility which rests upon this generation. We therefore affirm the following:

FIRST: Religious humanists regard the universe as self-existing and not created.

SECOND: Humanism believes that man is a part of nature and that he has emerged as a result of a continuous process . . .

FIFTH: Humanism asserts that the nature of the universe depicted by modern science makes unacceptable any supernatural or cosmic guarantees of human values . . .

SIXTH: We are convinced that the time has passed for theism . . .

EIGHTH: Religious Humanism considers the complete realization of human personality to be the end of man's life and seeks its development and fulfillment in the here and now . . .

NINTH: In the place of the old attitudes involved in worship and prayer the humanist finds his religious emotions expressed in a heightened sense of personal life and in a cooperative effort to promote social well-being.

TENTH: It follows that there will be no uniquely religious emotions and attitudes of the kind hitherto associated with belief in the supernatural.[203]

In 1973 Paul Kurtz and Edwin H. Wilson published *Humanist Manifesto II*. It reads, in part,

> As in 1933, humanists still believe that traditional theism, especially faith in the prayer-hearing God, assumed to live and care for persons, to hear and understand their prayers, and to be able to do something about them, is an unproved and outmoded faith. Salvationism, based on mere affirmation, still appears as harmful, diverting people with false hopes of heaven hereafter. Reasonable minds look to other means for survival. . . .
>
> Traditional dogmatic or authoritarian religions that place revelation, God, ritual, or creed above human needs and experience do a disservice to the human species . . .
>
> Promises of immortal salvation or fear of eternal damnation are both illusory and harmful. . . . Modern science discredits such historic concepts as the "ghost in the machine" and the "separable soul." Rather, science affirms that the human species is an emergence from natural evolutionary forces. . . . There is no credible evidence that life survives the death of the body . . .
>
> In the area of sexuality, we believe that intolerant attitudes, often cultivated by orthodox religions and puritanical cultures, unduly repress sexual conduct. The right to birth control, abortion, and divorce should be recognized. . . . Neither do we wish to prohibit, by law or social sanction, sexual behavior between consenting adults. The many varieties of sexual exploration should not in themselves be considered "evil." . . .
>
> We believe in the right to universal education. . . . The schools should . . . be open at all levels to any and all.[204]

Explain to me how these principles are not religious to their core. Tell me how they are anything but a frontal assault on the God of the Bible and His Word. And we had best realize the public school is the "church" of secular humanism.

The public education system is not a moral vacuum. It has its own religion prepared to fill the void once Christianity has at last been completely stripped of vitality.

An article in *Chronicles* magazine asks, "What 'new values' are educators trying to instill?" and gives this list from a North Carolina in-service workshop:

There is no right or wrong, only conditioned responses.

The collective good is more important than the individual.

Consensus is more important than principle.

Flexibility is more important than accomplishment.

Nothing is permanent except change.

All ethics are situational; there are no moral absolutes.

There are no perpetrators, only victims.[205]

It is a war. You and your God are the enemy. And your child's soul is at stake.

And the public universities are just as bad. As Charles Colson noted, within America's universities:

the very idea of truth had been called into question. . . . America was a victim of 'an education adrift in relativity that doubted all values, and a degraded science that shirked the spiritual issues.'

Universities responded by simply changing the goal of education. Where once the object of learning had been the discovery of truth, now each student must be allowed to decide truth for himself. Dogma, not ignorance, became the enemy.[206]

Thus the creation of thousands of spoiled millennials who have had everything handed to them on a silver platter, decrying the "injustice" of a nation that would expect them to repay their own student loans and seeking "safe spaces" to avoid having to endure the misery of opposing viewpoints.

3. HISTORY: THE UNHOLY ALLIANCE OF PUBLIC SCHOOLS AND SECULAR HUMANISM

Perhaps the two most influential figures in the development of public schools as we know them today were Horace Mann (1796–1859) and John

Dewey (1859–1952). Mann, known as the Father of American Public Schools, was famous for bringing the godless Prussian system of schooling from Germany to Massachusetts and thence to America as a whole. Ellwood Cubberley, the first dean of the Stanford School of Education, said of Mann, "No one did more than he to establish in the minds of the American people the conception that education should be universal, non-sectarian, and free, and that its aim should be social efficiency, civic virtue, and character, rather than mere learning or the advancement of sectarian ends."[207] But what Cubberley meant by "civic virtue, and character" is a far cry from a Christian conception of character. Mann's work brought an end to the Puritan idea of the schools as a means of teaching humanity about God and ushered in the idea that people need no God. Democracy, for Mann, was the ultimate means of human salvation, and being a good democratic citizen was the real display of civic virtue.

Mann intended to use the schools to pry children loose from the theistic ideals of their parents and teach them to embrace his ideal of salvation by democracy. He wrote, "We, then, who are engaged in the sacred cause of education are entitled to look upon all parents as having given hostages to our cause."[208]

Dewey is known as the Father of American Progressive Education. Dewey was an atheist and a signer of *Humanist Manifesto I*. Dewey sat on the board of Charles Francis Potter's First Humanist Society of New York and was a founding member of the Intercollegiate Socialist Society.

Dewey saw public education as the means to create not a more learned populace but a more collective society. He was "effusive in his praise of Vladimir Lenin . . . and believed that socialism was the ideal organization for society. Like the communist dictator, he believed that the goal of public education was to bring about 'state consciousness.'"[209] Caesar would replace God as the highest authority.

To that end, Dewey traveled to the new Soviet Union to report on how its schools were ushering in the new progressive state. "The schools are . . . the 'ideological arm of the Revolution. . . . That which distinguishes the Soviet schools . . . from the progressive schools of other countries (with which they have much in common) is precisely the conscious control of every educational procedure by reference to a single and comprehensive social purpose."[210] In other words, to the degree the Soviet schools were wholly geared toward the goal of creating an all-powerful state and subordinating the individual, they were superior to their less-progressive counterparts in America and elsewhere. "Their function is to create habits so that persons will act cooperatively and collectively as readily as now in capitalistic countries they act 'individualistically.'"[211]

Dewey and Potter—especially Potter—were devotees of Darwin's new theory of evolution. Dewey and Potter saw the public school as the training ground—the cathedral—of the religion of secular humanism. The public school would be the place where "science" would finally defeat supernaturalistic Christianity.

Here's Dewey himself: "There is no God and there is no soul. Hence, there are no needs for the props of traditional religion. With dogma and creed excluded, then immutable truth is also dead and buried. There is no room for fixed, natural law or moral absolutes."[212] We wonder why our kids don't believe in moral absolutes? They are being taught not to all day, every day, right under our noses.

Instead of the Christian God, Dewey promoted the god of the state: "Every teacher should realize the dignity of his calling; that he is a social servant set apart for the maintenance of proper social order. . . . In this way the teacher always is the prophet of the true God and the usherer in of the true kingdom of God."[213]

Potter put it quite presciently in his 1930 book *Humanism: A New Religion*: "Education is thus a most powerful ally of humanism, and every American school is a school of humanism. What can a theistic Sunday school's meeting for an hour once a week and teaching only a fraction of the children do to stem the tide of the five-day program of humanistic teaching?"[214]

Potter's thesis proved all too true (although he was wrong that humanism is a new religion; it is the oldest false religion, even older than humans themselves, as Isaiah tells us). The public schools are inexorably committed to the complete exclusion of God. And they have been frighteningly successful in defeating the church in the battle for the hearts of the younger generations.

As the great preacher J. Gresham Machen put it in the early 1900s,

> Our whole system of school and college education is so constituted as to keep religion and culture as far apart as possible and ignore the question of the relationship between them. On five or six days in the week, we were engaged in the acquisition of knowledge. From this activity the study of religion was banished. We studied natural science without considering its bearing or lack of bearing upon natural theology or upon revelation.[215]

Nor was this accidental. Now church leaders across America are searching desperately for a way to combat the vast amorality of the millennial generation, in particular the epidemic of young people leaving the faith. They look helplessly for ways to be relevant. New music, entertainment, seeker-friendly preaching, an emphasis on being nonjudgmental—anything and everything. Everything except facing the harsh reality—the public schools have stolen the hearts and souls of our children under our noses.

When millennials are asked their reasons for leaving the church, the answers mostly have nothing to do with "outdated" music or boring sermons. Instead, they reject the idea of being required to repress their sexual appetites, and they believe Christianity is a giant fairy tale, a religious experience wholly ungrounded in reality.

And no wonder. Potter was right. Our kids spend hours a day, five days a week, being inculcated endlessly with the ideas that people are just the product of natural, observable forces, that science believes in the real world, while the church is a fantasy world. Then we get the kids for an hour of Sunday school and tell them all about Adam and Eve and a talking snake, Noah getting two of every kind of animal on a boat, Jonah living inside a great fish for three days, Moses parting the Red Sea, and a god who rose from the dead. And we expect them to believe a word we say!

Using the schools as a means of religious indoctrination is nothing new or unique to America. Satan has always tried to pit "science" and "higher learning"—human reason—against divine revelation.

When Pharaoh's palace took Moses from his people, the Egyptians immediately began training him in the godless educational system of Egypt. Egypt of that day was considered the pinnacle of scientific knowledge, military prowess, and economic power. "Pharaoh's daughter took him up, and nourished him for her own son. And Moses was learned in all the wisdom of the Egyptians, and was mighty in words and in deeds. And when he was full forty years old, it came into his heart to visit his brethren the children of Israel" (Acts 7:21–23).

So completely did the Egyptian education succeed that it took Moses forty years to decide to visit his oppressed brethren, God's chosen people.

Likewise with Daniel and his three friends. When they were taken captive to Babylon, they immediately underwent an intensive religious reorientation program. Instead of the diet carefully planned by God, they were offered the king's wine and meat offered to pagan Babylonian idols: "The king spake unto Ashpenaz the master of his eunuchs, that he should bring certain of the children of Israel, and of the king's seed, and of the princes; Children in whom was no blemish, but well favoured, and skilful in all wisdom, and cunning in knowledge, and understanding science, and such as had ability in them to stand in the king's palace, and whom they might teach the learning and the tongue of the Chaldeans" (Daniel 1:3–4).

Even their names were changed. All four had Hebrew names that recognized Jehovah as God. *Daniel* means "God is my judge." *Hananiah* means "God has been gracious." *Mishael* means "Who is what God is?" and *Azariah* means "God has helped."

The pagan king changed those names. Daniel became Belteshazzar, a reference to the Babylonian goddess Beltis, meaning "Beltis protect the king." Hananiah became Shadrach, meaning "command of Aku" (the moon god), Mishael became Meshach, likely meaning "Who is what Aku is?" And Azariah became Abednego, likely meaning "slave of the god Nebo." All four Hebrews had names glorifying God, and all four were given names designed to strip them of their God and instead praise gods of wood and stone.

There was nothing coincidental about what the Babylonian schools were trying to do. And there is nothing coincidental about the history, the intent, or the devastating success of the American public school establishment in advancing the secular humanist religion.

We like to decry "the liberal media" or Democrats or homosexual activists or antigun liberals. We have entirely missed the enemy. Hear these words from Paul Blanshard in the *Humanist* magazine: "I think that the most important factor moving us toward a secular society has been the educational factor. Our schools may not teach Johnny how to read properly, but the fact that Johnny is in school until he is sixteen tends toward the elimination of religious superstition. The average American child now acquires a high school education, and this militates against Adam and Eve and all other myths of alleged history."[216]

Or consider the perspective of John J. Dunphy from one of the 1983 issues of *Humanist*:

> I am convinced that the battle for humankind's future must be waged and won in the public school classroom by teachers who correctly perceive their role as proselytizers of a new faith. . . . The classroom must and will become an arena of conflict between the old and new—the rotting corpse of Christianity, together with all its adjacent evils and misery, and the new faith of humanism, resplendent in its promise of a world in which the never-realized Christian ideal of "love thy neighbor" will finally be achieved.[217]

Those determined to root Christianity out of America as any sort of moving force know exactly what they're doing. But the church seems almost wholly ignorant. Tragically not only are we not fighting back; in far too many instances, Christians who have a financial interest in the education system are also the fiercest critics of those few who sound the warning. People who claim to be Christ followers are devotees of the religious system that has proven most effective in blunting the spread of the gospel—that has hastened the process of the salt losing its savor and relegated the church to our position of being laughed to scorn as unscientific Neanderthals and being "trodden under foot of men" (Matthew 5:13).

Martin Luther tried to warn us: "I am much afraid that the universities will prove to be the great gates of hell, unless they diligently labour in explaining the Holy Scriptures, and engraving them in the hearts of youth. I advise no one to place his child where the Scriptures do not reign paramount. Every institution in which men are not unceasingly occupied with the Word of God must become corrupt."[218]

Yet teaching children Scripture is exactly what Caesar's schools forbid! In 1980 in *Stone v. Graham*, the Supreme Court invalidated a law requiring the posting of the Ten Commandments in schools, even if paid for by private funds: "If the posted copies of the Ten Commandments are to have any effect at all, it will be to induce the schoolchildren to read, meditate upon, perhaps to venerate and obey, the Commandments. [This] is not a permissible state objective under the Establishment Clause."[219] And under *Edwards v. Aguillard*, the state cannot teach Genesis is true, that God created, that we are created in God's image instead of descended from monkeys. Rather, the schools not only can but *must* indoctrinate our children in the cry of the fool from Psalm 14:1: "There is no God!"

Speaker and author Voddie Baucham put it succinctly: "If we stop teaching our children in the faith, we will cease to exist as a community of faith. . . . We cannot continue to send our children to Caesar for their education and be surprised when they come home as Romans."[220]

It's bad enough that the schools are teaching moral relativism, premarital sex, free abortions, and the desirability of homosexuality. But the church had better deal with the harsh reality that our children are being trained to be fools, to be atheists, to be deniers of basic biblical truth, to be scorners of God and His Word. It is not a political problem. The public school and higher education establishment has become a false religion. But instead of "casting down imaginations, and every high thing that exalteth itself against the knowledge of God" (2 Corinthians 10:5), we defend the very system that is cutting out the souls of our kids, and we crucify those who sound the warning.

And a precious few have sounded the warning. In his book *Public Education against America*, the late conservative Christian talk radio host Marlin Maddoux wrote, "The public school system has done more to undermine the basic principles of freedom, free enterprise, patriotism, and Christianity than any other single institution."[221]

Maddoux continued,

> The steady stream of anti-Christian propaganda and the institutional bias against traditional values is having a devastating effect. Our children and young people are not prepared to counter highly developed psychological attacks. Bewildered parents watch helplessly from the sidelines as their children are marginalized and ridiculed by their peers for holding on to their Christian faith. Unable to effectively defend their faith, too often the students crumble under the intense psychological pressure to conform. The final blow comes when their biblical values are superseded by secular humanist values. At that point, rebellion sets in as the children inform their parents . . . that they don't have to live by their rules anymore, that they are free to choose their own values.[222]

Dan Smithwick runs a ministry called the Nehemiah Institute (NI). NI developed and administers its PEERS worldview test to students (evaluating their view of politics, economics, education, religion, and social issues). The PEERS test groups students by their responses into four groups across the worldview spectrum—biblical theism, moderate Christianity, secular humanism, and socialism. Scores of 70–100 are rated as a biblical theism worldview, while scores of 0–29 are rated as a secular humanist worldview. Scores of less than 0 are counted as a socialistic worldview.

In 2002 Smithwick wrote a frightening article detailing the findings of the PEERS test. The article was titled "One Generation to Go, Then the End."

Smithwick projected that evangelical kids in public schools—and Christian schools—would be firmly in the secular humanist camp by 2018.[223]

The article concluded, "Based on projections using the decline rate for Christian students, the church will have lost her posterity to hard-core Humanism between 2014 and 2018. . . . If these projections hold true . . . it will be the end of America as we have known it for over 200 years."[224] Smithwick wrote that the data projected that "we would have to officially label the 'next generation of Christian adults' as 'Committed Secular Humanists with leanings toward Socialism' between the years 2014 and 2018."[225]

Smithwick sent me a copy of the 2017 results of NI's PEERS test. The results were almost as bad as predicted. By 2017 Christian students in public schools were scoring at three, barely above socialism. Students in traditional Christian schools were scoring at twelve, in the lower half of the secular humanist ranking. These two groups make up more than ninety percent of Christian kids.[226]

The upshot is frightening. Ninety percent of professedly Christian high schoolers have a worldview that is the religion of the Enemy himself: secular humanism. The reality is stark. While professing Christ, we have lost our kids to the Enemy. And the public schools have driven the train. And we are generally unwilling to even consider a different educational paradigm. Perhaps we ourselves have changed gods.

4. SECULAR HUMANISM'S DISEASE: THE SEXUAL REVOLUTION SWALLOWS THE CHURCH

As much as many in the church are desperate to avoid the idea of a battle over "divisive social issues," perhaps the most desperate struggle going on in the schools today is the battle over sexual expression. As with the other battles going on in the schools, there is no way to take a neutral or amoral position. The battle, as always, is between God's command of "one man and one woman for one lifetime" and humanity's demand for absolute moral freedom to do as we please. And the other side is playing for keeps.

The LGBTQ lobby is increasingly unsatisfied with mere tolerance and has begun to demand absolute societal support and an end to public criticism. Chai Feldblum, a respected lesbian law professor and President Barack Obama's appointee to the Equal Employment Opportunity Commission, minces no words in drawing the battle lines between the LGBTQ movement and religion—particularly Christianity. In 2006 she told the *Weekly Standard* magazine that when sexual liberty and religious liberty are in conflict "I'm having a hard time coming up with any case in which religious liberty should win."[227] Like it or not, she's being honest.

As I was writing this book, the school board in Fairfax County in my home state of Virginia—the thirteenth-largest school district in America—was voting on a proposed new sex education program. The new proposed curriculum would replace "biological sex" with "sex assigned at birth"—as if the pink and blue "It's a Boy" and "It's a Girl" balloons that parents have taken home from the maternity ward for years were somehow just assigned by the obstetrician.

The purpose of the change? To "convey to students that they are accepted regardless of how they choose to identify," according to David Aponte, cochair of the advocacy group GLSEN NoVa, as paraphrased in the *Washington Post*.[228] That acronym stands for *Gay, Lesbian and Straight Education Network*. GLSEN seeks to create Gay-Straight Alliance clubs in schools across the country.

The new curriculum also removed the discussion of abstinence as the only 100 percent effective way to prevent sexually transmitted diseases.

Never mind the greater question of why schools arrogate to themselves the right to dictate sexual morality (or immorality) to our kids. The fact is, those who refuse to submit to any limits on sexual behavior imposed by anyone else are engaged in a great battle—and the hearts and minds of your kids are their target.

Don't take my word for it. According to another paraphrase from Mr. Aponte in the *Washington Post* article, "Northern Virginia and California have served as laboratories for policies regarding lesbian, gay, bisexual and transgender issues."[229] And in that laboratory, as Tony Perkins of the Family Research Council pointed out, "local children are the rats."[230]

The Fairfax County School Board voted ten to one to pass the new curriculum. And no, it wasn't because Fairfax County in the Washington, DC, suburbs is so liberal. In fact, the issue jammed the school board's comment line with 1,300 citizen comments: eighty-three percent opposed the "sex assigned at birth" change. And 100 percent—100 percent!—of comments opposed removing the discussion of abstinence as the only 100 percent effective way to prevent STDs.[231]

It's not about representing the values of the people. It's about revolutionizing the values of the people. It's about forcing immorality and license down the throats of the majority of citizens who still realize that some moral speed limits are good for a culture. Even when 100 percent of citizen comments take one position, GLSEN and its elite allies in the Fairfax public schools predetermined the outcome.

Don't think for a moment that the school system is neutral. The Fairfax schools ran an old-fashioned railroad job on their citizens, even in violation of state regulations. As Family Research Council's Cathy Ruse and her husband, Austin, president of the Center for Family and Human Rights, wrote,

> The sex-ed curriculum advisory committee that is responsible for drafting the lessons is supposed to be made up of stakeholders, namely parents. Any curriculum it devises must reflect "broad-based community involvement." These are mandates from the Virginia Department of Education.
>
> But the almost 40-member committee is made up mostly of people on the county payroll, not parents. There are even 4 high school students on the committee.[232]

Yes, Fairfax County Schools still teach about abstinence. They teach that students should abstain until they find a new steady sex partner. The word *marriage*, Cathy and Austin Ruse noted, is not mentioned one time in the new abstinence discussions.

"As a dad," Perkins wrote, "the idea that I wouldn't have control over what my children are learning at school is absolutely unacceptable. Parents—not teachers, state legislatures, school boards, or outside groups—should be the ultimate authority on what their kids learn and when. But, because of radical influences like GLSEN, teenagers growing up in Christian homes could be morally compromised because their parents don't know what they're hearing in class."[233]

Yes, they could be—and they have been.

Maddoux wrote,

> At the heart of their message to the children is the assumption of moral equivalence between homosexuality, bisexuality, and heterosexuality. Any natural aversion to homosexuality is portrayed as a personality defect or bigotry based on ignorance. . . . In most cases, children are subjected to these highly controversial courses and programs without parents knowing their content or even that they exist at all. In spite of what parents are being told, these presentations are vehicles for recruitment into the gay lifestyle . . .
>
> The pro-gay forces are all too willing to pick up on the signals of those few who do have confused feelings, preying upon their vulnerable state. They intensify the confusion and then zero in on those who are susceptible to their message. Like stalkers following their spoil, they watch for signs of weakness in the children, and then they pounce . . .
>
> The schools pride themselves at promoting diversity. Gay and lesbian counselors are made available for any teen that might show the slightest sign of sexual conflict or doubt. Closing the net, the school then funnels these confused children directly into the hands of veteran homosexuals who have already admitted to having a personal stake in seeing more teens "come out."[234]

The plan is devilishly simple. Apply the power of school authorities, plus peer pressure. Then,

> constant subjection to shocking sexual information slowly brings about a state of desensitization to bizarre and deviant human

sexual behavior. When that first stage of shock and desensitization is followed by even more shocking material, followed by even more desensitization, at some point nothing shocks the child anymore. The child is so overwhelmed and confused by the conflicting messages that he enters a state called "cognitive dissonance." The child's mind simply ceases to resist the emotional overload and gently succumbs to the sexual propaganda, thus accepting the abnormal as normal. The homosexual activists know that the earlier they can reach the children, the better their chances are of sowing confusion in their minds.[235]

I close this section with another real-life story in an effort to shock us from our complacency. Maddoux told of the Hayward Unified School District in California. The district crafted "a policy that allows school district employees to 'come out' in front of students." They allowed staff to talk about their sinful lifestyles during classroom time. The school board provided that no notice need be provided to parents, and parents were not given the chance to opt their children out of the propaganda.

It should be made abundantly clear that your children and grandchildren are in the crosshairs of the homosexual movement . . . The focus on children as sexual targets is not at the fringes of the homosexual movement. It is front and center in their political agenda. In fact, a significant goal of the gay rights movement is to have all laws against adults having sexual relations with children abolished.

A 1992 editorial in the *Sentinel*, San Francisco's premiere homosexual publication, stated that sex "between men and boys is at the foundation of homosexuality."[236]

When US Representative Nancy Pelosi marched in the 2001 Pride Parade in San Francisco, she marched three people away from Harry Hay. Who was Harry Hay? He was a very public advocate for pedophilia. At one New York University forum sponsored by a campus homosexual group, Hay stated, "If the parents and friends of gays are truly friends of gays, they would know from their gay kids that the relationship with an older man is precisely what thirteen-, fourteen-, and fifteen-year-old kids need more than anything else in the world."[237]

The website of NAMBLA, the North American Man-Boy Love Association, states, "Harry was a vocal and courageous supporter of NAMBLA and intergenerational sexual relationships."[238]

And the most powerful Democratic member of the House of Representatives marched proudly with him.

The schools serve perfectly as recruiting centers. They are coming for your kids. And how much better if they can use the schools to persuade them?

And don't buy for a moment the idea that homosexuality is just an alternative lifestyle. The homosexual lifestyle has been proven to be devastatingly unhealthy to its victims.

5. SECULAR HUMANISM'S DEATH SENTENCE: HOW SCHOOLS BECOME CLIENT FACTORIES FOR PLANNED PARENTHOOD

On January 16, 1992, Marlin Maddoux, then the host of *Point of View* radio talk show, interviewed Carol Everett. Everett had given her life to Christ after years as the wealthy owner of two abortion clinics.

Everett told Maddoux of her career of doing sex education presentations in schools and turning them into a pipeline of repeat customers. She told of making it her personal goal to get three to five abortions out of every girl between thirteen and eighteen years old. Her personal record was nine![239]

Everett told Maddoux that they couldn't naturally find enough thirteen-year-old pregnant girls. So, she said, they used sex education to stimulate the children's interest in sexual activity. Only then could they reap the bloody "rewards."[240]

In his book *Grand Illusions*, George Grant quoted one Planned Parenthood staffer: "Our goal is to be ready as educators and parents to help young people obtain sex satisfaction before marriage. By sanctioning sex before marriage, we will prevent fear and guilt."[241] He cited the language of a Planned Parenthood booklet:

Relax about loving, sex is fun and joyful, . . . and it comes in all types and styles, all of which are Okay. Do what gives pleasure, and enjoy what gives pleasure, and ask for what gives pleasure. Don't rob yourself of joy by focusing on old-fashioned ideas about what's *normal* or *nice.* Just communicate and enjoy!"[242]

Then, presumably, when the girl "has to" terminate an unplanned pregnancy, that will give great joy, too?

As Maddoux wrote, "The cold fact is that Planned Parenthood-style sex education produces *more* sexual activity among the kids, not less. . . . When your child enrolls in the sex ed course at school, the odds go up—*way up*—that he or she will have sex in the near future."[243]

6. THE DEUTERONOMY ETHIC: CHRISTIAN PARENTS OWE OUR KIDS A CHRISTIAN EDUCATION

We see it all the time. Americans' approval rating of Congress hovers around only twenty percent—and for good reason. Yet every two years, Americans almost uniformly reelect their same representative. We claim we're tired of the "good old boys," "the swamp," but we constantly reelect the same person. Hence, nothing ever changes.

The same thing happens with the broken public school system. American Christians will decry the barring of prayer, Bible reading, and the Ten Commandments from schools. They will grudgingly admit that there are problems with the system. But almost uniformly, the grudging admission is followed by a barrage of excuses for their local school. "I'm glad our school isn't like the others. My kid even has a couple of Christian teachers. I'm glad we have good schools here."

Unfortunately, even if your child has a Christian science teacher, that teacher has to teach your child that we are descended from monkeys and is forbidden from teaching any alternative, let alone "in the beginning God . . ." (Gen. 1:1). What, exactly, is the value of having a Christian teacher who is legally bound to teach your student that the Bible is untrue and that God is a liar?

The evidence is overwhelming that the American public school system—not the liberal media, not Hollywood, not Democrats—is the chief culprit in the loss of our kids' souls. But the vast majority of Christian parents, all the while claiming to worship God and love their kids, get defensive and even hostile at the suggestion that there may be a duty to God to do better for our kids. Most of us know instinctively that our kids would be better off with a distinctly Christian education. But there are innumerable excuses as to why we "cannot" do any better for our kids.

In 2002 Dr. James Dobson joined the chorus of lonely prophets urging Christian parents to pull their kids out of Caesar's schools. "This threat to kids is much, much broader than the homosexual movement," he warned. "It doesn't stop there. It is aimed at the very core of the Judeo-Christian system of values, the very core of scriptural values."[244]

Jesus gave us a plan to seek reconciliation with personal enemies in Matthew 18. It involves going to the offender personally, then with one or two witnesses, and finally taking the offense to the entire church if there is no repentance. Finally, if the offender refuses to listen even to the church as a whole, "let him be unto thee as an heathen man and a publican [tax collector]" (v. 17). Jesus was not advocating mistreating the publican; in fact, He personally ate with them in an effort to reach them with the gospel. But He essentially advised that when truth is consistently refused, the personal relationship is to be cut off.

Admittedly the pattern is given in reference to interpersonal relationships and is not advice specific to educating our kids. But I submit it is time for Christians to treat the public school system as "heathen"—it is—and as "a publican." In other words, just like the publican, the public school is a needy mission field. Christians can and indeed should serve there and seek to be salt and light. But there are endless places in which we should be salt and light but to whose care we should never leave our children. And at this critical juncture, the public schools have abundantly proven themselves to be such a place. The Bible promises, "He that walketh with wise men shall be wise: but a companion of fools shall be destroyed" (Proverbs 13:20) and "Do not be deceived: 'Bad company corrupts good morals'" (1 Corinthians 15:33, NASB). For too long we have left our kids to be destroyed. We *must* do better. Martin Luther was right; we have consigned our kids to the "gates of hell." It's time we take the gospel to the public schools but give our kids an unashamedly Christian education. If we do not, the trajectory is clear. And it will cost the souls of our kids.

It was the 2017 local school board race between Republican John Kinchen and his opponent that shone a spotlight on this issue for me. His opponent's campaign was based on increasing taxes to give more money to the schools. Kinchen chose a values-based approach, focusing on preventing taxpayer dollars from being used on transgender bathrooms and preventing any more articles glamorizing cross-dressing students in the local high school yearbook.

The race took on distinct overtones of a battle between "It is written" and "All these things I will give you, if you bow down and worship me." And even as the moderate Republican candidate for governor was winning 75 percent of the vote in the district (although he lost handily statewide), Kinchen fell seventy-three votes short. Undeniably large numbers of professing Christians had supported the transgender-friendly candidate who promised an expanded school budget. Kinchen even had professing Christians tell him he needed to repent for "picking on kids" by raising the issue.

That's when I realized where we are as a culture. If, in the very shadow of Liberty University, in an eighty percent Republican district, if a candidate cannot win on a values-based appeal over a purely financial appeal, something is desperately wrong. And unless and until the professing church of Jesus Christ begins to take the claims of Christ as authoritative again, all our political and cultural efforts are nothing more than a rear-guard action in a culture headed on the fast track to hell.

In early America the center of the village was the little white church with the steeple pointing up to God. The most respected people were the preachers. The Bible was seen as the way to societal happiness. God was the center and the giver of all that is.

Today the center of the village is the local public school. Cultural and civic life revolves around it. Instead of identifying by our church denomination, we identify by our school mascot. Education is seen as the way to societal happiness and achievement. And Caesar, the omnipotent state, is the center, the giver of all that is.

It's time the church took a stand. It's time we fulfilled our Deuteronomy 6 mandate:

> These words, which I command thee this day, shall be in thine heart:
>
> And thou shalt teach them diligently unto thy children, and shalt talk of them when thou sittest in thine house, and when thou walkest by the way, and when thou liest down, and when thou risest up.
>
> And thou shalt bind them for a sign upon thine hand, and they shall be as frontlets between thine eyes.
>
> And thou shalt write them upon the posts of thy house, and on thy gates. (vv. 6–9)

It's time for the church to get over our inferiority complex. Christ has commanded us to "[teach] them to observe *all things* whatsoever I have commanded you" (Matthew 28:20). We do so on the basis that "all authority has been given unto [him] in heaven and in earth" (v. 18). We have the Book that gives us "*all things* that pertain unto life and godliness" (2 Peter 1:3). We "have an anointing from the Holy One, and . . . know *all things*" (1 John 2:20 NKJV).[245] Why do we agree to speak only on how to get to heaven and consent to be silent on everything else He commands? Worse, why does so much of the church spend so much effort on supporting our local schools instead of evangelizing our local schools? "What agreement hath the temple of God with idols?" (2 Corinthians 6:16). It is time we offered our nation Truth instead of moral relativism. Holiness instead of tolerance of abominations. Life instead of death. The freedom of the gospel instead of bondage to the omnipotent state.

"He that is not with me is against me; and he that gathereth not with me scattereth abroad" (Matthew 12:30). American Christianity has surrendered the battle for the hearts and minds of our kids. And the younger generations have been scattered abroad, away from Him.

It's time we boldly proclaimed Truth and accepted the mandate to teach it to our children. Caesar will never do it for us.

CHAPTER 10

RIGHTLY DIVIDING BIBLE BUZZWORDS

For years I've heard from pulpit and pew about the desirability of unity, oneness in Christ, being together in the gospel, and so forth. But my mind has struggled to balance these correct-sounding terms with reality. This came home to me with the election of President Barack Obama. Obama became the first US president to endorse homosexual "marriage." As an Illinois senator, he actually voted against a ban on so-called partial-birth abortion, the act of murdering a partially born baby. But he attended Trinity United Church of Christ in Chicago, and when some suggested he was Muslim, he stoutly insisted that he was a Christian.

And I watched many African American friends, folks whose churches I knew, vote for him in droves for the chance to elect an African American president. I watched as preachers in the news prayed that God would help the president enact his agenda. But I could see how so much of the president's voting record was not merely godless but downright murderous.

I was continually backed, again and again, into a quandary. How in this world could I claim the same gospel as folks who would knowingly vote for a man with principles so antithetical to God's Word? How could these folks and I all be in church at eleven o'clock Sunday morning, singing many of the same hymns and hearing preaching in many ways similar? How could this be squared?

* * * * *

Perhaps every generation of the church has its emphasis and its Bible buzzwords to teach that emphasis. Often that emphasis is formed to address a problem the church sees that needs addressing. I have observed that oftentimes that emphasis can be so all consuming that it tends to minimize or even ignore other important biblical truths that we ought to be teaching. The emphasis itself—and the Bible buzzwords themselves—may be entirely true. But if considered in a vacuum, these truths may not present the whole truth. The church has seen numerous times in its history that these partial truths, presented in the relative absence of the rest of Scripture, tend to actually lead to error. That is my concern in writing this chapter.

GRACE

Martin Luther and the Reformers spent a huge amount of time talking about salvation by grace alone. The emphasis was born out of a reaction against the Catholic idea of salvation by works. Luther's seminal ninety-five theses were a response to the idea that the pope could sell indulgences, whereby people could purchase forgiveness of sins.

I love Southern Gospel music. The genre has its roots in the early 1900s. It tends to include many songs about poverty, how hard life on earth is, and how our troubles will end in heaven. The genre is a child of a time in the agrarian age and the Great Depression, and the lyrics tend to be adapted to the experience of the people at the time.

When I was a child in the 1970s, the church had a strong emphasis on the soon return of Christ. Songs about heaven and the rapture, like Bill and Gloria Gaither's "The King Is Coming," were hugely popular.

Today the evangelical church seems to spend a huge amount of time back in Luther's day. We seem terribly concerned that people will fall for the false gospel of salvation by works. A primary Bible word used today is *grace*. We are "grace-centric," "grace-focused," "grace-filled" churches. We should be.

But are we minimizing or even ignoring much of what God says in the Bible? Are we truly giving out "the whole counsel of God" (Acts 20:27 ESV)? Are we even perhaps risking slipping into error through a hyperfocus on a single truth?

Throughout the Bible, God is presented as Someone too big for our human minds to completely grasp. Scripture presents attributes of God as settled facts. Yet, to our minds, some of these attributes seem exclusive of each other. How can the same Jesus be the "Prince of Peace" (Isaiah 9:6) yet say, "I came not to send peace, but a sword" (Matthew 10:34)? How can it be that "God is love" (1 John 4:8) yet that God is "holy, holy, holy" such that He cannot "look on iniquity" (Isaiah 6:3; Habakkuk 1:13)? How can He be "not willing that any should perish" (2 Peter 3:9) and still say, "Depart from me, ye that work iniquity" (Matthew 7:23)? How can it be true that those "whom he did predestinate, them he also called" (Romans 8:30) yet that "whosoever will" may come (Revelation 22:17)?

I submit that these things that seem contradictory to us simply describe a God who is "all in all" (1 Corinthians 15:28), who is self-existent, uncreated, perfect, and in need of nothing, "the fulness of the Godhead" (Colossians 2:9), while we ourselves are by definition imperfect, incomplete, and needy. And if we focus only on one aspect of His nature, without giving due appreciation to His other attributes, we risk not giving Him the honor He is due. We even risk misleading others as to His true nature.

I fear the modern church has done just that with our emphasis on grace. I believe it's high time we reassess whether we are speaking the whole truth and whether the medicine we are prescribing even fits the current raging cultural disease.

It is true "the plural of *anecdote* is not *data*." I understand my thoughts are reactions to my own experiences. But the problem seems to me to be so widespread, I believe a reexamination is needed across the spectrum of the professing church of Jesus Christ, certainly in America and perhaps across much of the world.

I submit that there are three grace-centric messages at work in the church— the one being preached, the one being heard, and the one being twisted to fit our sinful nature and actually practiced.

Grace-centric preachers, in vast numbers, preach basically this message: "Because Jesus came, because of Calvary, I am no longer under the law but under grace. Before, we were obligated to keep the law, and because we could not, Christ came, and now we no longer have to. The law kept us bound; grace sets us free."

That is almost entirely true—as far as it goes. Almost.

The grace-centric position is supported by verses like the following:

- "A man is justified by faith without the deeds of the law" (Romans 3:28).
- "That no man is justified by the law in the sight of God, it is evident: for, The just shall live by faith" (Galatians 3:11).
- "Christ hath redeemed us from the curse of the law" (Galatians 3:13).
- "By grace are ye saved through faith; and that not of yourselves: it is the gift of God: not of works, lest any man should boast" (Ephesians 2:8–9).
- "If we confess our sins, he is faithful and just to forgive us our sins, and to cleanse us from all unrighteousness" (1 John 1:9).

It is indeed a central tenet of biblical Christianity that "our righteousnesses are as filthy rags" (Isaiah 64:6) and that it is impossible for sinful people to earn their way into heaven. I would never dispute this point, because I know I cannot earn my way in and apart from grace I have no hope of eternal life. And if we could be saved by our works, there was no need for Jesus to die, and God murdered His own sinless Son to no purpose.

The problem is that sinful human beings *love* to hear that we are now free from laws and rules and no longer have to live by all those exhausting Old Testament commands. Accordingly, we take the heavily emphasized almost truth and twist it into something false.

When the grace-centric message is preached, what we far too often hear, even if it is not the intent of the grace-centric preacher, is this: "We are sinful, hopelessly depraved human beings. We can do nothing to earn God's favor. The Old Testament law proved this, because they kept having to do the same sacrifices over and over again. But now Jesus has come and paid our penalty. Now we are freed from the responsibility to keep the law. All our sins are forgiven—past, present, and future. We are 'positionally' sanctified, even though until we get to heaven, we will always still sin. There is no righteousness in us, but when God sees us, He sees the righteousness of His Son, which is imputed to us. God loves us and forgives us unconditionally because of what Jesus did, not because of what we do. All our sins are 'under the blood.' Our obligation is just to keep confessing them, pleading the blood of Jesus Christ, and claiming 1 John 1:9 over them, and one day He will come and take us to a place free from sin.' "

Again, this is almost entirely true. But the vast amount of Scripture we leave out of this equation leaves us vulnerable to the third grace-centric message, the one we hear but then twist to fit our sinful human nature and actually live by.

Here is how this third message goes: "I am hopelessly depraved and can't do any good myself anyway. I'm positionally righteous in Christ no matter what I do. God doesn't love me any more or less because of what I do. Once I am saved, I'm always saved. 'No man is able to pluck them out of my Father's hand' [John 10:29]. I'm free from the law. The law is a curse. The law is bondage. Now 'all things are lawful for me' [1 Corinthians 10:23]. 'Why is my freedom judged by another's conscience?' [1 Corinthians 10:29 NASB]. *I'm free in Christ!*"

This partial truth ends up basically turning the death of Christ into a "get out of jail free" card, a license to do just as I please, with "biblical" justification. In essence, because Christ came and died, because of grace, I can live however I wish, I need not change my ways or make sacrifices, and I'm all set for heaven—even if I live like the devil until I get there.

Sinful human beings don't need much excuse to live in sin. We're perfectly happy to use the Bible to justify it. And a steady diet of grace-centric preaching salves the conscience pretty nicely.

I submit that this focus is only partial truth, that the nature of God encompasses much more, and that Scripture demands much more. I submit that grace-centric preaching, in the almost complete absence of sermons on the holiness of God, the wrath of God, sin, and repentance, has left the church almost morally bankrupt, with a defiled conscience and a polluted witness. I submit that the Word that, in its entirety, is "sharper than any a twoedged sword" (Hebrews 4:12) has been dulled to the point of near uselessness and that the saving gospel of Jesus Christ has been replaced with a half gospel that cheapens grace and risks damning souls to eternal hell.

Tozer said,

> The coming of Jesus Christ to the world has been so sentimentalized that it means now something utterly alien to the Biblical teaching concerning it. Soft human pity has been substituted for God's mercy in the minds of millions, a pity that has long ago degenerated into self-pity. The blame for man's condition has been shifted to God, and Christ's dying for the world has been twisted into an act of penance on God's part . . .
>
> This is humanism romantically tinted with Christianity, a humanism that takes sides with rebels and excuses those who by word, thought and deed would glorify fallen men and if possible overthrow the glorious high Throne in the heavens.[246]

Let's examine the Scriptures for some less-popular verses and see whether the Word has answers.

The starting point for me is the apostle Paul, deservedly known as "the apostle of grace." Paul foresaw the problem and worked hard to address it. In the midst of his stirring ode to grace in Romans 5–8, he attempted to preemptively attack the message American Christianity lives by.

Paul ended chapter five with this encouragement: "Where sin abounded, grace did much more abound" (v. 20). But presciently he opened chapter six with a reply to those who would turn grace into license: "What shall we say then? Shall we continue in sin, that grace may abound?" (v. 1).

His answer comes in language just about as strong as the Bible uses: "God forbid." He added, "How shall we, that are dead to sin, live any longer therein?" (v. 2). In verses 6–7, he elaborated: "Knowing this, that our old man is crucified with him, that the body of sin might be destroyed, that henceforth we should not serve sin. For he that is dead is freed from sin."

In verses 11–13, he continued his exposition: "Likewise reckon ye also yourselves to be dead indeed unto sin, but alive unto God through Jesus Christ our Lord. Let not sin therefore reign in your mortal body, that ye should obey it in the lusts thereof. Neither yield ye your members as instruments of unrighteousness unto sin: but yield yourselves unto God, as those that are alive from the dead, and your members as instruments of righteousness unto God."

Let not doesn't translate well from Greek to English. In the Greek it is essentially equivalent to the Hebrew language in the Ten Commandments, "Thou shalt not." It is a direct command: "Thou shalt not let sin reign in your mortal body." Sounds familiar, doesn't it?

Then he nailed the door shut with verse 14: "For sin shall not have dominion over you: for ye are not under the law, but under grace." That derails the train looking to turn grace into license, doesn't it? We must not let sin have dominion over us, *because* we are now under grace! Because of grace, we need no longer be subject to sin.

Paul continued: "Know ye not, that to whom ye yield yourselves servants to obey, his servants ye are to whom ye obey, whether of sin unto death, or of obedience unto righteousness? . . . Being then made free from sin, ye became the servants of righteousness" (vv. 16–18). "Servants of righteousness"? What about being "free in Christ"?

We are. We are now free from sin! "Now being made free from sin, and become servants to God, ye have your fruit unto holiness, and the end everlasting life" (v. 22).

Why don't we hear the rest of the chapter preached? And why don't we see it when we read it? I submit, because it's not what our sinful nature wants to hear.

As for "the curse of the law" (Galatians 3:13), let's consider that a bit more carefully. Was Paul saying God's law is a curse? Galatians 3:10 and 13 might be cited: "As many as are of the works of the law are under the curse: for it is written, Cursed is every one that continueth not in all things which are written in the book of the law to do them . . . Christ hath redeemed us from the curse of the law, being made a curse for us: for it is written, Cursed is every one that hangeth on a tree."

But look a little deeper. Let's return to Romans: "Wherefore the law is holy, and the commandment holy, and just, and good. . . . For I delight in the law of God after the inward man" (7:12, 22).

The existence of the law is not the curse. Nor is the requirement to keep His law the curse. The curse is our inability to keep the law—and the judgment of the law on those who fail to keep it. "Cursed is every one that that continueth not in all things which are written in the book of the law to do them" (Galatians 3:10). But the law itself is not the curse. Paul took the previous quote from Deuteronomy 27:26, where God's people were warned of the curses of disobedience. God was offering His people a choice—obedience and blessing, or disobedience and a curse: "I call heaven and earth to record this day against you, that I have set before you life and death, blessing and cursing: therefore choose life, that both thou and thy seed may live" (30:19).

In the very next chapter after the curse Paul quoted, we see the promised blessings for obedience: "It shall come to pass, if thou shalt hearken diligently unto the voice of the LORD thy God, to observe and to do all his commandments which I command thee this day, that the Lord thy God will set thee on high above all nations of the earth: and all these blessings shall come on thee, and overtake thee, if thou shalt hearken unto the voice of the Lord thy God" (Deuteronomy 28:1–2).

And Paul said that under grace we *can* keep God's commandments: "There hath no temptation taken you but such as is common to man: but God is faithful, who will not suffer you to be tempted above that ye are able; but will with the temptation also make a way to escape, that ye may be able to bear it" (1 Corinthians 10:13). While we will not achieve sinless perfection in this life, grace provides us the enabling power to keep the law and to experience the blessings of obedience instead of the curses of disobedience.

God's law is not drudgery. Psalm 119 is David's song of praise to God for providing His law.

- "Blessed are the undefiled in the way, who walk in the law of the Lord" (v. 1).
- "Open thou mine eyes, that I may behold wondrous things out of thy law" (v. 18).
- "Give me understanding, and I shall keep thy law; yea, I shall observe it with my whole heart. Make me to go in the path of thy commandments; for therein do I delight" (vv. 34–35).
- "Behold, I have longed after thy precepts: quicken me in thy righteousness" (v. 40).
- "So shall I keep thy law continually for ever and ever. And I will walk at liberty: for I seek thy precepts" (vv. 44–45). (Just as in the New Testament—to walk in God's law is to be free.)
- "I will delight myself in thy commandments, which I have loved. My hands also will I lift up unto thy commandments, which I have loved; and I will meditate in thy statutes" (vv. 47–48).
- "Let thy tender mercies come unto me, that I may live: for thy law is my delight" (v. 77).
- "O how love I thy law! it is my meditation all the day. Thou through thy commandments hast made me wiser than mine enemies: for they are ever with me. I have more understanding than all my teachers: for thy testimonies are my meditation. I understand more than the ancients, because I keep thy precepts. I have refrained my feet from every evil way, that I might keep thy word" (vv. 97–101).
- "I hate vain thoughts: but thy law do I love" (v. 113).
- "I opened my mouth, and panted: for I longed for thy commandments" (v. 131).
- "Thy word is very pure: therefore thy servant loveth it" (v. 140).

- "Thy righteousness is an everlasting righteousness, and thy law is the truth. Trouble and anguish have taken hold on me: yet thy commandments are my delights" (vv. 142–43).
- "Consider how I love thy precepts: quicken me, O Lord, according to thy lovingkindness" (v. 159).
- "I have longed for thy salvation, O Lord; and thy law is my delight" (v. 174).

Some curse indeed. And it's not just the Old Testament. First John 5:3 tells us, "This is the love of God, that we keep his commandments: and his commandments are not grievous."

The cheap-grace gospel is, at its heart, a sinful concession to sinful human nature, using the blood of Christ as a cover for the sin it was shed to take away. It is blasphemous. Consider the apostle James, the half brother of Jesus and leader of the Jerusalem church. James hammered home the point that "faith without works is dead" (James 2:26).

> Be ye doers of the word, and not hearers only, deceiving your own selves.
>
> For if any be a hearer of the word, and not a doer, he is like unto a man beholding his natural face in a glass:
>
> For he beholdeth himself, and goeth his way, and straightway forgetteth what manner of man he was.
>
> But whoso looketh into the perfect law of liberty, and continueth therein, he being not a forgetful hearer, but a doer of the work, this man shall be blessed in his deed. (1:22–25)

"The law of liberty," James said? But weren't law and liberty in Christ supposed to be opposites?

> Even so faith, if it hath not works, is dead, being alone.
>
> Yea, a man may say, Thou hast faith, and I have works: shew me thy faith without thy works, and I will shew thee my faith by my works.
>
> Thou believest that there is one God; thou doest well: the devils also believe, and tremble.

But wilt thou know, O vain man, that faith without works is dead?

Was not Abraham our father justified by works, when he had offered Isaac his son upon the altar?

Seest thou how faith wrought with his works, and by works was faith made perfect?

And the scripture was fulfilled which saith, Abraham believed God, and it was imputed unto him for righteousness: and he was called the Friend of God.

Ye see then how that by works a man is justified, and not by faith only.

Likewise also was not Rahab the harlot justified by works, when she had received the messengers, and had sent them out another way?

For as the body without the spirit is dead, so faith without works is dead also. (2:17–26)

James here declared that much of what passes for belief in Jesus is no more saving faith than the demons have. They believe that Jesus is God and that He determines eternal destiny. Accordingly, they shudder. But there is no repentance of sin. In that respect, the demons and much of the evangelical church in America share a similar "faith."

James directly stated that Abraham was "justified by works," that "faith wrought with his works, and by works was faith made perfect? And the scripture was fulfilled which saith, Abraham believed God, and it was imputed unto him for righteousness" (vv. 21–23).

Was James contradicting Paul? Not at all. After all, it was Paul who said in Romans 6:22, "Now being made free from sin, and become servants to God, ye have your fruit unto holiness, and the end everlasting life."

James presented a chilling question: "What doth it profit, my brethren, though a man say he hath faith, and have not works? can faith save him?" (2:14). He didn't answer his own question. He presumed he didn't need to. James was making a simple point that countless evangelical pulpits spend countless Sundays attempting to deny. Faith, unaccompanied by works, is mere mental assent. One can believe from the evidence that the historical Jesus died, was buried, and rose again to pay the price for sin. That is the gospel. But mere mental assent to the historical facts of the gospel never got anyone to heaven. Hell is going to have a large population of people who assent to the historical facts of the gospel. That is not enough.

But don't take my word for it. Ask Jesus. "After that John was put in prison, Jesus came into Galilee, preaching the gospel of the kingdom of God, and saying, The time is fulfilled, and the kingdom of God is at hand: repent ye, and believe the gospel" (Mark 1:14–15).

And *that* is where the modern cheap-grace movement misses the entire point. We ask people whether they believe Jesus died and rose from the dead to pay for their sins. If so, we pronounce them regenerated by the Holy Spirit. *Nonsense.* "The devils also believe, and tremble" (James 2:19). But the demons don't repent. And tragically untold numbers of people with "demon faith" will share the corridors of hell with those demons, because we failed to tell them that Jesus requires repentance of sin.

Paul's own words give the death knell to the cheap grace spilling from pulpits across America. Second Corinthians 5:17 is the clincher verse. It is full of absolute, declarative statements. Paul was a lover of reasoned argument, and in this verse he used what students in logic classes recognize as a classic if/then syllogism: "If any man be in Christ, he is a new creature: old things are passed away; behold, all things are become new." If I am in Christ, then I *am* a new creature. If I am in Christ, then old things *are* passed away. If I am in Christ, then all things *are* become new. This is not some ethereal "positional" language. Nor is it futuristic—an assurance that someday in heaven all things *will* become new. No, it is a past-tense statement of accomplished fact.

And an if/then syllogism also has a reverse side, as logic students will also recognize. If I am *not* a new creature, if old things are *not* passed away, if all things are *not* become new, Paul said, *I am not in Christ.*

It is 100 percent true. I am not in Christ because I changed myself to become new. It is by grace through faith. And it is equally true that if old things have not passed away, I have not been made new in Christ. It is 100 percent true—no one who dies an unrepentant sinner will ever enter heaven, no matter how many theological boxes that person correctly checks.

This is why Paul warned us later to "examine yourselves, whether ye be in the faith; prove your own selves. Know ye not your own selves, how that Jesus Christ is in you, except ye be reprobates?" (2 Corinthians 13:5). In other words, if you habitually live like the devil, you have proven that you are *not* in Christ.

In 1 John the "beloved apostle" offers us a path to assurance of our salvation. He also tells us how we can know that we are not in Christ.

Just three verses before the much more popular verse, he wrote, "If we say that we have fellowship with him, and walk in darkness, we lie, and do not the truth" (1:6).

He hammered the theme home in the next chapter: "Hereby we do know that we know him, if we keep his commandments. He that saith, I know him, and keepeth not his commandments, is a liar, and the truth is not in him. But whoso keepeth his word, in him verily is the love of God perfected: hereby know we that we are in him" (2:3–5).

The way we are saved is all of faith and not of works. The proof of whether we are saved—or not—is just as surely our works. "The Bible tells me so."

John made it clear in the rest of his epistle he is not suggesting we can achieve sinless perfection in this life. But he made it clear in the verses here we cannot simultaneously live an ongoing life of unrepentant sin and be on the way to heaven. By preaching cheap grace, by allowing for the possibility to both "have fellowship with him, and walk in darkness, we lie, and do not the truth" (1:6). I cannot be a "gay Christian" or a "Christian adulterer" or a "Christian thief," proud of my sin, demanding its acceptance by others, and defining myself by my sin of choice. I can be a Christian tempted by a particular sin, but if my identity—my "boasting," which Paul said should be in Christ (1 Corinthians 1:31)—is instead in my sin, I can rest assured I am *not* in Christ. John made it painfully clear that the Holy Spirit cannot reside in the temple of idols.

In Chapter 6 we dealt with the issue of idolatry in the church and how it is not just an Old Testament issue. Both John and James warned earnestly of the danger of idolatry and brought it right into our modern headlines: "Love not the world, neither the things that are in the world. If any man love the world, the love of the Father is not in him" (1 John 2:15). "Ye adulterers and adulteresses, know ye not that the friendship of the world is enmity with God? whosoever therefore will be a friend of the world is the enemy of God" (James 4:4).

James here used the exact analogy for people in the professing church that God used for His people in idolatrous Israel—the accusation that His people have committed adultery against Him. James nuked the suggestion that I can "do the Jesus thing" on Sundays, while my Monday through Saturday is indistinguishable from the world around me, and still be heaven bound. It is difficult to look at America, spending seven minutes a day on religious activities and five hours on television,[247] and not see the adultery, the idolatry. Our language is not much different from the world around us. Our entertainment is not much different. Our marriage success rates are not much different. We had best dispense with our glib assumption that "all things are become new" (2 Corinthians 5:17), even where there is no evidence of repentance, and "examine [ourselves], whether [we] be in the faith" (2 Corinthians 13:5).

As Os Guinness put it,

> In an age when comfort and convenience are unspoken articles of our modern bill of rights, the Christian faith is not a license to entitlement, a prescription for an easy-going spirituality, or a how-to manual for self-improvement. The cross of Jesus Christ runs crosswise to all our human ways of thinking. A rediscovery of the hard and the unpopular themes of the gospel will therefore be such a rediscovery of the whole gospel that the result may lead to reformation and revival.[248]

I pray—and believe—that he is right.

As a final witness, let us call the Lord Jesus Christ:

- "If ye love me, keep my commandments" (John 14:15).
- "If a man love me, he will keep my words: and my Father will love him, and we will come unto him, and make our abode with him. He that loveth me not keepeth not my sayings: and the word which ye hear is not mine, but the Father's which sent me" (John 14:23–24).
- "He that entereth in by the door is the shepherd of the sheep. To him the porter openeth; and the sheep hear his voice: and he calleth his own sheep by name, and leadeth them out. And when he putteth forth his own sheep, he goeth before them, and the sheep follow him: for they know his voice. And a stranger will they not follow, but will flee from him: for they know not the voice of strangers. . . . My sheep hear my voice, and I know them, and they follow me. And I give unto them eternal life; and they shall never perish, neither shall any man pluck them out of my hand" (John 10:2–5, 27–28).
- "Whosoever heareth these sayings of mine, and doeth them, I will liken him unto a wise man, which built his house upon a rock: and the rain descended, and the floods came, and the winds blew, and beat upon that house; and it fell not: for it was founded upon a rock. And every one that heareth these sayings of mine, and doeth them not, shall be likened unto a foolish man, which built his house upon the sand: and the rain descended, and the floods came, and the winds blew, and beat upon that house; and it fell: and great was the fall of it" (Matthew 7:24–27).

The world knows two—and only two—Bible verses: "Judge not, that ye be not judged" (Matthew 7:1—perhaps the world's favorite verse) and "He that is without sin among you, let him first cast a stone" (John 8:7).

Let's look at the rest of the "judge not" passage from Matthew 7: "Judge not, that ye be not judged. For with what judgment ye judge, ye shall be judged: and with what measure ye mete, it shall be measured to you again" (vv. 1–2).

This is not a prohibition against making moral judgment calls. It is not a wink and nod to those who would live as they please. It is a double warning—a warning to use God's standard as our standard and to be mindful to apply God's standard first to ourselves. How do we know this? From the rest of the same chapter:

> Enter ye in at the strait gate: for wide is the gate, and broad is the way, that leadeth to destruction, and many there be which go in thereat:
>
> Because strait is the gate, and narrow is the way, which leadeth unto life, and few there be that find it . . .
>
> Ye shall know them by their fruits. Do men gather grapes of thorns, or figs of thistles?
>
> Even so every good tree bringeth forth good fruit; but a corrupt tree bringeth forth evil fruit.
>
> A good tree cannot bring forth evil fruit, neither can a corrupt tree bring forth good fruit.
>
> Every tree that bringeth not forth good fruit is hewn down, and cast into the fire.
>
> Wherefore by their fruits ye shall know them. (vv. 13–20)

Too many churches like the "Barney the purple dinosaur" message: "I love you; you love me; we're a happy family."[249] I'm okay; you're okay. But Jesus obliterates our subjective human idea that we can live as we please and that as long as we don't hurt anybody (much), we're good.

In John 12:47 He offered these comforting words: "I came not to judge the world, but to save the world."

Then, in case we cheapen grace, come the next verses:

> He that rejecteth me, and receiveth not my words, hath one that judgeth him: the word that I have spoken, the same shall judge him in the last day.

For I have not spoken of myself; but the Father which sent me, he gave me a commandment, what I should say, and what I should speak.

And I know that his commandment is life everlasting. (vv. 48–50)

Imagine that. In the age of grace, no less. We will be judged in the last day by whether we kept God's commandments. "His commandment is life everlasting" (v. 50). Jesus never ever suggested that He abolished the law of God.

But the truth is even more amazing. While He was on earth, Christ the God-man perfectly kept the law. And had He not, His death would be powerless to save. "Christ also hath once suffered for sins, the just for the unjust, that he might bring us to God" (1 Peter 3:18). He was "made . . . sin for us, who knew no sin; that we might be made the righteousness of God in him" (2 Corinthians 5:21). Just the slightest deviation from the law of God, and Christ's death would have been a colossal waste.

But He came, and He perfectly kept God's law, and He died, and He rose again. That is life changing, life giving.

Now what? What does Christ's perfect fulfillment of God's law mean for me?

Did God send His only begotten Son to earth to be beaten and crucified by sinful men, to pay the penalty for all my sin, so I could continue to live as I please until I die? Did God really execute His sinless Son to buy me the freedom to "continue in sin" (Romans 6:1)? Let us say with Paul, "God forbid" (v. 2)!

We assume that the reason Jesus died is to save us from hell and take us to heaven. But does the Bible ever say this? Certainly salvation from hell is a benefit. But is that the purpose? I can't find much evidence to that effect. Why, then, does the Bible say He came and died?

- "Thou shalt call his name JESUS: for he shall save his people from their sins" (Matt. 1:21).
- "I am not come to call the righteous, but sinners to repentance" (Matt 9:13).
- "He died for all, that they which live should not henceforth live unto themselves, but unto him which died for them, and rose again" (2 Cor. 5:15).

- "He that committeth sin is of the devil; for the devil sinneth from the beginning. For this purpose the Son of God was manifested, that he might destroy the works of the devil" (1 John 3:8).

This is it! This is the glorious truth, the gospel! Jesus came to save us *from* our sin, not *unto* sin. He died that we should live *not* unto ourselves but unto Him whose death and resurrection purchased us.

And again, in Titus 2:14: "[He] gave himself for us, that he might redeem us from all iniquity, and purify unto himself a peculiar people, zealous of good works."

Life eternal is a side benefit. The purpose of Christ's death is to save us from sin. It is to radically transform our nature and our actions. Our works must necessarily change 180 degrees as a result. The chief difference between heaven and earth is not the absence of death. Death is just the symptom. The chief difference is the absence of *sin*. And for those who love sin, heaven seems an undesirable destination. There is none there. We had better recheck our blithe idea we can live like the devil in this life and walk straight into a sinless eternity.

The sine qua non of salvation is a changed life. And if there is no change, the Lord has a stern warning: "It is impossible for those who were once enlightened, and have tasted of the heavenly gift, and were made partakers of the Holy Ghost, and have tasted the good word of God, and the powers of the world to come, if they shall fall away, to renew them again unto repentance; seeing they crucify to themselves the Son of God afresh, and put him to an open shame" (Heb. 6:4–6).

These are chillingly sobering words. It is possible for those who mentally assent to the gospel, who make a profession of faith, who check all the right theological boxes, to become "impossible . . . to renew . . . again unto repentance." Whoa.

That is the Bible's answer to cheap grace. That is the Bible's answer to the idea that because Christ came, I am free in Christ, with all my sins forgiven— past, present, and future—and no one can judge my sin, and I don't have to judge myself either. To hold this position is to "crucify . . . the Son of God afresh," to "put him to an open shame."

The law of grace is not a lesser standard than the Old Testament law. In fact, the standard is higher. And is it not fitting, for those bought and paid for by Christ's sacrifice, that more and not less should be expected?

For those who doubt this statement, we call Jesus Christ back to the stand.

"Ye have heard that it was said by them of old time, Thou shalt not commit adultery: but I say unto you, That whosoever looketh on a woman to lust after her hath committed adultery with her already in his heart" (Matthew 5:27–28). It isn't that hard to avoid committing the physical act of adultery. That's all Moses demanded. I'm okay there. But Christ's standard is infinitely harder to live. "Ye are not under the law, but under grace" (Romans 6:14). Ouch.

"Ye have heard that it was said of them of old time, Thou shalt not kill; and whosoever shall kill shall be in danger of the judgment: but I say unto you, That whosoever is angry with his brother without a cause shall be in danger of the judgment: and whosoever shall say to his brother, Raca, shall be in danger of the council: but whosoever shall say, Thou fool, shall be in danger of hell fire" (Matthew 5:21–22). It isn't that hard not to murder someone. That's all Moses demanded. And again, I'm okay. But "whosoever is angry with his brother without a cause shall be in danger of the judgment"? Christ's standard is far harder to live. "Not under the law, but under grace" (Romans 6:14). Ouch.

We like to preach "there is therefore now no condemnation to them which are in Christ Jesus" (Romans 8:1). And on the level of an individual soul, that's true. But it does not apply to nations or to churches. While my individual soul may be promised eternity, America—and the American church—need not think they can escape condemnation just because we are post-Calvary.

Consider the testimony of Christ Himself to the seven churches in Revelation. Notice there's no hint of the "no condemnation" language in Christ's words to the church at Ephesus. Or Laodicea. Or the others. No. In fact, the Lord berated several of them for failing to work the works of repentance.

Christ sent His message "to the angel of the church" (i.e., the messenger, the pastor, of the church). To five of the seven churches, Christ's message to the pastor is not "preach grace" but "preach repentance."

Let's take Ephesus first: "I have somewhat against thee, because thou hast left thy first love. Remember therefore from whence thou art fallen, and repent, and do the first works; or else I will come unto thee quickly, and will remove thy candlestick out of his place, except thou repent" (2:4–5).

Whoa! What happened to "no condemnation"? I thought works didn't matter after Calvary. "Repent, and do the first works." Or else? "I . . . will remove thy candlestick out of his place."

Christ went on to warn Pergamos: "So hast thou also them that hold the doctrine of the Nicolaitanes, which thing I hate. Repent; or else I will come unto thee quickly, and will fight against them with the sword of my mouth" (vv. 15–16).

On to Thyatira: "I have a few things against thee, because thou sufferest that woman Jezebel, which calleth herself a prophetess, to teach and to seduce my servants to commit fornication, and to eat things sacrificed unto idols. And I gave her space to repent of her fornication; and she repented not. Behold, I will cast her into a bed, and them that commit adultery with her into great tribulation, except they repent of their deeds" (vv. 20–22).

Sardis is next: "I know thy works, that thou hast a name that thou livest, and art dead. Be watchful, and strengthen the things which remain, that are ready to die: for I have not found thy works perfect before God. Remember therefore how thou hast received and heard, and hold fast, and repent. If therefore thou shalt not watch, I will come on thee as a thief, and thou shalt not know what hour I will come upon thee" (3:1–3).

And, of course, Laodicea: "I know thy works, that thou art neither cold nor hot: I would thou wert cold or hot. So then because thou art lukewarm, and neither cold nor hot, I will spue thee out of my mouth. . . . As many as I love, I rebuke and chasten: be zealous therefore, and repent" (vv. 15–19)

Perhaps the most sobering reality for "the church of America" is this. The God of grace went a perfect seven for seven. Every one of those seven churches eventually had its candlestick removed. Because their *works* did not please God. Because they failed to repent. No doubt many folks from those churches are in heaven today, but the churches died, and their impact on the culture died with them. These seven churches were all within modern-day Turkey, a Muslim nation. If we think for a moment that the American church is superior to the Ephesian church, that it is immune to having its candlestick removed, we are fools. The fact is, we're probably overdue for removal.

It is time to tackle the question we asked at the outset of this chapter: What is the real biblical meaning of our buzzword *grace?* Paul gave a concise and clear answer: "The grace of God that bringeth salvation hath appeared to all men, teaching us that, denying ungodliness and worldly lusts, we should live soberly, righteously, and godly, in this present world" (Titus 2:11–12).

Those who try to make law and grace enemies try to set God at war with Himself. God is both Lawgiver and Grace giver. Psalm 119:29 puts it beautifully: "Remove from me the way of lying: and grant me thy law graciously." The gift of God's law is an act of grace. And the greater act of grace is sending His Son to die and His Holy Spirit to indwell, in order that I now can keep the law that I was powerless to keep.

Peter gave us instruction in how to live in light of grace: "Gird up the loins of your mind, be sober, and hope to the end for the grace that is to be brought unto you at the revelation of Jesus Christ; as obedient children, not fashioning yourselves according to the former lusts in your ignorance: but as he which hath called you is holy, so be ye holy in all manner of conversation; because it is written, Be ye holy; for I am holy" (1 Peter 1:13–16).

SOVEREIGNTY

Another often-misused buzzword is *sovereignty.* "God is sovereign," we are told, and "the king's heart is in the hand of the LORD" (Proverbs 22:1). It's not our job as Christians to call out the world for its sin or to try to influence policy. God is sovereign, and if He wanted abortion outlawed, He could do it in a heartbeat. Therefore, it's not my responsibility that it continues.

I have seen God's sovereignty used as an excuse for our sin until I've become disgusted: "God is sovereign; therefore, unless He mystically changes reality through some miracle, I guess He expects me to live in the current reality."

Here I return to the examples of Corrie ten Boom and the Underground Railroad. "God is sovereign, and the heart of the king is in the hand of the Lord, so if God wants the Jews saved, He can raise up a new leader to replace Hitler. Until then, I'll rest in His sovereignty, and the Jews can do the same." Or "God is sovereign, and if He wanted slavery ended, He could do so in a moment. If He doesn't want it ended or want this particular fugitive slave to be free. I don't see any mystical, miraculous change in the Fugitive Slave Act. I guess it's predestined to be this way. After all, in the last days, things will wax worse and worse!"

It must really turn God's stomach to hear us blaspheme His Word this way. As with the Laodiceans, surely He is about ready to "spue [us] out of [His] mouth" (Revelations 3:16). Do we even consider what the word *sovereignty* means? The dictionary defines it as "the quality or state of being sovereign, or of having supreme power or authority" and "the status, dominion, power, or authority of a sovereign; royal rank or position; royalty."[250]

We've turned sovereignty upside down. "Because God is sovereign, I'm absolved of all responsibility." I often wonder where we get this notion. No, if God is sovereign, He has "supreme power or authority"—"the status, dominion, power, or authority of a sovereign; royal rank or position." God's sovereignty does not *negate* human responsibility; it defines and mandates it!

And what does our Sovereign say?

- "If you love Me, you will keep My commandments" (John 14:15 NASB).
- "Whoever denies Me before men, I will also deny him before My Father who is in heaven" (Matthew 10:33 NASB).
- "Whoever then annuls one of the least of these commandments, and teaches others to do the same, shall be called least in the kingdom of heaven; but whoever keeps and teaches them, he shall be called great in the kingdom of heaven" (Matthew 5:19 NASB).

- "Go therefore and make disciples of all the nations, baptizing them in the name of the Father and the Son and the Holy Spirit, *teaching them to observe all that I commanded you*" (Matthew 28:19–20 NASB, emphasis added).

And somehow we've tortured that into the devilish idea that because God is sovereign, I'm a free agent, wholly unaccountable for what goes on in the culture around me.

Let's call our Sovereign back to the stand for the verdict on this point. How are the people of the Sovereign to live in the age of grace? "Be ye therefore perfect, even as your Father which is in heaven is perfect" (Matthew 5:48).

GOSPEL

The word *gospel* literally means "good news." Truly the gospel is the best news almighty God ever gave fallen humanity. But the American church has shrunk the gospel so badly we risk depriving it entirely of its power to give eternal life.

We take a couple of verses that are true, as far as they go, and then make sure to subtract the meaning from them, lest they offend the culture. "If thou shalt confess with thy mouth the Lord Jesus, and shalt believe in thine heart that God hath raised him from the dead, thou shalt be saved" (Romans 10:9). "Believe on the Lord Jesus Christ, and thou shalt be saved" (Acts 16:31). It's very simple. It's a free gift. In fact, you can't earn it anyway. It's easy. Nothing to it.

As far as much of the modern American church is concerned, salvation is a "head thing." You have to give mental assent to three historical facts. A historical figure named Jesus, who is the Son of God, died on the cross to pay for our sins. He was buried. He rose again. And then you pray a prayer telling Him that you believe these things about Him and that you want Him to come into your heart and take you to heaven someday. And that's it. It's by grace alone, through faith alone. You just have to believe the historical facts and pray to show your belief, and you have your "get out of hell free" card.

I have five words for you: *that is not the gospel!* Never mind that you can go to evangelical churches your entire life and never be told this truth. That is *not* the gospel! And we have many witnesses to this.

First, let us call John the Baptist. "He came into all the country about Jordan, preaching the baptism of repentance for the remission of sins" (Luke 3:3).

Next, we call Jesus to the stand. Perhaps *He* can tell us what the gospel is. Christ never offered only an evangelical half gospel. "Jesus came into Galilee, preaching the gospel of the kingdom of God, and saying, The time is fulfilled, and the kingdom of God is at hand: repent ye, and believe the gospel" (Mark 1:14–15).

He likewise commissioned His followers to preach the whole gospel, not the half-truth modern evangelical version. In Luke's version of the Great Commission, Christ laid out the whole gospel to His witnesses:

> Then opened he their understanding, that they might understand the scriptures,
>
> And said unto them, Thus it is written, and thus it behooved Christ to suffer, and to rise from the dead the third day:
>
> And that repentance and remission of sins should be preached in his name among all nations, beginning at Jerusalem.
>
> And ye are witnesses of these things. (24:45–48)

All across American evangelicalism, you see churches defining themselves as "gospel-centered," "gospel-focused," "gospel-driven" churches. But we do not "understand the scriptures." Often the "gospel-centered" church seems to position itself as focused on Christ's ability to save from hell as opposed to focusing on "externals" or "legalism" or "rules." It's all about "the gospel," not about some requirement that people must have their very nature changed.

Yet that precisely *is* the message of the gospel. Repentance is the sine qua non of salvation. That is, without repentance there can be no salvation. Regardless of how much "faith," how much mental assent to historical facts and even to theological truths. The gospel *requires* repentance.

> Despisest thou the riches of his goodness and forbearance and longsuffering; not knowing that the goodness of God leadeth thee to repentance?

But after thy hardness and impenitent heart treasurest up unto thyself wrath against the day of wrath and revelation of the righteous judgment of God;

Who will render to every man according to his deeds:

To them who by patient continuance in well doing seek for glory and honour and immortality, eternal life:

But unto them that are contentious, and do not obey the truth, but obey unrighteousness, indignation and wrath,

Tribulation and anguish, upon every soul of man that doeth evil, of the Jew first, and also of the Gentile. (Romans 2:4-9)

And the surest evidence—the only real evidence—that salvation has occurred will be a changed life: "If any man be in Christ, he is a new creature: old things are passed away; behold, all things are become new" (2 Cor. 5:17). If your "gospel-centered" church is not hammering the need for repentance, it's time to admit it's not a gospel-centered church.

This makes logical sense as well. What is the value of the gospel if I don't *need* to change? What is the value of being saved if I am not hopelessly lost? What is the use of heaven if I am not by nature and by choice bound for hell? A "gospel" without a major emphasis on repentance tells the world that Jesus's death was unnecessary, an exercise in futility. What good did it do me that He took "our sins in his own body on the tree" (1 Peter 2:24) if I don't need to forsake those sins anyway?

We call Peter to the stand. Interrogated by the Pharisees, he boldly preached the gospel story: "The God of our fathers raised up Jesus, whom ye slew and hanged on a tree. Him hath God exalted with his right hand to be a Prince and a Saviour, for to give repentance to Israel, and forgiveness of sins" (Acts 5:30-31).

We call the apostle Paul to the stand. He testified before King Agrippa about his call to preach the gospel:

I said, Who art thou, Lord? And he said, I am Jesus whom thou persecutest.

But rise, and stand upon thy feet: for I have appeared unto thee for this purpose, to make thee a minister and a witness both of these things which thou hast seen, and of those things in the which I will appear unto thee . . .

Whereupon, O king Agrippa, I was not disobedient unto the heavenly vision:

But shewed first unto them of Damascus, and at Jerusalem, and throughout all the coasts of Judaea, and then to the Gentiles, that they should repent and turn to God, and do works meet for repentance. (26:15–20)

And again, "I kept back nothing that was profitable unto you, but have shewed you, and have taught you publicly, and from house to house, testifying both to the Jews, and also to the Greeks, repentance toward God, and faith toward our Lord Jesus Christ" (20:21). Repentance and faith are inseparable. Without repentance, faith in Jesus Christ is nothing more than mental assent, utterly without eternal significance.

Romans 10:9 and Acts 16:31 are not untrue. But neither verse in itself contains the entirety of the gospel. And the modern evangelical church fails even to report the entirety of those verses. Let's consider each.

Romans 10:9 says, "If thou shalt confess with thy mouth the Lord Jesus, and shalt believe in thine heart that God hath raised him from the dead, thou shalt be saved." This verse is one of the "Romans Road" verses we use to create a "formula" for "getting saved"—if you will, a box to check. Likewise with Acts 16:31: "Believe on the Lord Jesus Christ, and thou shalt be saved."

But we leave out the word that changes the whole meaning of these verses. The word is *Lord*. We are not called to simply believe in historical facts about a historical figure. But we are asked to "believe on" and "confess with [our] mouth" Jesus as *Lord*. And that makes all the difference. If He is Lord, what does that make me? An inferior creature. A dependent creature. A creature obligated to a higher authority, the Lord.

What happens if I confess Him as Lord? It means I come down off the throne of my life and acknowledge a new Sovereign. The only proper response is that of the humble child Samuel: "Speak; for thy servant heareth" (1 Samuel 3:10). Or, just as appropriately, that of Paul on the Damascus Road: "Lord, what wilt thou have me to do?" (Acts 9:6). That's why Paul didn't imagine that these verses would ever be taken as suggesting mere formulaic mental assent. He had seen the risen Christ. And he immediately changed masters. He was radically, permanently, functionally, fundamentally changed. No mere mental assent here.

To confess Him as Lord means I am obligated to keep His commands. And His command is to "Repent . . . and believe the gospel," for "the kingdom of God is at hand" (Mark 1:15).

Christ Himself destroyed the idea that just checking the box of confessing Him as Lord offers any hope of eternal life:

> Not everyone who says to Me, "Lord, Lord," will enter the kingdom of heaven, but he who does the will of My Father who is in heaven will enter. Many will say to Me on that day, "Lord, Lord, did we not prophesy in Your name, and in Your name cast out demons, and in Your name perform many miracles?" And then I will declare to them, "I never knew you; depart from Me, you who practice lawlessness." (Matthew 7:21–23 NASB)

Many or all these folks presumably give mental assent to the death, burial, and resurrection of the One in whose name they claim to prophesy and work miracles. They even call Him "Lord." But they fail to keep His commandments.

Believing on the Lord Jesus Christ is a total life commitment. A mental assent alone has no effect on eternity. Ask Him.

> If any man come to me, and hate not his father, and mother, and wife, and children, and brethren, and sisters, yea, and his own life also, he cannot be my disciple.
>
> And whosoever doth not bear his cross, and come after me, cannot be my disciple. . . .
>
> So likewise, whosoever he be of you that forsaketh not all that he hath, he cannot be my disciple. (Luke 14:26–27, 33)

The One whose blood wrote the gospel story certainly has the right to define that story. And His Word does so clearly:

Hereby we do know that we know him, if we keep his commandments.

He that saith, I know him, and keepeth not his commandments, is a liar, and the truth is not in him.

But whoso keepeth his word, in him verily is the love of God perfected: hereby know we that we are in him.

He that saith he abideth in him ought himself also so to walk, even as he walked. (1 John 2:3–6)

Salvation is a work of the Holy Spirit of God, accompanied always by repentance. It cannot be gained by checking boxes or praying formula prayers, any more than it can be attained by any other human work.

Modern evangelicalism's cheap-grace, formulaic half gospel is nothing more than what Paul warned of, "a form of godliness, but denying the power thereof" (2 Timothy 3:5). It knows nothing of "the power of God unto salvation" (Romans 1:16). Here is the function of the gospel, according to its Author: "To open their eyes, and to turn them from darkness to light, and from the power of Satan unto God, that they may receive forgiveness of sins, and inheritance among them which are sanctified by faith that is in me" (Acts 26:18).

It's time our churches started either taking up Christ's message and preaching the gospel of "repentance for the forgiveness of sins" (Luke 24:47 ESV) or ending the charade of being a gospel-centered church. The evangelical half gospel is without power to save and may indeed be convincing the damned that they are saved. If so, in the name of helping the lost, we are only their executioners. Let us truly be gospel centered, not gospel free.

It is not enough to tell *some* truth. "Rightly dividing the word of truth" is not easy. That is why Paul tells us to "study to shew thyself approved unto God, a workman that needeth not to be ashamed, rightly dividing the word of truth" (2 Tim. 2:15). The evangelical half gospel has done far too much damage already. It's time the church returns to preaching "the whole counsel of God" (Acts 20:27).

CHAPTER 11

BETRAYED BY THE PULPITS

For years I have believed that if the pulpits would just challenge the culture and encourage the folks in the pews to do the same, the gospel would begin again to have an impact on the culture. I've been endlessly frustrated at how seldom I hear the challenge. But on a few occasions, I have seen it, and I have seen it work.

A couple of years back, my wife planned to take our older kids about an hour west to a protest at a Planned Parenthood death center in Roanoke. She drew up posters with creative messages and prepped the kids for the experience.

Of course, my whole extended family is pro-life. So my wife began asking others in my family (her family lives in Arizona, a bit too far for that commute) to accompany her to the protest. But, like us, they all had busy lives, and one by one they explained that they didn't have Saturday the next week available.

But the next Sunday, at my parents' church, Timberlake Baptist, pastor Bryan Ferrell spoke from the pulpit about the protest. Christians, he said, ought to pray, but they ought to do more than pray. He was going to the protest himself, he said, along with others from the pastoral staff. And he encouraged the church to go as well.

Saturday came. My wife and the kids arrived for the protest. When she arrived, there were numerous members of my family, signs in hand. "But I thought you couldn't come," my wife said.

"Well, Pastor Ferrell encouraged us on Sunday and said we should come. We managed to move some things around so we could come."

Years ago, when I attended Timberlake, former pastor Jim Alley always used to say, "It takes three to thrive." He repeatedly encouraged folks to make all three services—Sunday morning, Sunday evening, and Wednesday night. As a result of his regular hammering of the topic, as surrounding churches began giving up Sunday night services for lack of attendance, Timberlake didn't have a huge letdown from Sunday morning to Sunday night. And attendance dropped only a bit more on Wednesday nights. Since Pastor Alley left, Timberlake still gets decent Sunday night attendance but not like the percentage it used to get under Pastor Alley.

Everything rises and falls on leadership—both within the church and without. Where leaders will lead, the people will follow. When leaders fail to lead or lead in failure, so also goes the church.

* * * * *

Many evangelicals are passingly familiar with the verse "Judgment must begin at the house of God" (1 Peter 4:17). Very few take it seriously.

When history paints a picture of a corrupted culture, at the core of the rot is usually a compromised church (or in Old Testament times, corrupted priests and prophets).

THE BIBLICAL EXAMPLE: CORRUPTED PULPITS CAUSE CORRUPTED CULTURES

Consider the story of the rebellion of Korah in Numbers 16. Korah, a Levite, theoretically charged with leading the people in worship, instead led them in rebellion against Moses, God's chosen leader. The rebellion spread like wildfire until finally "the LORD spake unto Moses and unto Aaron, saying, Separate yourselves from among this congregation, that I may consume them in a moment" (vv. 20–21). Only the fervent prayer of Moses and Aaron stayed God's hand.

God dealt with the disobedient leader swiftly, as the earth opened up and swallowed Korah and his fellow ringleaders. But the damage they had done was so engrained that, even after seeing Korah's fate, "on the morrow all the congregation of the children of Israel murmured against Moses and against Aaron, saying, Ye have killed the people of the Lord" (v. 41). God's patience finally ran out, and a plague ensued among the people. Aaron took incense off the altar and ran through the camp, and "the plague was stayed" (v. 48). But the disobedience of one spiritual leader cost the lives of 14,700 of the people.

Or consider the nearly pagan Israel in young Samuel's day. The people were far from God. The sons of the high priest Eli—Hophni and Phinehas—were having immoral relations with women who came to the tabernacle to offer sacrifices (1 Samuel 2:22). Their undisciplined father failed to discipline them. God slew both sons before the Philistines. But the rot in the "pulpit" led to the loss of thirty thousand Israelite soldiers, besides the faithless priests (4:10).

Or consider the book of Judges. In one truly sordid story, a Levite from the country of Ephraim (theoretically a leader of worship of Jehovah) and his concubine were traveling through the land of Benjamin. They stopped at a house to rest for the night, and the men of the city began to riot outside, demanding that the homeowner turn the Levite over to them, just as the men of Sodom had demanded that two angels be given to them to satisfy their lust (Genesis 19:1–5).

The Levite gave the men his concubine instead. They had their way with her all night, and the Levite found her dead on the doorstep the next morning (Judges 19:1–28). A truly sordid story.

But in the previous two chapters, we read the real reason the culture had decayed so badly. It was a failure of those who should have been spiritual leaders.

We read the story of Micah and the men of the tribe of Dan. Micah crafted an idol of silver and hired a traveling Levite to be his personal "priest." "Micah said unto him, Dwell with me, and be unto me a father and a priest, and I will give thee ten shekels of silver by the year, and a suit of apparel, and thy victuals. So the Levite went in. . . . And Micah consecrated the Levite; and the young man became his priest, and was in the house of Micah. Then said Micah, Now know I that the Lord will do me good, seeing I have a Levite to my priest" (17:10–13).

This Levite was content to "speak for God" for hire in the home of a man who had created a god in his own image. Soon enough, the military forces of the tribe of Dan came along, on their way to attack the city of Laish to enlarge their territory.

While Micah had tempted the Levite with money, the Danites tempted him with popularity: "Hold thy peace, lay thine hand upon thy mouth, and go with us, and be to us a father and a priest: is it better for thee to be a priest unto the house of one man, or that thou be a priest unto a tribe and a family in Israel? And the priest's heart was glad, and he took the ephod, and the teraphim, and the graven image, and went in the midst of the people" (18:19–20).

The graven image stolen from Micah was set up by the Danites in the captured city, which they renamed Dan. The moment began an unbroken tradition of idolatry (vv. 27–30). Later on, after the kingdom was taken from Solomon's son Rehoboam, King Jeroboam set up a golden calf at Dan to keep the people from traveling back to the temple in Jerusalem to worship (1 Kings 12:26–30).

The Bible repeatedly refers to the wicked ways of "Jeroboam the son of Nebat, who made Israel to sin" (1 Kings 22:52; 2 Kings 10:29; 14:24). King after king, in both Israel and Judah, "walked in all the way of Jeroboam . . . to provoke the Lord God of Israel to anger" (1 Kings 16:26).

In Revelation, the final book of the Bible, John tells of the future story of the 144,000 chosen servants of God, twelve thousand from each tribe of Israel. Joseph and his son Manasseh are each mentioned among the twelve tribes. Dan is conspicuously absent. Numerous scholars have suggested that the complete idolatry of the tribe of Dan led to their being wiped from the nation by God.

How might the story have been different if the one Levite had stood for the claims of Jehovah God instead of being ensnared by the wealth and fame offered by Micah and the Danites? And how he could have been a light to the dark culture of his day instead of helping spread the idolatry and wickedness that we read about in the next chapter of Judges.

In the idolatrous days of Ahab, the king kept a handy stable of "prophets," his own personal preachers who, as in today's America, told their audience pretty much what he wanted to hear. They put on quite the show, and their message was quite popular.

"Zedekiah the son of Chenaanah made him horns of iron: and he said, Thus saith the Lord, With these shalt thou push the Syrians, until thou have consumed them. And all the prophets prophesied so, saying, Go up to Ramothgilead, and prosper: for the Lord shall deliver it into the king's hand" (1 Kings 22:11–12).

Only the lone Micaiah, the only true prophet of God, prophesied that Ahab would be killed in battle and the backslidden Israelites badly defeated (vv. 15–23). Of course, he was proven right.

In the days of Ezra the priest, the priests helped lead the nation away from God by intermarrying with heathen women from the lands round about, in direct violation of the law of Moses. "Among the sons of the priests there were found that had taken strange wives" (Ezra 10:18). "Also of the Levites . . . " (v. 23). "Of the singers also . . . " (v. 24). And the people followed the spiritual misleaders. "Moreover of Israel . . . " (v. 25). The common man followed the example of the religious leaders and violated God's law. The example of the "worship leaders" corrupted the whole nation.

Time and time again, those claiming to speak for God—and even those legitimately charged with the responsibility to speak for God—not only prophesied falsely but actually helped lead the nation into rebellion and judgment.

MANY AMERICAN PULPITS OPENLY DENY BASIC BIBLICAL TRUTHS

Today in America the pulpit is at worst openly antagonistic to Scripture, in most cases painfully silent on the ills of a dying culture, and at best focused on half truths such as the "grace-centric" preaching we referenced in the previous chapter. As a result, the American pulpit that has produced the likes of Jonathan Edwards, Dwight Moody, A. W. Tozer, J. Gresham Machen, and Adrian Rogers is largely impotent—either at war with the Word of God or not preaching it fully.

In 2004 the Episcopal Church made V. Gene Robinson the first openly homosexual bishop in a major US Christian denomination. Robinson's most shocking "contribution" to "preaching" may be his blasphemous assertion that Jesus and John, "the disciple whom Jesus loved" (John 21:20), may have been homosexuals.[251] Little more need be said.

Judy Peterson, an ordained minister in the Evangelical Covenant Church and pastor at its North Park University in Chicago, officiated at a gay "marriage" of two men in April 2017.[252] Peterson is just one of untold Christian clergy to have done the same. Noted clergyman and Bill Clinton's spiritual adviser Tony Campolo said, "We in the Church should actively support such families."[253]

Others have decided to turn God's story of redemption of sinful humanity from "the snare of the devil" (2 Timothy 2:26) into a feminist revolution. "Feminist theologians" have reinterpreted the story of Creation, the Fall, and Calvary as Jesus stepping in to liberate women from the oppression of men started by Adam and his male buddy, the serpent, in the Garden of Eden. The damage this does to the saving work of Christ needs no elaboration.

Then there are the blatantly false teachers like Joel Osteen, who isn't quite sure whether Jesus is the only way to heaven, as he explained to Larry King in 2005:

> KING: What if you're Jewish or Muslim, you don't accept Christ at all?
>
> OSTEEN: You know, I'm very careful about saying who would and wouldn't go to heaven. I don't know . . .
>
> KING: If you believe you have to believe in Christ? They're wrong, aren't they?
>
> OSTEEN: Well, I don't know if I believe they're wrong. I believe here's what the Bible teaches and from the Christian faith this is what I believe. But I just think that only God will judge a person's heart. I spent a lot of time in India with my father. I don't know all about their religion. But I know they love God. And I don't know. I've seen their sincerity. So I don't know.[254]

THE SUBTLE BUT PERHAPS GREATER DANGER: PIETISM

But much of the damage done to Christianity by its spiritual leaders is much more subtle—and sometimes even well intentioned—and done by leaders who would generally be considered well within orthodox Christianity. For example, there is what I call Christian pacifism, Radical Two Kingdoms (R2K) theology, or the neo-Reformed movement. This movement would include such scholars as David VanDrunen and Michael Horton of Westminster Seminary California, Meredith Kline, Darryl Hart (author of *A Secular Faith*), and John MacArthur of Master's Seminary.

The Radical Two Kingdoms theology holds that Christians are citizens of two kingdoms, a heavenly and an earthly. The heavenly kingdom is under the dominion of Christ and is, of course, the ultimate destination of believers. The earthly kingdom is under the thumb of Satan, the prince of this world, and he governs the world system. The Christian's calling is simply to practice personal evangelism (and, presumably, personal spiritual growth) in order to convert as many people as possible from Satan's kingdom to Christ's.

The R2K theologians agree with their critics that when Christ returns, He will overthrow Satan and unify the two kingdoms under His sole control. But in the meantime, in the words of MacArthur, Christian political and civic activism is irrelevant: "The moral, social, and political state of a people is irrelevant to the advance of the gospel."[255] He went on to a fairly direct attack on Christians who are deeply involved in proclaiming truth to the culture in the public square: "Using temporal methods to promote legislative and judicial change, and resorting to external efforts of lobbying and intimidation to achieve some sort of 'Christian morality' in society is not our calling—and has no eternal value."[256]

MacArthur is wrong on this, both biblically and by the weight of church history. His language sets up straw men that he can knock down without facing the reality of the positions actually taken by those he criticizes.

I'm not certain who is using "intimidation" to achieve "Christian morality." And "using temporal methods to promote legislative . . . change" is precisely how Queen Esther saved her people. Admittedly she didn't send anyone to heaven by arming the Jews for self-defense, but she saved many lives. Surely she *was* fulfilling her calling.

A crucial mistake MacArthur and far too many others make is creating a false dichotomy between the sacred and the secular. This false dichotomy assumes that Jesus is concerned only with getting souls to heaven and that anything else is a carnal weapon that is at best a waste of time. If this is true, Jesus wasted a lot of time on carnal weapons. He fed people, healed people, raised people from the dead. Many of those He fed and healed did not end up in heaven. In the R2K false dichotomy, all this work was wasted and was a distraction from what Jesus should have been doing, which is just telling people how to get to heaven.

I use the term *neo-Reformed*, because Calvin, Knox, and the other actual Reformers spoke an entirely different language from the neo-Reformers. And there are plenty of modern Reformed theologians who have carried on the tradition of Calvin and Knox—Cornelius Van Til and John Frame, to name just a couple. As I say, the R2K position is not the historic position of Christianity generally nor of Reformed Christianity. Calvin himself headed up the Geneva experiment in creating a Christian commonwealth, and—echoing Esther's efforts centuries before—Knox helped the Protestants in Scotland literally take up arms to resist Scotland's Roman Catholic queen regent.[257] Mary, Queen of Scots, reportedly confessed, "I fear the prayers of John Knox more than all the assembled armies of Europe."[258]

"The Reformers resisted the view that only those in clerical ranks were called into the service of God; they insisted that all who were God's through Christ were so called. The sphere in which this calling is exercised is not limited to the Church; it extends to every area in which Christian people work, to the whole range of responsibilities they assume. And the more power that is attached to a calling, they maintained, the greater the responsibility that has to be exercised in its discharge."[259] Indeed, John Calvin himself stated that the "civil magistracy" (involvement in civil government) is the second highest calling of God, second to that of the pastorate.[260]

By contrast, R2K theology has the practical effect of isolating the church inside its walls. We all get together and make sure every fine point of theology is nailed down. Meanwhile, more than sixty million babies have died from legal abortion. As God told Jeremiah, "My people hath been lost sheep: their shepherds have caused them to go astray" (Jeremiah 50:6).

Theologian Jay Rogers gave an excellent description of the debate over the proper relationship of the Christian to civil government. He described the contenders as Pietism (R2K theology) and Puritanism (the more faithful to traditional Reformed views). I offer Rogers's explanation of the positions here:

> "There are essentially two views of government that have been held to by two groups of evangelical Christians in modern times—the Puritan or Reformed view (based on the ideals of the Protestant Reformation), and the Pietist view.
>
> 1. **The Puritan view of government**: All people are under a two-fold theocratic form of government (ecclesiastical and civil). The church legislates the moral law of God through the preaching of blessings and curses found in God's Word (the Bible); the state enforces the moral law of God through a system of reward and punishment. Believers obey the moral law of God out of love and are subject to church discipline; sinners obey out of constraint and fear of punishment by civil judges. But both classes of men are to be ruled by the moral law of God. Human government is an institution given by God to be cared for and reformed by men. The Puritan historical view of government is providential, with Jesus Christ leading believers in His train as a captain leads an army to victory over the anti-Christian power bases of the world. The ultimate destiny of government is to establish Christ's dominion over all the earth with God's people ruling in positions of power. Christ will return to the earth when all things are subject to Him

under His feet (the church). The role of the elect is to occupy the power bases of both ecclesiastical and civil forms of government until He comes to establish greater justice.

2. **The Pietist view of government**: Christians are under the authority of both church and civil government; sinners are under the authority of civil government only. The moral law of God rules over Christians; but since sinners are doomed to hell, they are free to do whatever they please. Civil government is a part of the world system which is controlled by Satan. It is no surprise to the pietist that so many governments are unjust and evil. The Pietist historical view of government is conspiratorial. Government is a part of the world system which is controlled by Satan and his cohorts. The conspiracy will end in a one-world government ruled by an anti-Christ figure who will control the hearts and minds of men for a dispensational time period. The only job for the church is to preach the gospel so that some may be saved. The job of Christians in civil government is limited since politics is evil. Christians have to wait until Christ returns to the earth with cataclysmic judgment before they can rule as the elect.[261]

Although I believe the Pietist end times eschatology is more biblical, I believe the Puritan view of the Christian's relationship to civil government is much more so.

Pietism sees the Bible as primarily related only to the individual believer's personal relationship with God, and Pietism is not greatly concerned with how that relationship works itself out in the wider world. Pietism tends to be confined inside the walls of the church and views activity in the culture, beyond evangelism, as beside the point. In the R2K view, Christians ought not to waste time seeking civil office, as this has no effect on saving souls. On the other hand, Christians should pray that our leaders would make godly decisions and would themselves be saved. But the R2K approach really can't be supported biblically and doesn't work practically.

Look at two commands from Christ, fo.
to be sent into the harvest (Luke 9:38), anᴅ
and preach the gospel" ourselves (Mark 16:15 N.
practical action. Why would Christ command u
earth, as it is in heaven" (Matthew 6:10), then forbᵢ

The Pietist preachers would agree, once we haᵥ
ourselves ought to go into the harvest field. But then ma
civic involvement to praying that heathen leaders woulᴅ   ᴜke godly
decisions in government, without the necessary corollary thᴇ ᴄʜristians ought to
take practical action—as if faith without works counted for something. Why do
we never preach against using "carnal weapons" when it comes to offering food
and shelter to disaster victims? We don't limit ourselves to prayer and preaching—
and of course, neither did Christ. We seldom hear criticism of using "temporal
methods" like holding a Super Bowl party in a church to reach the lost. Only in
the world of government—one of three human institutions created directly by
God—do so many preachers insist on prohibiting practical Christian involvement.

It is intellectually dishonest. It is also useless to pray that heathen
politicians would make godly decisions: "The natural man receiveth not the
things of the Spirit of God: for they are foolishness unto him: neither can he
know them, because they are spiritually discerned" (1 Corinthians 2:14). Why
pray for what God has already told us won't happen?

Practically R2K doesn't work either. If Christians aren't supposed to be involved,
other than to pray for wisdom and salvation for wicked officials, what happens
when our prayers get answered? If Christians shouldn't be involved in government,
as soon as wicked officials receive Jesus Christ in answer to our prayers for their
salvation, they would need to step down, since Christians shouldn't be involved.

It is R2K's false dichotomy of secular versus sacred, the kingdom of God
versus the kingdom of the world, that hamstrings the church. This conception
simply isn't biblical. Either Christ is Lord *of all*, or He is not Lord *at all*. Christ
is not somehow meddling in Satan's kingdom until the Rapture, when God
will take the keys from Satan and give them to Christ.

victorious risen Christ proclaimed, "All power is given unto ___ and in earth. Go ye therefore, and teach all nations, baptizing them ___ name of the Father, and of the Son, and of the Holy Ghost: teaching them to observe all things whatsoever I have commanded you" (Matthew 28:19–20).

Christ's victory cry is not some futuristic hope. It is a present-tense declaration of a victory already won. "All power is given unto me." Not "will be given at some future point." No—"it is finished" (John 19:30). And on the basis of that present-tense authority, we are to go into all the world.

As we quoted from Simon Greenleaf in Chapter 5,

> The religion of Jesus Christ aims at nothing less than the utter overthrow of all other systems of religion in the world; denouncing them as inadequate to the wants of man, false in their foundations, and dangerous in their tendency.... If [these claims] are well founded and just, they can be no less than the high requirements of heaven, addressed by the voice of God to the reason and understanding of man, concerning things deeply affecting his relations to his sovereign, and essential to the formation of his character and of course to his destiny, both for this life and for the life to come.[262]

My favorite quote of all time regarding the Christian's relationship to civil government—and I believe the most biblical also—is this statement made by Dutch Reformed theologian (and prime minister, incidentally) Abraham Kuyper: "There is not a square inch in the whole domain of our human existence over which Christ, who is Sovereign over *all*, does not cry: 'Mine!'"[263] Either Christ is Lord *of all*, or He is not Lord *at all*.

OUR AMERICAN HERITAGE: A MISSION-DRIVEN CHURCH HOLDING CULTURE ACCOUNTABLE

Thankfully for all of us, the Founding Fathers subscribed to a more Puritan view of the responsibility of the church to direct the culture. Pastors played such a crucial role in preaching a Bible-inspired vision of freedom that the British called them the "black-robed regiment."

"John Adams credited six people in his writings as being key influencers of American independence. Five of the six people were preachers (Reverends John Wise, Jonathan Mayhew, Samuel Cooper, George Whitefield, and Charles Chauncy), because many of the ideas that made their way into our Constitution were first being preached in the pulpit during the Great Awakening."[264] "Historians have documented that every right set forth in the Declaration of Independence was first preached from the pulpit at some time or another before 1763."[265]

"Rev. George Whitefield urged us to separate from Great Britain and also came up with the first American military flag, motto, and banner.[266] The first troops to go into battle in the American Revolution stopped by his church, where a sermon was preached to the troops." Though Whitefield had died by this time, the troops actually took a piece of his clothing into battle with them, as a testament to his influence on the cause of liberty.[267]

"Though all men being created equal was a radical concept at the time, it really only became revelation to the colonists when preachers like Edwards, Whitefield, and John Wesley taught it."[268] Though Wesley opposed American's secession from Britain, his preaching had helped develop the spine of spiritual steel America needed to sustain itself against the greatest superpower of that day.

Preachers like Edwards, Wesley, and Whitefield were used by God to inspire revival and save souls in a way that dwarfs what any of our preachers today can claim. Yet they did not fall for the Pietist/R2K false dichotomy between secular and sacred. They instead applied the Bible to the arena of culture and human government and helped give us the freest nation in history. It is astonishing that some modern preachers suggest that those like Whitefield were somehow in rebellion against Romans 13 by supporting independence.

As President Calvin Coolidge, himself a devout Christian, put it many years later, "The sturdy old divines of those days found the Bible a chief source of illumination for their arguments in support of the patriot cause.

They knew the Book. They were profoundly familiar with it, and eminently capable in the exposition of all its justifications for rebellion" against the British tyrant George III.[269] Coolidge also said, "The principles of human relationship which went into the Declaration of Independence . . . are found in the texts, the sermons, and the writings of the early colonial clergy who were earnestly undertaking to instruct their congregations in the great mystery of how to live."[270]

"Founding pastors taught a practical Christianity. Not a by-and-by one like the when-we-all-get-to-Heaven theology we hear so often today. Pastors preached on social issues like slavery, executions, military, elections, politics, and war."[271] They bequeathed us a Christian nation, with its Constitution, political system, and legal system founded on the Solid Rock.

THE PIETIST SURRENDER COMPROMISES EVEN THE GOSPEL WITNESS

By contrast, the Pietist preachers of our day have silenced the church's voice in the public square, leaving us defeated and impotent. "If the salt have lost his savour . . . it is thenceforth good for nothing, but to be cast out, and to be trodden under foot of men" (Matthew 5:13). Truly we have been and continue to be. And the preaching of today is at the root of the blame.

A 2014 study by George Barna surveyed pastors to ask whether they believe the Bible speaks to the political issues of our day. What he found is truly shocking.

Barna said, "When we ask [pastors] about all the key issues of the day, [90 percent of them are] telling us, 'Yes, the Bible speaks to every one of these issues.' Then we ask them: 'Well, are you teaching your people what the Bible says about those issues?' and the numbers drop . . . to less than 10 percent of pastors who say they will speak to it."[272]

On August 7, 2014, pastor (and former Constitution Party presidential candidate) Chuck Baldwin wrote an article entitled "New Research: Pastors Deliberately Keeping Flock in the Dark." Baldwin excoriated the ninety percent:

It would have been one thing if the pastors had said that these political issues were not relevant to scripture. . . . But the pastors are admitting that, yes, they KNOW that the scriptures DO relate to our current political issues, but they are deliberately choosing to NOT teach those scriptural principles.[273]

Baldwin added, "We are not dealing with IGNORANT pastors; we are dealing with DELIBERATELY DISOBEDIENT pastors."[274]

He then concluded, "It is time for Christians to acknowledge that these ministers are not pastors; they are CEOs. They are not Bible teachers; they are performers. They are not shepherds; they are hirelings."[275]

In 1993 David Wells, professor at Gordon-Conwell Theological Seminary, wrote a brilliant book entitled *No Place for Truth: Or Whatever Happened to Evangelical Theology?*

While Wells did not make the Puritan/Pietistic distinction, the problems he found in the disappearing theology of evangelicalism are particularly apparent in Pietism/R2K. Wells noted that while many people in church still profess many of the biblical doctrines, those inside the church are becoming secularized along with the culture. Thus,

> theology . . . has become peripheral and remote. Even 'those who count themselves as believers, who subscribe to the tenets of a Church, and who attend services regularly . . . nevertheless operate in a social space in which their beliefs about the supernatural are rendered in large part irrelevant.' Wherever modernity has intruded upon the Church . . . the beliefs of [Christians] will have been pushed to the margins of life, the central and integrating role they once had commandeered by other interests.[276]

Wells added, "While these items of belief are professed, they are increasingly being removed from the center of evangelical life where they defined what that life was, and they are now being relegated to the periphery where their power to define what evangelical life should be is lost."[277]

A "theology" that touches only on the hereafter, that eschews and denigrates any role for the church in the culture other than institutional evangelism, forcibly relegates *itself* to the periphery of its members' lives. Those lives involve difficult marriages, rearing children, relating to civil government and community, concerns over international relations, work and professional life. The hereafter happens only after we're gone, but all else has been banished from the pulpits. Scripture certainly speaks to all these, and a healthy theology would address them all. It is not the left, the liberal media, or Hollywood that has forced the church out of the culture. It is misguided pulpits and truncated theology that have forced us out! It is the rebellious determination to teach only a "Half Great Commission" theology—"We'll tell you how to go to heaven while refusing to teach you all things our Sovereign has commanded"—that has left the church powerless and defeated.

As we noted in previous chapters, the culture has attacked the very foundations of absolute truth and scriptural authority. And except in the context of how to get to heaven, the pulpits have spectacularly failed in giving us any ammunition to fight back. And in direct consequence of that failure, we are losing the war for the souls of our neighbors.

As we discussed earlier, the culture has called the tune, and the church has largely danced to it.

"Today, there is a large and flourishing establishment of professional scholars dedicated to the refinement and dissemination of biblical knowledge, but reflection on what all of that means in the contemporary world is largely left to others."[278] Or, I might say, ignored altogether. "Evangelical faith is pursued as a matter of internal fascination but abandoned as a matter of external and public relevance."[279] We did it to ourselves, and the world is only too thrilled to accommodate our folly. As British writer Dorothy Sayers said, "How can anyone remain interested in a religion which seems to have no concern with nine-tenths of his life?"[280]

The world is happy to accept a private, inoffensive Christianity. And apparently our pulpits are eager to gratify the world. And what is ignored by the pulpit is actively excused by the sinful pews. Wells noted that "evangelicals who were once cognitive dissidents within the culture are rapidly becoming amicable partners with it."[281] And God's judgment has been poured on our land as a result of our disobedience.

> "Shall I not punish these people?" declares the LORD,
> "On a nation such as this
> Shall I not avenge Myself?"
> An appalling and horrible thing
> Has happened in the land:
> The prophets prophesy falsely,
> And the priests rule on their own authority;
> And My people love it so!
> But what will you do at the end of it? (Jeremiah 5:29–31 NASB)

Some pulpits have openly sold themselves for financial gain. I have watched pastors oppose candidates who strongly espoused biblical truth in favor of candidates who instead offered more taxpayer dollars to the local government school system. Sometimes this is even due to family members profiting from the pagan world system. On these preachers Micah 3:11 passes judgment: "The heads thereof judge for reward, and the priests thereof teach for hire, and the prophets thereof divine for money: yet will they lean upon the LORD, and say, Is not the Lord among us? none evil can come upon us."

But I believe far more are not intentionally selling out the gospel for money. Far too many are engaged in a well-intentioned—but devastating— retreat to a purely private, church gospel that is utterly impotent.

I have sought desperately to understand *why*. Is it cowardice? Ignorance? A desperate drive to avoid conflict? I don't know. All I can offer are guesses.

Perhaps this Pietism is a tactical retreat from a culture war that seems unwinnable. It is cloaked in the premillennial idea that "things will just wax worse and worse until Jesus comes back to take us all out of here." This cloak allows us to process our frustration when the gospel seems to have lost its power and preaching seems to change nothing. Rather than considering the preaching itself may need to change, we have perhaps adopted a sanctified fatalism.

Perhaps this retreat is based on the common misconception that Christianity needs to be nice—and showing pictures of aborted babies to a murderously selfish culture is not nice. Perhaps it is rooted in the fear that the vast engine of church programs can't afford to lose volunteer hours to cultural battles.

Regardless, the R2K/Pietism "Half Great Commission" preaching has borne the illegitimate children of cultural decay and institutionalized sin, as surely as the Puritan perspective of our Founders unleashed both historic human liberty and the great early American missionary movement.

REDEEMING THE PULPITS—PREACHING THE WHOLE COUNSEL OF GOD

This must change. The church can no longer wait for the pulpits to lead. We must demand change or find new leaders.

> Genuine leadership in the Church . . . is not a matter of finding out what everyone wants and already knows and articulating it; genuine leadership is a matter of teaching and explaining what has not been so well grasped, where the demands of God's truth and the habits of the culture pull in opposite directions. . . .
>
> Genuine leaders often have to be different. They often have to articulate the truth of God's Word among those who do not fully understand its demands and implications. . . . In the evangelical world, there are many organizers and many managers but only a very few leaders . . . because there can be no leadership without a vision, and the ability to see is now in very scarce supply.
>
> And seeing is what theology is all about. It is about seeing the truth of God, seeing the gaping chasm that lies between that truth and the nostrums of modernized society, seeing how to practice that truth in this world.[282]

Way back in 1922, Charles Brown wrote, "When we think of the weak, inefficient preaching that is being perpetrated on a patient, trusting public, we marvel that the Christian religion has stood up under it without being annihilated. . . . If our faith had not been divine in its origin and essence it would have collapsed long ago."[283] Imagine if Brown could see the Christianity of today.

In a very real sense, even in Bible-believing churches, there is "a famine in the land, not a famine of bread, nor a thirst for water, but of hearing the words of the Lord" (Amos 8:11). America, "thy prophets have seen vain and foolish things for thee: and they have not discovered thine iniquity, to turn away thy captivity" (Lamentations 2:14).

The Old Testament prophets had choice words for the priests, the shepherds, who failed to diligently "feed the flock of God" (1 Peter 5:2).

> Therefore, O ye shepherds, hear the word of the LORD;
>
> Thus saith the Lord God; Behold, I am against the shepherds; and I will require my flock at their hand, and cause them to cease from feeding the flock; neither shall the shepherds feed themselves any more; for I will deliver my flock from their mouth, that they may not be meat for them.
>
> For thus saith the Lord God; Behold, I, even I, will both search my sheep, and seek them out.
>
> As a shepherd seeketh out his flock in the day that he is among his sheep that are scattered; so will I seek out my sheep, and will deliver them out of all places where they have been scattered in the cloudy and dark day. (Ezekiel 34:9–12)

It is time the pulpits ended their rebellion—and began again to fulfill the *whole* Great Commission: "teaching them to observe *all things* whatsoever I have commanded you" (Matthew 28:20, emphasis added).

"By whom is this task of transforming the unwieldy, resisting mass of human thought until it becomes subservient to the gospel—by whom is this task to be accomplished? To some extent, no doubt, by professors in theological seminaries and universities. But the ordinary minister of the gospel cannot shirk his responsibility."[284]

On September 11, 1934, Dietrich Bonhoeffer wrote to Erwin Sutz, "We must finally stop appealing to theology to justify our reserved silence about what the state is doing—for that is nothing but fear. 'Open your mouth for the one who is voiceless'—for who in the church today still remembers that that is the least of the Bible's demands in times such as these?"[285]

There is a path back to national cultural renewal. It is finding men for the pulpits who will themselves repent—and preach repentance to the rest of us. The prophet Joel's appeal to a nation under divine judgment rings too true today:

> Therefore also now, saith the LORD, turn ye even to me with all your heart, and with fasting, and with weeping, and with mourning:
>
> And rend your heart, and not your garments, and turn unto the Lord your God: for he is gracious and merciful, slow to anger, and of great kindness, and repenteth him of the evil.
>
> Who knoweth if he will return and repent, and leave a blessing behind him; even a meat offering and a drink offering unto the Lord your God?
>
> Blow the trumpet in Zion, sanctify a fast, call a solemn assembly. . . .
>
> Let the priests, the ministers of the Lord, weep between the porch and the altar, and let them say, Spare thy people, O Lord, and give not thine heritage to reproach, that the heathen should rule over them: wherefore should they say among the people, Where is their God?
>
> Then will the Lord be jealous for his land, and pity his people. (Joel 2:12–15, 17–18)

It is worth praying for, is it not?

CHAPTER 12

"WHERE THERE IS NO VISION, THE PEOPLE PERISH": EVANGELICALISM'S FAILURE TO TEACH A CHRISTIAN WORLDVIEW

At twenty-one years of age, after nearly a decade in the family construction business, I decided to pursue a degree at Liberty University. I had been involved in conservative activism and support for conservative Christian candidates for five years at that point.

I knew I was a Christian, and I knew I was a political conservative, and I believed the two to be connected, but I was not articulate in connecting the dots. I knew Christians should be pro life. I knew we should support candidates who believed in the definition of marriage Jesus gave in Matthew 19—one man for one woman for one lifetime. But I felt that the Bible must speak to many other issues, if only because my conscience kept telling me so.

It was in my Government 200 class that a professor finally began to connect the dots for me. Dr. Kevin Clauson (now at Christendom Bible College in Ohio) was famous for saying, "The Bible speaks to everything from A to Z, agriculture to zoning." He had a huge reading list for the class, books like Frédéric Bastiat's The Law *and others, that showed me that the Bible was so much more than a two-issue book. If we read it carefully, it is a manual for all of life, containing "everything pertaining to life and godliness" (2 Peter 1:3 NASB). In Dr. Clauson's class I finally began to gather the intellectual ammunition to defend what I had always thought but not known how to defend.*

* * * * *

While finishing this book, I picked up Nancy Pearcey's book *Total Truth* from our church library "by accident." Within a few pages, I realized that it is the single best book I have found dealing with the failure of the modern church to reach the culture. With appreciation to Pearcey, I use her book as the foundational resource for this chapter.

Pearcey combined an encyclopedic knowledge of church history and world history with an excellent framework for developing a Christian worldview.

CONSTRUCTING A CHRISTIAN WORLDVIEW

Pearcey posited Scripture actually includes two "Great Commissions." One is the familiar command of Matthew 28, to "teach all nations" (v. 19). The other, she said, is the Cultural Mandate, God's original command to His human creation.

> How do we go about constructing a Christian worldview? The key passage is the creation account in Genesis, because that's where we are taken back to the beginning to learn what God's original purpose was in creating the human race. With the entrance of sin, humans went off course. . . . But when we accept Christ's salvation, we are . . . restored to our original purpose. Redemption is not just about being saved *from* sin, it is also about being saved *to* something—to resume the task for which we were originally created.
>
> And what was that task? In Genesis, God gives what we might call the first job description [I would add, the first Great Commission]: "Be fruitful and multiply and fill the earth and subdue it." The first phrase, "be fruitful and multiply," means to develop the *social* world: build families, churches, schools, cities, governments, laws. The second phrase, "subdue the earth," means to harness the *natural* world: plant crops, build bridges, design computers, compose music. This passage is sometimes called the Cultural Mandate because it tells us that our original purpose was to create cultures, build civilizations—nothing less.
>
> This means that our vocation or professional work is not a second-class activity. . . . It is the high calling for which we were originally

created. The way we serve a Creator God is by being creative with the talents and gifts He has given us.[286]

Pearcey is right. And if we will carefully read the second Great Commission, we will hear Christ echo the first. We are both to "preach the gospel to every creature" (Mark 16:15) *and* to "[teach] them to observe *all things* whatsoever I have commanded you" (Matthew 28:20, emphasis added). This can be nothing less than a reiteration of the command to shape the culture. And the great failing of the Pietist movement in the American church is its rebellion against both the first and second Great Commissions.

THE FALSE DICHOTOMY: SECULAR VERSUS SACRED, SCIENCE VERSUS RELIGION, REASON VERSUS FAITH

Pearcey also grappled with the destructive false dichotomy between the secular and the sacred. We dealt with the Pietism/Puritanism debate in Chapter 10. But Pearcey revealed that the debate is not just theological but philosophical as well.

Pearcey attacked the secular world's "two-realm theory of truth." The upper story includes things that are nonrational or noncognitive. Consigned to the upper story are personal preferences, feelings, and, of course, religious views, since these are "subjective" and not "factual." The lower story includes things like economics, politics, government, science, mathematics, and other disciplines in the realm of reason and logic. The upper story is merely values, while the lower story has to do with facts.[287]

A quick consideration shows why this two-story dualism is so effective against Christianity. Evolution is "science," "factual," and therefore objective, empirical, and not subject to challenge. Ideas that prevail in the lower story can, by virtue of their "factual" basis, be imposed by law and public opinion.

Belief in God, or a god, however, is subjective, not rational, and not "factual." So are ideas of morality and values. Any "truth" about things in the upper story is relative; your truth may not be my truth. And upper-story truth is inappropriate for public discourse and may never be imposed by law or public opinion. Thus, the secularist creates a badly skewed playing field, where the favored team is given a set of rules under which it cannot lose.

The scheme is pretty much foolproof. If the secularist can get "science" to say that homosexuality is inborn, the church just has to deal with it in individual persuasion with our "opinions." But we fear to fight for our beliefs in the public square, because the "scientific" view is acceptable for the public discourse but our personal, subjective, internal religious views on the subject are not.

And, as Pearcey suggested, much of Protestantism has largely accepted this basic premise.[288] We believe Jesus is the only way to heaven, but we can't impose that view on others, because it's just our belief. (I agree we can't impose it on others but for a different reason: no one is converted by application of force.) We relinquish to "science" the ability to determine what's true in the secular world, six days a week, because it's "factual." We consign Creation to Sundays, because it's "opinion."

> The reason it's so important for us to learn how to recognize this division is that it is the single most potent weapon for delegitimizing the biblical perspective in the public square today. Here's how it works: . . . [Secularists] consign religion to the *value* sphere—which takes it out of the realm of true and false altogether. Secularists can then assure us that of course they "respect" religion, while at the same time denying that it has any relevance to the public realm.[289]

This "divided concept of truth," Pearcey wrote, referring to a warning from Lesslie Newbigin, "is the primary factor in 'the cultural captivity of the gospel.'"[290] Thus, "the barred cage that forms the prison for the gospel in contemporary western culture is [the church's] accommodation . . . to the fact-value dichotomy."[291]

Worse yet, the Pietistic view attempts to endow the two-story, "two kingdoms" narrative with biblical and theological endorsement, effectively surrendering the argument. "Secularists reinforce this split mentality by claiming that their theory does not reflect any particular philosophy—that it is just 'the way all reasonable people think.' They thus promote their own views as unbiased and rational, suitable for the public square, while denouncing religious views as biased or prejudiced."[292] And unfortunately, we absorb and accept the world's paradigm. "This tactic has often cowed Christians into being defensive about our faith, which in turn has taken a steep toll on our effectiveness in the broader culture."[293]

But, as with Marxism, anti-Christian ideas are themselves religious. "Every system of thought begins with some ultimate principle. . . . Every alternative to Christianity is a religion."[294] This includes modern American secularism. Pearcey noted that the secular revolution

> affected every part of American culture—not only higher education but also the public schools, politics, psychology, and the media. In each of these areas, Christianity was privatized as "sectarian," while secular philosophies like materialism and naturalism were put forth as "objective" and "neutral," and therefore the only perspectives suitable for the public square.
>
> Of course, they were nothing of the sort. There is nothing neutral about the claim that the only way to get at truth is to deny God's existence. That is a substantive religious claim, just as it is to affirm God's existence.[295]

The difference is that one claim is true and the other is false. How dare we be more timid about speaking the truth than the world is about speaking what is false?

Pearcey referenced historian Martin Marty's idea that every religion serves two functions: "First, it is a message of personal salvation, telling us how to get right with God; and second, it is a lens for interpreting the world. Historically, evangelicals have been good at the first function—at 'saving souls.' But they have not been nearly as good [I would say, we have been a colossal failure] . . . at providing . . . a lens to give a biblical view of areas like science, politics, economics, or bioethics . . . In fact, many no longer think it's even the *function* of Christianity to provide an interpretation of the world."[296]

Marxism, Darwinism, feminism, postmodernism—each anti-Christian view gives its adherents a comprehensive worldview. Each counsels its adherents how to confront society in order to bring about societal change. In modern America, only Christianity fails to do the same. So guess which worldviews are prevailing and which one is failing?

THE BIRTH OF THE "TWO KINGDOMS" VIEW: NOT THE BIBLE BUT PAGAN GREEK PHILOSOPHERS

Pearcey argued that the roots of this dichotomy come not from Scripture but from pagan Greek philosophers. The early church was born in a world pervaded by Greek culture. The classical Greek philosophers were considered the opinion leaders in that society. Even in the church, some pagan Greek ideas held currency.

An especially strong dualistic view, she said, was Plato's notion of the Forms. For Plato, "everything is composed of Matter and Form—raw material ordered by rational ideas. . . . Matter on its own was regarded as disordered and chaotic. The Forms were rational and good, bringing about order and harmony."[297] Plato thought both Matter and Forms to be eternal. The Forms were, in essence, the "upper story," while Matter was the "lower story."[298]

Of course, Scripture teaches that only God is eternal and that matter as originally created by God was not disordered or chaotic: "God saw every thing that he had made, and, behold, it was very good" (Genesis 1:31).

But the early Christian father Augustine, himself a converted Platonist, retained much of the Platonic thought he had learned. "Most important, he retained an adapted notion of the double creation, teaching that God first made the Platonic intelligible Forms, and afterward made the material world in imitation of the Forms."[299]

"This dualistic view of creation led naturally to a dualistic view of the Christian life."[300] Accordingly, Augustine taught that the material world was inherently inferior to the "spiritual." He urged drastic self-denial in things material, pronouncing marriage as inferior to celibacy, and "secular work" as inferior to a monastic lifestyle focused exclusively on the "spiritual."[301]

Augustine's Platonic dichotomy dominated Christian thought until the Reformation. And its effects were pernicious. "The problem with this radical dichotomy was that it divided human nature itself in half."[302] Thus, "by a sagacious division of labor that the Gospel had not foreseen," wrote Jacques Maritain tongue in cheek, "the Christian will be able to serve two masters at once, God for heaven and Mammon for the earth, and will be able to divide his soul between two obediences each alike absolute and ultimate—that of the Church, for heaven, and that of the State, for the earth."[303] This same trap permeates the teaching of too many modern Christian leaders such as Russell Moore. It is not inconsequential; the trap, in practical effect, elevates Caesar to God-status.

The Reformers attacked this false dichotomy. "One of the driving motives of the Reformers was to overcome this medieval dualism and to recover the unity of life and knowledge under the authority of God's Word. . . . Rejecting monasticism, they preached that the Christian life is not a summons to a state of life *separate from* our participation in the creation order of family and work, but is *embedded within* the creation order."[304] Therefore, "the Reformers contrasted the monastic call *from* the world with the biblical call *into* the world. . . . Calvin taught that Christ was the Redeemer of every part of creation, including culture, and that we serve him in our everyday work."[305]

Unfortunately the modern evangelical church has largely fallen back into the Platonic trap. The current state of the church is similar to the state of the medieval church: "In practical terms, . . . dualism implied that we need *spiritual* regeneration in the upper story of theology and religion, but we don't need *intellectual* regeneration in order to get the right view of politics, science, social life, morality, or work. In these areas, human reason is treated as religiously neutral, and we can all go ahead and accept whatever the secular experts decree. It should come as no surprise, then, that this dichotomy led believers to accommodate with the world in these areas."[306]

We talked in Chapter 3 about how the world sees a schizophrenic church—claiming to believe the Bible's teaching on the afterlife while rejecting its teachings in this life—and they simply mock us. "The crucial challenge is to present Christianity as a unified, comprehensive truth that is not restricted to the upper story. We must have the confidence that it is true on *all* levels—that it can stand up to rigorous rational and historical testing, while also fulfilling our highest spiritual ideals."[307]

If we are not on offense, we are unavoidably on defense. "In order to resist the spirit of the world, we must recognize the form it takes in our own day. Otherwise, we will fail to resist it, and indeed may even unconsciously absorb it ourselves."[308] I submit we have absorbed the world's spirit—wholesale.

A HOUSE BUILT ON SAND: THE MODERN EVANGELICAL MISTAKE

Pearcey undertook a thorough historical review of American evangelicalism's birth during the revivals and camp meetings of the 1700s and 1800s. She devoted a good deal of time to praising evangelicalism's efforts at soul winning but offered some critique as well.

> The focus on an intense conversion experience was highly effective in bringing people to faith. But it also tended to redefine religion in terms of emotion, while contributing to a neglect of theology and doctrine and the whole cognitive element of belief. This tendency did enormous damage by reinforcing a conception of Christianity as a noncognitive upper-story experience.[309]

Pearcey suggested that evangelicalism allowed itself to be influenced by American political ideals of individualism. America's move to political independence foreshadowed a move toward anti-historical religious individualism as well, favoring subjective conversion experiences over doctrinal confessions that were seen as old and dead. She contrasted this movement with the earlier, covenantal form of church involvement familiar to the Puritans.

> In early New England, to become a member of a church, a candidate went through a long process of learning the Bible, the creeds, the Lord's Prayer, the Ten Commandments, the catechism. Then he or she was required to submit to an initial examination by the church elders and minister. After that, he had to present a credible narrative of his conversion experience before the entire congregation. Next came an investigation of the candidate's life and moral conduct. . . . Only if the candidate passed these various tests was he or she received into the covenant.[310]

In its rush to match American Christianity with American individualism, Pearcey suggested, evangelicalism deemphasized doctrine. Instead, too many seem to be proudly anti-intellectual. "God said it; I believe it; that settles it (even if I can't tell you where God said it)" has replaced the ability to "give an answer to every man that asketh you a reason of the hope that is in you" (1 Peter 3:15). Evangelicalism has become "theologically broad to the point of incoherence," and we can observe a troubling "disappearance of doctrine."[311]

This trend only assisted the secularists' efforts to pigeonhole Christianity to the "upper story," the nonfactual, subjective, experiential, private realm.

> Churches and seminaries . . . largely *withdrew* from intellectual confrontation with the secular world, limiting their attention to the realm of practical Christian living. . . . They *gave up* the idea that Christianity gives a comprehensive framework to interpret all of life and scholarship, allowing it to become boxed into the upper story. . . . In the process, they *abandoned* an entire range of intellectual inquiry to the lower story. They gave in to the demand that the academic disciplines must be religiously and philosophically autonomous, without realizing that it was just a cover to introduce *new* philosophies like positivism and naturalism.[312]

The anti-intellectual view of many evangelicals threatens to make the world's accusation of "blind faith" an accurate assessment. We believe in something we know little about. We all call Christ "Savior," but our lack of knowledge of the great doctrines leads to failure to follow Him as Lord.

Pearcey cited a 1970s survey of Lutherans. In the survey, "75 percent of Lutherans agreed that belief in Jesus Christ was absolutely necessary for salvation. But 75 percent also agreed that all roads lead to God and it does not matter which way one takes."[313] But these two positions are at mortal odds with each other! The world's lexicon and the world's values have so totally corrupted our own that we cannot see our own incoherence, our own schizophrenia. We are content with "having a form of godliness, but denying the power thereof" (2 Timothy 3:15). Is it any wonder that "the Glory has departed" (1 Samuel 4:21 NIV)?

Jesus warned us that if we hear His words but fail to do them, we are building on the sand and risking complete failure (Matthew 7:26–27). "My people are destroyed for lack of knowledge," God cried in Hosea 4:6. "Because thou hast rejected knowledge, I will also reject thee, that thou shalt be no priest to me: seeing thou hast forgotten the law of thy God, I will also forget thy children." The message of God to the churches in Revelation cries out to the church in America today: "Remember therefore from whence thou art fallen, and repent, and do the first works" (Revelation 2:5). "Remember therefore how thou hast received and heard, and hold fast, and repent" (Revelation 3:3).

CHAPTER 13

REVIVAL OR RUIN? CALLING THE CHURCH TO CHALLENGE THE CULTURE

One afternoon in 1806, five students from Williams College in Massachusetts met in a field to pray for foreign missions. A thunderstorm blew in before the students could find shelter. They eventually took shelter in a haystack.

But the prayer meeting continued in the haystack as the five students sought God and asked His help in taking His Word to the whole world. The leader of the group, Samuel Mills, said to his companions, "We can do this, if we will."

Mills and several of the other students eventually were instrumental in founding the first American mission board. Their board sent missionaries all over the world.[314] *Its missionaries taught the Word, opened hospitals, and established translations of the Bible in languages that did not have the Scriptures yet.*

God used five committed college students to have a great impact on large portions of the world. Why could He not do it again?

* * * * *

I realize that most of this book has been written in a distinctly minor key. I may be wrong, but I don't think my perspective is unduly negative; I think it is a realistic view if one is informed as to the bankrupt nature of American culture and the decayed state of the American church.

But I don't want to end on that note. If I were convinced that there were no hope for "one nation under God," I would still have tried to sound the warning.

I believe Truth is precious enough to shout from the housetops for its own sake, even if no one listens.

But my hope and prayer in sounding the warning is that a remnant few may listen. One thing proven by history is that God seldom works through majorities. Whether Christ's twelve apostles, Daniel in the lions' den, the roughly forty percent of the American colonists that supported independence from England, the tiny Jewish nation against the world, Luther and the Reformers standing against king and pope, or lonely missionaries like Adoniram Judson, John Paton, and Amy Carmichael all alone against impossible odds, God usually uses a remnant.

Who would have thought Gideon could free his people with just three hundred men (Judges 7)? Who would have thought that 102 Pilgrims could start an experiment in 1620 that would lead to freedom for hundreds of millions for four hundred years? Who would have thought Wilberforce and a small minority could capture the conscience of a nation and be the driving force to end British slavery?

But that has always been how God works. And that is why, when the hour is darkest, I believe God is calling most urgently that we "let [our] light so shine before men" (Matthew 5:16)—not just through church functions but also in the rough and nasty world of societal debate.

PRESCRIPTION FOR REVIVAL: CALLING THE CHURCH FROM SELFISHNESS TO SACRIFICE

One thing is clear to me. Unless the church intentionally and prayerfully seeks a massive course correction, the result, America's epitaph, is already written across our headlines. If we continue to try to appease the world through cowardly and misbegotten "tolerance," if churches continue to fail to train our people in a truly biblical worldview, if we continue down the Pietistic path of withdrawing from the culture, if we fail to repent of our individual and corporate sins and continue operating as if Christ died to allow us not to have to change, we are history. The definition of insanity is to keep repeating the same actions and expecting different results. *It isn't working*; we must "repent, and do the first works" (Revelation 2:5).

We need a revival of spiritual understanding. It is time for the church to pursue "the knowledge of the holy," which "is understanding" (Proverbs 9:10). Wisdom, the knowledge of God, is not gained by accident. "If thou seekest [wisdom] as silver, and searchest for her as for hid treasures; then shalt thou understand the fear of the LORD, and find the knowledge of God" (Proverbs 2:4–5). We must no longer acquiesce to the disappearance of doctrine. We are promised, "Ye shall seek me, and find me, when ye shall search for me with all your heart" (Jeremiah 29:13). We must "study to shew [ourselves] approved unto God" (2 Timothy 2:15) rather than settling for checking a half-dozen theological boxes.

In their book *How Now Shall We Live?* Charles Colson and Nancy Pearcey highlighted some of the same problems this book raises. At the end of their book, they proposed concrete steps Christians can take to again contend for the faith in a culture adrift. I will borrow some of those here and add others we have argued for in earlier chapters.

1. TREAT GOD'S WORD AS AUTHORITATIVE AGAIN

I contend that those who claim the name of Christ in America are morally obligated to again consider His eternal Word to be authoritative from cover to cover, in all times, places, and circumstances, no matter how much an "enlightened" culture may oppose God's Word or how uncomfortable it may be. If we are basically practical atheists, our "witness" will be ignored, or worse, our worldly philosophies will speed our country's destruction.

As the great British theologian Os Guinness put it, "The church may fall captive to this culture or that ideology, to this philosophy or that fashion. But when the Word of the Lord speaks and is listened to, the church wakes up to be herself and the captivity can be thrown off."[315] Guinness encouraged a constant resort to Scripture and a constant comparison of Scripture to the culture and to our own lives to be sure that we have not sacrificed the eternal in order to be "relevant" to a dying culture.[316]

Of course, if we hold Scripture to be authoritative, we have to confess absolute truth. And we must advocate in society for that absolutism. We are ambassadors for a holy heavenly King, in a depraved earthly country. We are not here to be comfortable in that country; we are here to defend and advance the interests of our King.

We understand, though, that not all will bring "into captivity every thought captive to the obedience of Christ" (2 Corinthians 10:5). However, this is utterly irrelevant to the divine mandate to do so ourselves and to diligently teach our children to do the same (Deuteronomy 6). It is also crucial that we recall the Great Commission. We are to be "teaching them to observe *all things* whatsoever [Christ has] commanded" (Matthew 28:20, emphasis added), whether they wish to hear or not. We are instructed to "earnestly contend for the faith" (Jude 1:3). This presumes that we will have to *contend*. We like to think we can just share our faith. Some folks don't want us to share it. Some are committed to making certain that our faith be confined, cloistered, banned from public discourse. But because "all power is given unto [Christ] in heaven and in earth" (Matthew 28:18), they have no authority to stop us from proclaiming His Truth. They can mock. They can try to silence. Christ even warned us they may "kill the body" but in the same breath commanded us to "fear not" (Matthew 10:28). The gospel is intolerant. Jesus is the only way. And as John told King Herod at great cost, just because something is legal does not mean it is lawful (Matthew 14:1–11). We must constantly confront Caesar with the reality of his limited, delegated, inferior authority and his ultimate accountability to "the King eternal" (1 Timothy 1:17).

2. FOLLOW CHRIST'S EXAMPLE: REACH HUMAN NEEDS OUTSIDE THE CHURCH

Colson and Pearcey argue that "Christians must carry out their civic duty in every walk of life."[317] Just as Jesus healed lepers, opened blind eyes, fed the hungry, and delivered those oppressed by evil spirits, so the church must do *far* more to reach beyond our walls and our self-focused programs. As an attorney, when I am appointed to represent kids who were taken from their drug-addicted parents, I have nothing to offer but the government's Department of Social Services. These folks try hard and do a lot of great work, but they can't tell the kids of the Jesus who loves the little children and "brings justice to victory" (Matthew 12:20 ESV). And the church simply has no options to offer and even little realization of the nature of the problem. It is time we used more of the resources God has loaned to His church to carry the gospel to the rougher parts of town.

3. TEACH A BIBLICAL WORLDVIEW IN THE CHURCHES AND SEMINARIES

As Colson and Pearcey wrote, "Christians [and, I would argue, especially pastors] must be engaged directly in politics."[318] God's commands to human government are lengthy and direct. We need to be His messengers to the government chosen to serve as "God's ministers" (Romans 13:6). How else will they know what He expects of His ministers? Churches must again teach their people what God actually says throughout Scripture about civic involvement and must encourage us to be salt and light in the deep, dark recesses of government and the electoral process.

Our seminaries must reject the two-story, two-kingdoms narrative borrowed from the pagan Greek philosophers and impart a comprehensive biblical answer to the cultural challenge.

The current popular generation of two-kingdoms preachers should be replaced with a new generation of John the Baptists, Tozers, and Wesleys. The pulpits must again blaze with the power of the God who makes all things new.

Proverbs 29:18 tells us, "Where there is no vision, the people perish: but he that keepeth the law, happy is he." The pulpits must again proclaim and teach "the *whole* counsel of God" (Acts 20:27 ESV, emphasis added), a comprehensive biblical vision that addresses our whole life.

4. APPLY THE AUTHORITY OF THE WORD TO CULTURE AGAIN

The church must act as the conscience of society, as a restraint against the misuse of governing authority. Corporately, the church must zealously guard its independence [I might add, including from the anti-God government education complex], keep its prophetic voice sharp, and resist the allure of worldly power. It should hold government morally accountable to live up to its delegated authority from God (along with holding all other spheres of society accountable to fulfill the functions ordained to them by God).[319]

Colson and Pearcey are correct. Scripture is the story of God's creation, humanity's fall through sin, and Christ's redemption. We must tell and retell that story. We must let sinners know that they are lost and that there is only one way. Tolerating sin will *never* convict them that they need a Savior.

5. REJECT PIETISM'S SELF-FULFILLING FATALISM

We must get over the irresponsible fatalism of Pietism. Jesus knew He was going to the cross. Later, so did Peter. But they were not fatalistic. Peter warned of persecution to come, but he also reminded people of God's "exceeding great and precious promises" (2 Peter 1:4). We must remember "for ever, O Lord, thy word is settled in heaven" (Psalm 119:89) and "I am the Lord, I change not" (Malachi 3:6). It is still true that "righteousness exalteth a nation: but sin is a reproach to any people" (Proverbs 14:34). Today our sin has brought us into reproach. But "if my people, which are called by my name, shall humble themselves, and pray, and seek my face, and turn from their wicked ways; then will I hear from heaven, and will forgive their sin, and will heal their land" (2 Chronicles 7:14).

Therefore also now, saith the LORD, turn ye even to me with all your heart, and with fasting, and with weeping, and with mourning:

And rend your heart, and not your garments, and turn unto the Lord your God: for he is gracious and merciful, slow to anger, and of great kindness, and repenteth him of the evil.

> Who knoweth if he will return and repent, and leave a blessing
> behind him? (Joel 2:12–14)

Certainly, we are living in the last days. But Peter knew he was in "the last days" too (Acts 2:17). And see how many revivals God has brought to lands around the globe since then. See America's own Great Awakening, as sinful professing Christians began to seek God and repent and a nation was revolutionized. See the explosion of Christianity in our own lifetimes in South Korea. God is still in the business of changing lives and changing cultures. "Them that honour me I will honour" (1 Samuel 2:30). Let us honor Him with our lives and allow our light to shine that those around us may "glorify [our] Father which is in heaven" (Matthew 5:16).

We must avoid the temptation to turn the only religion backed by the power of God into a monastic, academic pursuit that doesn't touch the world around us. Instead, we must embrace the vision of John Winthrop.

As the Puritans were preparing to establish a colony in Massachusetts, John Winthrop, who would become the first governor, preached a sermon to inspire his people to remember that, in establishing this new land, they were on a mission for the King.

> We must consider that we shall be as a city upon a hill. The eyes of
> all people are upon us. So that if we shall deal falsely with our God
> in this work we have undertaken, and so cause Him to withdraw
> His present help from us, we shall be made a story and a by-word
> through the world . . . till we be consumed out of the good land
> whither we are going . . .
>
> "Beloved, there is now set before us life and death, good and
> evil," in that we are commanded this day to love the Lord our
> God, and to love one another, to walk in his ways and to keep his
> Commandments and his ordinance and his laws, and the articles
> of our Covenant with Him, that we may live and be multiplied,
> and that the Lord our God may bless us in the land whither we go
> to possess it. But if our hearts shall turn away, so that we will not

obey, but shall be seduced, and worship other Gods, our pleasure and profits, and serve them; it is propounded unto us this day, we shall surely perish out of the good land whither we pass over this vast sea to possess it.

Therefore let us choose life,
that we and our seed may live,
by obeying His voice and cleaving to Him,
for He is our life and our prosperity.[320]

The vision of men like Winthrop, the understanding these men had of being on a divine mission, gave us the freedom we have enjoyed for four hundred years. That vision has been lost, trampled into the ground by modern "nice Christianity," where the unpardonable sin is to be offensive to anyone. We must reject the irresponsible Pietism that has invaded the modern church. We must reject the counsel of surrender offered by Russell Moore and others and instead appropriate the courage of Daniel and the vision of Winthrop. We must reject the culture's demands that we confine Christ to Sunday and to the church building. We must understand that the world is demanding we play a game where the world has written the rules and the victor is predetermined. We must forcefully reject the Enemy's demand that we "live and let live." We must reject his demand that we relegate Jesus to one hour of contrived emotion on Sunday while we pretend for the other six days that we somehow hold no responsibility for the babies being slaughtered, the marriages being destroyed, and our neighbors being oppressed by a lawless Caesar who demands our silence while he seeks to make himself god on earth.

6. RUTHLESSLY ROOT OUT AND REJECT OUR OWN IDOLS

The sixth requirement may be the most difficult. True worship of Jehovah always demands that His people throw down their idols. In Genesis 35 Jacob was returning to his homeland after many years away to escape Esau. God commanded him to go to Bethel, where God had met with him as he fled from

Esau, and build an altar to meet again with God. When he received this command, "Jacob said to his household and to all who were with him, 'Put away the foreign gods which are among you, and purify yourselves and change your garments'" (v. 2 NASB). Jacob's own family, under the spiritual leadership of the patriarch, had allowed idolatry to creep in. Before Jacob could meet with God again and receive His blessing again, the idols had to be done away with. God was—and still is—"a jealous God" (Exodus 20:5). "I am the Lord, that is My name; I will not give My glory to another, nor My praise to graven images" (Isaiah 42:8 NASB).

Every time in Scripture that you see God's people turn to Him from idols, the life change had to be total. There were no half measures. As far as God was concerned, if idols were worshipped, He was not being honored as God. Elijah's question of his people is critically relevant today: "How long halt ye between two opinions? if the Lord be God, follow him: but if Baal, then follow him" (1 Kings 18:21). When the people chose God, they killed the 450 prophets of Baal (vv. 22, 40). When Moses destroyed the golden calf, he ground it to powder, threw the dust into the water, and made the people drink it (Exodus 32:20). When Gideon accepted God's call to free his people from the Midianites, the first thing he did was to throw down the altar his father had built to Baal and cut down the grove of trees that surrounded the altar (Judges 6:25–27). When the high priest found the book of the law in the temple and King Josiah heard God's pronouncement of judgment on his land, he tore his clothes and wept before God (2 Kings 22:18–19). His very next repentant move was to remove the objects of Baal worship from the temple and burn them (23:4).

The departed glory will never return to America, unless we the American church admit our idolatry, remove idols completely from our lives, and make a radical reorientation, devoting to God and His Truth the time, treasure, and effort we have been pouring into the swollen coffers of our idols.

Pearcey's words are incisive: "In a world of moral relativism, where everything is reduced to personal choice, simply saying no is in itself a very hard teaching. *If it does not seem hard, then we are probably accommodating to the world without realizing it.*[321]

We need not oppose education. But we must recognize that its end is to know God, to understand Truth, and to equip us to proclaim that. We must reject our delegation of education to Caesar and rededicate ourselves and our children to the "fear of the Lord [that] is the beginning of wisdom" (Proverbs 9:10). If we believe in the God of eternity, it is time we stopped devoting so much effort to "fatten[ing our] hearts in a day of slaughter" (James 5:5 ESV) and began devoting that time and effort to "lay[ing] up . . . treasures in heaven" (Matthew 6:20).

We must end the rebellion of the pulpits and demand that those claiming to speak for God again preach "the whole counsel of God" (Acts 20:27 ESV) and not a truncated gospel. We must demand that our leaders train us in the whole Great Commission, both the preaching of salvation by repentance through faith and the teaching to "observe all things whatsoever [Christ has] commanded" (Matthew 28:20). "The crying need of the Western church today is for reformation and revival."[322]

THE HISTORICAL RECORD: PREACHING JUDGMENT TO COME PRODUCES REVIVAL

But there is hope. Despite the self-fulfilling prophecies of the "wax worse and worse" preachers, history—both biblical history and church history since Christ—is full of examples of things getting *better* when God's people preach the whole Book. In particular, revival has happened when preachers began to remind people in no uncertain terms of the wrath and judgment of God.

As bad as things are in America, the situation is not unprecedented. Jonah was called to preach to Nineveh that it would be destroyed in forty days (Jonah 3:4). And the Ninevites certainly deserved it. Nineveh was the capital of Assyria, and the Assyrians were the ancient version of ISIS (Islamic State of Iraq and Syria). They conquered much of the world through fear and brutality. Ancient Assyrian records reveal horrific torture of captured enemies. They enjoyed skinning captives alive, impaling them on poles, cutting off hands and tongues, gouging out eyes.

Yet when Jonah told this depraved city that judgment was coming, the king and people humbled themselves and repented, literally in sackcloth and ashes (Jonah 3:5–9). Eventually the empire returned to its old ways, but God's judgment was delayed for many years through repentance.

In the fifteenth and sixteenth centuries, the Catholic Church was by far the dominant church in the world. It had grown extremely powerful but extremely corrupt. It had banned private ownership of the Bible. Bibles were often chained to pulpits and the public was kept largely illiterate, thus giving only the church leaders access to God—and not coincidentally, keeping power in the hands of the papacy as well. The church had reached the point that its leaders were selling indulgences, with which a person could supposedly buy forgiveness from sin.

But one man, Martin Luther, beset by awareness of his sin and fear of the wrath of God, found salvation by grace. Having found salvation, he set out to challenge the corrupt Catholic practices. His brave stand, initiated by his posting ninety-five theses in Wittenberg, Germany, was not appreciated by the church. When put on trial for his faith and ordered to recant, Luther reportedly made this famous statement: "Here I stand. God helping me, I can do no other." The Protestant Reformation he started swept through Europe and had a profound impact on the Pilgrims and Puritans who founded our nation.

The first true Christians to come to America's shores were the Pilgrims in 1620 and the Puritans shortly thereafter. The Pilgrims believed that the Church of England had failed to follow the teachings of the Bible. Their refusal to participate in the king's denomination led to persecution, and eventually the Pilgrims fled to Holland, then to America. But even while in Holland, they did not give up their attempt to spread the truth of the Word in England. They established a printing press and used it to print illegal Separatist and Puritan books for distribution in England.[323] Their steadfast commitment to live according to the dictates of the Bible as they saw it— and their unwillingness to accept the state's prohibition of their religious practices—birthed our great country.

England, before the Wesleyan revival, was in spiritual straits perhaps as desperate as those of today's America. "In 18th century England, poverty was widespread and endemic. The nation was on the verge of revolution. One out of every four women were prostitutes, many of them as young as eight years old. Thousands died annually from syphilis and gonorrhea. Crime abounded. Slavery was widespread and brutal."[324]

How did Wesley respond? Not with "your best life now."[325] Not with an emphasis on meek and mild Jesus. No, he preached the wrath of God and the necessity of "flee[ing] from the wrath to come" (Luke 3:7). Wesley's Methodist revival unleashed "revival power which ultimately changed a nation. During this prolonged period of cultural transformation, a thought provoking question was consistently asked. . . . That question . . . was as follows: '*Do you desire to flee from the wrath to come, and to be saved from your sins?*' For many today, notions of 'the wrath of God' may seem outdated, questionable, or even backward. Nonetheless, the theme of *God's wrath* permeates all of Scripture and was a central theme in the DNA of the Wesleyan revival."[326] The revival swept through England and crossed the Atlantic to America.

"Why would John Wesley ask people, '*Do you desire to flee from the wrath to come?*' John Wesley would ask people that question because he put his confidence in what was *true* over what was *popular*; and God honored the message as masses turned to faith in God's justifying grace in Jesus Christ."[327]

In the mid-1780s, a young member of Parliament named William Wilberforce became "convinced . . . of wealth's emptiness, Christianity's truth, and his own failure to embrace its radical demands. Outwardly he looked ever confident, but inwardly he agonized. 'I was filled with sorrow,' he wrote. 'I am sure that no human creature could suffer more than I did for some months.'"[328]

After counsel from John Newton (former slave trader and author of "Amazing Grace"), Wilberforce decided that his Christianity required action. "He . . . increasingly felt the burden of his calling: 'A man who acts from the principles I profess,' he later wrote, 'reflects that he is to give an account of his political conduct at the judgment seat of Christ.'"[329] That sense of accountability was to dominate the rest of his life.

He determined to do "nearer the throne what Wesley [had] accomplished in the meeting and among the multitude."[330] "He also summed up what became his life mission: 'God Almighty has set before me two great objects, the suppression of the slave trade and the reformation of manners' (i.e., morality)."[331]

In April 1797 Wilberforce published a book entitled *A Practical View of the Prevailing Religious System of Professed Christians, in the Higher and Middle Classes in This Country, Contrasted with Real Christianity*. It was a call for a revival of true, vibrant Christianity in the face of cultural decay and a prevailing "Christianity" that he believed had become an impotent shell because of a lack of commitment to the Bible's demands for sacrificial Christian living.

From 1787, convinced it was a Christian duty, Wilberforce championed the cause of abolishing slavery in the British Empire. The economic system of Britain depended on slave trade, and the fight was a lonely one. Ill health forced him from Parliament in 1825, but in 1833, just three days before he died, Wilberforce heard Parliament had the votes to force the abolition of slavery in the British Empire.

Here in our own country, the greatest historical example of the centrality of repentance to moral and political renewal is the Great Awakening. The most famous sermon of the Awakening was delivered by Jonathan Edwards and entitled "Sinners in the Hands of an Angry God." Many of us have heard that the sermon had an unusual impact on its original audience, but few of us have read it. I did. Even to me, Edwards's language was shocking. I recommend it to the reader. You will find no soft promises to sinners that "God loves you and has a wonderful plan for your life."

Edwards's sermon is so politically incorrect that it is nearly impossible to imagine it preached today in America. Preaching to professing Christians, Edwards began his sermon with ten observations:

1. There is no want of power in God to cast wicked men into hell at any moment.
2. They deserve to be cast into hell.

3. They are already under a sentence of condemnation to hell.

4. They are now the objects of that very same anger and wrath of God that is expressed in the torments of hell.

5. The devil stands ready to fall upon them, and seize them as his own, at what moment God shall permit him.

6. There are in the souls of wicked men those hellish principles reigning that would presently kindle and flame out into hell fire, if it were not for God's restraints.

7. It is no security to wicked men for one moment that there are no visible means of death at hand.

8. Natural men's prudence and care to preserve their own lives, or the care of others to preserve them, do not secure them a moment.

9. All wicked men's pains and contrivance which they use to escape hell, while they continue to reject Christ, and so remain wicked men, do not secure them from hell one moment.

10. God has laid Himself under no obligation by any promise to keep any natural man out of hell one moment.[332]

Edwards told his congregation, "God is a great deal more angry with great numbers that are now on earth: yea, doubtless, with many that are now in this congregation, who it may be are at ease, than He is with many of those who are now in the flames of hell."[333]

Harsh stuff. Suffice it to say, Edwards wasn't losing sleep over being seeker friendly or catering to the false fatalistic view that "I can't please God anyway, so what's the use?" Edwards warned "unconverted persons in this congregation,"

All your righteousness . . . would have no more influence to uphold you and keep you out of hell, than a spider's web would have to stop a falling rock. . . .The sun does not willingly shine upon you to give you light to serve sin and Satan; the earth does not willingly yield her increase to satisfy your lusts; nor is it willingly a stage for your wickedness to be acted upon; the air does not willingly serve you for breath to maintain the flame of life in your vitals, while you spend your life in the service of God's enemies.[334]

The Reverend Stephen Williams was there that day and reported on the effect of Edwards's words on the church full of professing Christians:

> Before the sermon was done there was a great moaning and crying out through the whole house—"What shall I do to be saved?" "Oh, I am going to hell!" "Oh what shall I do for Christ?" and so forth—so that the minister was obliged to desist. [The] shrieks and cries were piercing and amazing. After some time of waiting, the congregation were still, so that a prayer was made . . . and after that we descended from the pulpit and discoursed with the people, some in one place and some in another. And amazing and astonishing: the power [of] God was seen and several souls were hopefully wrought upon that night, and oh the cheerfulness and pleasantness of their countenances that received comfort.[335]

That sort of preaching would never be welcome in today's evangelical churches. But it is exactly what fueled the Great Awakening. And it was the Great Awakening that birthed our War of Independence and our Declaration of Independence, which declares our belief that "all men . . . are endowed by their Creator with certain unalienable Rights."

God has done it before. He *can* do it again. But "no man can serve two masters" (Matthew 6:24). The church in America has a stark choice. Yes, there *is* hope. God is "the same yesterday, and to day, and for ever" (Hebrews 13:8). But He "stand[s] at the door, and knock[s]" (Revelation 3:20). He allows us to choose between "life and death, blessing and cursing" (Deuteronomy 30:19). He calls us to choose "to serve the LORD . . . or the gods of the Amorites, in whose land [we] dwell" (Joshua 24:15). And He "will not give [His] glory to another" (Isaiah 42:8 NASB).

We have a choice. We can repent and return. We can "do the first works" (Revelation 2:5). We can go back to preaching the law of God and Christ's demand to "repent: for the kingdom of heaven is at hand" (Matthew 4:17). Scripture and history tell us it works.

Or we can continue to demand the right to keep our idols along with Christ. We can allow the majority of our kids' lives to be spent being indoctrinated that the Bible is false, because it's convenient and affordable and we're "free in Christ" and nobody can judge us. We can. And the results are painfully obvious all around us and within us. And they won't change. Because we won't change. The sine qua non of Christianity is repentance and a changed life. And we don't want that. Not really. Not if it means paying a price.

By and large, the professing church of Jesus Christ in America treats Jesus as an afterthought, a helpful add-on to our busy lives. Jesus is not—and will not be—a helpful add-on. We can no longer be satisfied to live lives that take His name in vain. It is time for radical, wholesale changes to our day planners, our bank account statements, our choices regarding the things we allow to invade our hearts and minds.

British revivalist Henry Varley once said to Dwight L. Moody, "Moody, the world has yet to see what God will do with a man fully consecrated to him."[336]

I submit that Jesus has had His fill of sanctified fandom. He has more fans than He ever needed. Jesus is looking for bondservants. If we Jesus fans decided to be bondservants of Jesus Christ, I have little doubt that America would experience genuine revival, a genuine cultural awakening.

"Judgment must begin at the house of God" (1 Peter 4:17). And "if we would judge ourselves, we should not be judged" (1 Corinthians 11:31). Let us say with the broken King David, "Thou desirest not sacrifice; else would I give it: thou delightest not in burnt offering. The sacrifices of God are a broken spirit: a broken and a contrite heart, O God, thou wilt not despise" (Psalm 51:16–17).

America is like the heathen sailors on the ship with Jonah. Our countrymen are adrift on an unknown sea in the midst of a storm that threatens to destroy everything they know. They do not know our God. They do not understand how to have eternal life. They are wracked by addiction, ridden with guilt for slaughtering their own children, seeking desperately for love and fulfillment in perverse lifestyles, trusting the fickle mercies of government to provide security for this life while trying desperately not to think about the next, drowning in fear and anger.

And we are Jonah. We are called by God to preach the message of Jesus: "Repent: for the kingdom of heaven is at hand" (Matthew 4:17). But we don't want to sacrifice. We have other priorities. We are pursuing everything but that divine call. And as a result, we and our countrymen are in mortal danger. Whether they know it or not, the only hope of our fellow Americans lies in the cry of the shipmaster to Jonah: "What meanest thou, O sleeper? arise, call upon thy God, if so be that God will think upon us, that we perish not" (1:6). At least Jonah was wise enough that he didn't blame his situation on the heathen sailors around him. He accepted responsibility and repented. We should be wise enough to do the same.

The key to restoration—to national revival—is in the same place it has always been: "If my people . . . " (2 Chronicles 7:14). If we—you and I—would pray and seek His face and, yes, turn from *our* wicked ways, healing is still available. "Behold, the Lord's hand is not shortened, that it cannot save; neither his ear heavy, that it cannot hear: but your iniquities have separated between you and your God, and your sins have hid his face from you, that he will not hear" (Isaiah 59:1–2).

God will always—*always*—hear a prayer of repentance. If He withheld judgment from vicious, wicked Nineveh when they repented (John 3:5–10), we know there is hope for us. But He has promised that He will not hear the prayers of the unrepentant. It is painfully simple. We have two options: revival or ruin. We must repent. And we must return. Then—and only then— we can have confidence that the Great Physician will restore our broken land.

WORLDVIEW TREND CHART

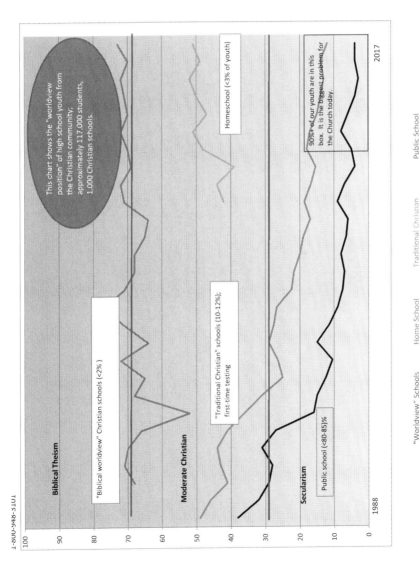

This chart shows the "worldview position" of high school youth from the Christian community; approximately 117,000 students, 1,000 Christian schools.

Biblical Theism

"Biblical worldview" Christian schools (<2%)

Moderate Christian

"Traditional Christian" schools (10-12%); first-time testing

Homeschool (<3% of youth)

Secularism

Public school (<80-85)%

90% of our youth are in this box. It is the biggest problem for the Church today.

"Worldview" Schools   Home School   Traditional Christian   Public School

1988   2017

THE "PEERS WORLDVIEW" GRID

This chart summarizes four major worldview perspectives on five key spheres of life. It can be read in two ways: ACROSS, to see a single worldview's perspective on each of the five spheres, or DOWN, to compare the various worldviews' perspectives on each sphere. The chart serves as an aide to the PEERS Test and its follow-up course, PILLARS. Information on both products can be found at website below.

	Politics	Economics	Education	Religion	Social Issues
Biblical Theism (God is God)	Law originates with God. In all spheres of government (family, church, and civil), man's law must align with divine law in order to be valid. God's Law is His word, as written in the Holy Scriptures.	God has ordained productive labor and private property ownership. The first rule of economics is "You shall not steal." The second is to maintain honest weights and measures. The third is: If you don't work, you don't eat, with certain exceptions for the truly disabled.	The purpose of education is that we might know God and obey his commands. Parents are primarily responsible for the education of their children, through both direct instruction and the optional procurement of instruction by others of their choosing.	Everyone is born in sin and needs a Savior. Salvation comes through confession of faith in the atoning work of Jesus Christ, as evidenced by genuine repentance. God is knowable only through Christ, and his Holy Scriptures are authoritative for all of life. All who die without Christ will spend eternity in the fires of Hell.	The Ten Commandments and the Sermon on the Mount are the ethical basis for personal conduct, interpersonal relations, social order, and public policy. They are God's standard for all people, in all cultures, in all generations.
Moderate Christian (God/Man is God)	New Testament Grace supersedes Old Testament Law, and has little to contribute to modern political discussion, other than to encourage fairness and integrity. Public policy should be conducted according to natural law.	Individual responsibility is good, but Christian love requires us to help others unconditionally. Both private charity and government aid are good.	Spiritual and secular education are distinct. Children receive academic training at school, whereas spiritual instruction is the responsibility of the family and the Church.	Christianity is a relationship with Jesus Christ, not a religion with set requirements. Repentance - if it is necessary - is secondary to grace.	Love emphasizes tolerance. Calling the private or public actions of others sinful is judgmental, since only God knows men's hearts.

RECOMMENDED READING
(an asterisk marks the books most highly recommended)

GOD'S LAW

*Bahnsen, Greg L. *By This Standard: The Authority of God's Law Today*. Powder Springs, GA: American Vision, 2008.

Rushdoony, Rousas John. *Institutes of Biblical Law*. Nutley, NJ: Craig Press, 1973.

Titus, Herbert W. *God, Man, and Law: The Biblical Principles*. Oak Brook, IL: Institute in Basic Life Principles, 1994.

THE PROBLEM WITH GOVERNMENT-CONTROLLED EDUCATION

Gatto, John Taylor. *The Underground History of American Education: A Schoolteacher's Intimate Investigation into the Problem of Modern Schooling*. Gabriola Island, BC: New Society, 2005.

*Gunn, Colin, and Joaquin Fernandez. *IndoctriNation: Public Schools and the Decline of Christianity*. Green Forest, AR: Master Books, 2012.

*Maddoux, Marlin. *Public Education against America: The Hidden Agenda*. New Kensington, PA: Whitaker, 2006.

Barton, David. *America: To Pray or Not to Pray?* Aledo, TX: WallBuilders, 1994.

Noebel, David. *Clergy in the Classroom*. Manitou Springs, CO: Summit, 2007.

Shortt, Bruce N. *The Harsh Truth about Public Schools*. Vallecito, CA: Chalcedon Foundation, 2004.

THE PROBLEM IN THE PULPIT

Baldwin, Alice M., and Joel McDurmon. *The New England Pulpit and the American Revolution: When American Pastors Preached Politics, Resisted Tyranny and Founded a Nation on the Bible*. Braselton, GA: Devoted Books, 2019.

Frame, John. *Cornelius Van Til: An Analysis of His Thought.* Philipsburg, NJ: P&R, 1995.

*—. *The Escondido Theology.* Lakeland, FL: Whitefield Media Productions, 2011.

*Guinness, Os. *Prophetic Untimeliness: A Challenge to the Idol of Relevance.* Grand Rapids, MI: Baker Books, 2003.

Kuyper, Abraham. *Christianity: A Total World and Life System.* Marlborough, NH: Plymouth Rock Foundation, 1996.

*Machen, J. Gresham. *Christianity and Liberalism.* Grand Rapids, MI: Eerdmans, 2009.

*Mammen, Neil. *Jesus Is Involved in Politics! Why Aren't You? Why Isn't Your Church.* San Jose, CA: Rational Free Press, 2016.

*McIlhenny, Ryan C. *Kingdoms Apart.* Philipsburg, NJ: P&R, 2012.

Sandoz, Ellis, ed. *Political Sermons of the American Founding Era.* Indianapolis: Liberty Fund, 1991.

Van Til, Cornelius. *Christian Apologetics.* Philipsburg, NJ: P&R, 2012.

*Wells, David. *No Place for Truth: Or Whatever Happened to Evangelical Theology?* Grand Rapids, MI: Eerdmans, 1993.

Wilberforce, William. *A Practical View of Christianity.* Peabody, MA: Hendrickson, 2006.

ABSOLUTE TRUTH

*Guinness, Os. *Time for Truth: Living Free in a World of Lies, Hype & Spin.* Grand Rapids, MI: Baker Books, 2000.

*Ham, Ken, and Britt Beemer. *Already Gone: Why Your Kids Will Quit Church and What You Can Do to Stop It.* Green Forest, AR: Master Books, 2009.

Lutzer, Erwin. *Christ among Other Gods: A Defense of Christ in an Age of Tolerance.* Chicago: Moody, 2016.

*Tozer, A. W. *Voice of a Prophet.* Bloomington, MN: Bethany House, 2014.

THE FALSE RELIGION OF "TOLERANCE"

*Tozer, A. W. *Man: The Dwelling Place of God.* Chicago: Moody, 2018.

GOD AND CAESAR

Baldwin, Timothy, and Chuck Baldwin. *Romans 13: The True Meaning of Submission.* Kalispell, MT: Liberty Defense League, 2011.

*Barton, David. *Original Intent*. Aledo, TX: WallBuilders, 2008.

*Trewhella, Matthew J. *The Doctrine of the Lesser Magistrates: A Proper Resistance to Tyranny and a Repudiation of Unlimited Obedience to Civil Government*. Self-published, CreateSpace, 2013.

Zacharias, Ravi, and Vince Vitale. *Jesus among Secular Gods: The Countercultural Claims of Christ*. New York: FaithWords, 2017.

AMERICA'S CHRISTIAN HERITAGE

*Barton, David. *America's Godly Heritage*. Aledo, TX: WallBuilders, 1992.

Beliles, Mark A., and Stephen K. McDowell. *America's Providential History*. Charlottesville, VA: Providence Foundation, 1989.

*Boyer, Marilyn. *For You They Signed*. Green Forest, AR: Master Books, 2009.

DeMar, Gary. *America's Christian History*. Powder Springs, GA: American Vision, 2005.

Eidsmoe, John. *Christianity and the Constitution: The Faith of Our Founding Fathers*. Grand Rapids, MI: Baker Book House, 1995.

Federer, William J. *America's God and Country: Encyclopedia of Quotations*. St. Louis, MO: Amerisearch, 2000.

Kelly, Douglas F. *The Emergence of Liberty in the Modern World: The Influence of Calvin on Five Governments from the 16th through 18th Centuries*. Philipsburg, NJ: P&R, 1992.

Kennedy, D. James. *What If America Were a Christian Nation Again?* Nashville: Thomas Nelson, 2003.

*Wooten, Allen. *America, Christianity, and the Forgotten Link*. Self-published, Lulu, 2013.

TOWARD A CHRISTIAN WORLDVIEW

*Bastiat, Frederic. *The Law*. Mansfield Centre, CT: Martino, 2011.

Colson, Charles. *Kingdoms in Conflict: An Insider's Challenging View of Politics, Power, and the Pulpit*. Grand Rapids, MI: Zondervan, 1987.

Colson, Charles, and Nancy Pearcey. *How Now Shall We Live?* Carol Stream, IL: Tyndale, 1999.

Dobson, James. *Marriage under Fire: Why We Must Win This Battle.* Sisters, OR: Multnomah, 2004.

Kinnaman, David, and Gabe Lyons. *Good Faith: Being a Christian When Society Thinks You're Irrelevant and Extreme.* Grand Rapids, MI: Baker Books, 2016.

Lockman, Vic. *Biblical Economics in Comics.* Ramona, CA: V. Lockman, 1985. Geared toward children but useful for adults as well.

Morecraft, Joe. *With Liberty and Justice for All.* Sevierville, TN: Covenant House Books, 1995.

Noebel, David A. *Understanding the Times: The Collision of Today's Competing Worldviews.* Manitou Springs, CO: Summit Ministries, 2006.

*Pearcey, Nancy. *Total Truth: Liberating Christianity from Its Cultural Captivity.* Wheaton, IL: Crossway Books, 2009. If you read only one book, read this one.

Phillips, W. Gary, William E. Brown, and John Stonestreet. *Making Sense of Your World: A Biblical Worldview.* Salem, WI: Sheffield, 2008.

*Rose, Tom. *Economics: The American Economy from a Christian Perspective.* Mercer, PA: American Enterprise, 1985.

Rutherford, Samuel: *Lex Rex (The Law Is the King).* Edinburgh: Robert Ogle and Oliver & Boyd, 1644.

*Schaeffer, Francis A. *A Christian Manifesto.* Wheaton, IL: Crossway Books, 2005.

*Schanzenbach, Donald J. *Advancing the Kingdom: Declaring War on Humanistic Culture.* Minneapolis, MN: River City, 2001.

CHRISTIAN ACTIVISM

Kennedy, D. James, and Jerry Newcombe. *How Would Jesus Vote? A Christian Perspective on the Issues.* Colorado Springs, CO: WaterBrook, 2013.

*McDurmon, Joel. *Restoring America One County at a Time.* Braselton, GA: Devoted Books, 2019.

Staver, Mathew. *Take Back America.* Orlando: New Revolution, 2011.

ENDNOTES

CHAPTER 1

1   "2017 Governor Election," Virginia.gov, accessed February 4, 2019, http://historical.elections.virginia.gov/elections/view/87708; Alissa Smith, "Rypkema, Phillips, Miller Win Campbell County School Board Seats," *New and Advance* (Lynchburg, VA), November 8, 2017, www.newsadvance.com/news/local/rypkema-phillips-miller-win-campbell-county-school-board-seats/article_b6dada4e-c447-11e7-91c8-b39f3ee21837.html.

CHAPTER 2

2   "Sexual Risk Behaviors: HIV, STD, & Teen Pregnancy Prevention," Centers for Disease Control and Prevention, June 14, 2018, www.cdc.gov/HealthyYouth/sexualbehaviors.

3   "Sexual Risk Behaviors."

4   William J. Bennett, "Sex and the Education of Our Children," (address, National School Boards Association Meeting, Washington, DC, January 1987), 2, https://files.eric.ed.gov/fulltext/ED284148.pdf.

5   Rachel E. Morgan and Jennifer L. Truman, *Criminal Victimization*, 2017 (Washington, DC: Bureau of Justice Statistics, 2018), 2.

6   "Crime in the United States by Metropolitan Statistical Area, 2012," FBI: UCR, 2012, https://ucr.fbi.gov/crime-in-the-u.s/2012/crime-in-the-u.s.-2012/tables/6tabledatadecpdf/table-6.

7   Steven A. Camarota, "Births to Unmarried Mothers by Nativity and Education," Center for Immigration Studies, May 5, 2017, https://cis.org/Camarota/Births-Unmarried-Mothers-Nativity-and-Education.

8   *Family Matters: Substance Abuse and the American Family* (New York: National Center on Addiction and Substance Abuse at Columbia University, March

2005), 3, www.centeronaddiction.org/addiction-research/reports/family-matters-substance-abuse-and-american-family.

9 "Facts and TV Statistics," Parents Television Council, accessed February 4, 2019, http://w2.parentstv.org/main/Research/Facts.aspx.

10 Parents Television Council, *TV's Newest Target: Teen Sexual Exploitation*, July 2013, 10, http://w2.parentstv.org/MediaFiles/PDF/General/sexploitation_report_20130709.pdf.

11 Parents Television Council, *TV's Newest Target*, 12.

12 Obergefell v. Hodges, 135 S. Ct. 2584, 2599 (2015).

13 *Obergefell*, 135 S. Ct. at 2599.

14 "The Trends Redefining Romance Today," Barna, February 9, 2017, www.barna.com/research/trends-redefining-romance-today.

15 David Kinnaman, "The Porn Phenomenon," Barna, February 5, 2016, www.barna.com/the-porn-phenomenon.

16 "Pornography Survey Statistics," Proven Men, accessed February 4, 2019, www.provenmen.org/pornography-survey-statistics-2014/#.

17 LifeWay Research, *Study of Women Who Have Had an Abortion and Their Views on Church*, 2015, 32, http://lifewayresearch.com/wp-content/uploads/2015/11/Care-Net-Final-Presentation-Report-Revised.pdf.

18 LifeWay Research, *Study*, 4, 36.

19 "The End of Absolutes: America's New Norm," Barna, May 25, 2016, www.barna.com/research/the-end-of-absolutes-americas-new-moral-code.

CHAPTER 3

20 "Answers with Ken Ham: Did God Create in 6 Literal Days, Part 1," video, 14:44, www.youtube.com/watch?v=h2w-phgOAOo.

21 Laura Schlessinger, "Addiction May Be Grounds to End Marriage," *Deseret News*, October 17, 1997, www.deseretnews.com/article/589566/Addiction-may-be-grounds-to-end-marriage.html.

22 Roy Moore, quoted in Eyder Peralta, "Federal Judge Orders Ala. Official to Issue Marriage Licenses to Gay Couples," NPR, February 12, 2015, www.npr.org/sections/thetwo-way/2015/02/12/385835809/federal-judge-orders-alabama-official-to-hand-out-same-sex-marriage-licenses. Later in 2015, after

the Obergefell decision, Moore wrote, *"Obergefell* is particularly egregious because it mandates submission in violation of religious conscience." Quoted in Moore v. Alabama Judicial Inquiry Commission (2017), https://cases.justia.com/alabama/supreme-court/2017-1160002.pdf?ts=1492718728.

23 Russell Moore, quoted in David Roach, "Moore: SCOTUS Will 'Probably' OK Gay Marriage," Baptist Press, February 12, 2015, www.bpnews.net/44212/moore-scotus-will-probably-ok-gay-marriage.

24 A. W. Tozer, "In Praise of Dogmatism," in *Man: The Dwelling Place of God* (Chicago: Moody, 2018), chap. 27.

25 "Welcome to Q Christian Fellowship," Q Christian Fellowship, accessed February 5, 2019, www.qchristian.org.

26 Jonathan Merritt, "Eugene Peterson on Changing His Mind about Same-Sex Issues and Marriage," Religion News Service, July 12, 2017, https://religionnews.com/ 2017/07/12/eugene-peterson-on-changing-his-mind-about-same-sex-issues-and-marriage.

27 Kate Shellnutt, "Actually, Eugene Peterson Does Not Support Same-Sex Marriage," *Christianity Today*, July 13, 2017, www.christianitytoday.com/news/2017/july/eugene-peterson-actually-does-not-support-gay-marriage.html.

28 Greg Carey, "Rob Bell Comes Out for Marriage Equality," Huffington Post, March 18, 2013, www.huffingtonpost.com/greg-carey/rob-bell-comes-gay-marriage_b_2898394.html.

29 Dan Haseltine, quoted in Alexandra Bolles, "Christian Band 'Jars of Clay' Frontman Comes Out as Ally in 3 Days of Tweeting," GLAAD, April 24, 2014, www.glaad.org/blog/christian-band-jars-clay-frontman-comes-out-ally-3-days-tweeting.

30 Mark Twain, *The Wit and Wisdom of Mark Twain*, ed. Alex Ayres (New York: HarperCollins, 2005), 24.

31 Smith, Samuel, "SBC Pres. JD Greear says he'll refer to trans individuals by their preferred pronouns," Christian Post, available at https://www.christianpost.com/news/sbc-president-jd-greear-says-he-will-refer-to-transgender-individuals-by-their-preferred-pronouns.html.

32 Smith, Samuel, "SBC Pres. JD Greear says he'll refer to trans individuals by their preferred pronouns," Christian Post, available at https://www.christianpost.com/news/sbc-president-jd-greear-says-he-will-refer-to-transgender-individuals-by-their-preferred-pronouns.html

33 Joel Osteen, interview by Larry King, *Larry King Live*, CNN, June 20, 2005, www.cnn.com/TRANSCRIPTS/0506/20/lkl.01.html.

34 Osteen, interview.

CHAPTER 4

35 R. C. Sproul, "What Is Truth? Ravi Zacharias, Os Guiness, RC Sproul," *The Truth Project*, video, 1:21, www.youtube.com/watch?v=9AARDtGay5w.

36 Barna Group, "Competing Worldviews Influence Today's Christians," Barna, May 9, 2017, www.barna.com/research/competing-worldviews-influence-todays-christians.

37 Barna Group, "Competing Worldviews Influence Today's Christians."

38 Barna Group, "Competing Worldviews Influence Today's Christians."

39 Barna Group, "Competing Worldviews Influence Today's Christians."

40 Barna Group, "Competing Worldviews Influence Today's Christians."

41 Barna Group, "Competing Worldviews Influence Today's Christians."

42 Barna Group, "The End of Absolutes: America's New Moral Code," Barna, May 25, 2016, www.barna.com/research/the-end-of-absolutes-americas-new-moral-code.

43 Barna Group, "The End of Absolutes."

44 Barna Group, "The End of Absolutes."

45 Barna Group, "The End of Absolutes."

46 Barna Group, "The End of Absolutes."

47 Barna Group, "The End of Absolutes."

48 Barna Group, "The End of Absolutes."

49 Barna Group, "The End of Absolutes."

50 Barna Group, "Americans Are Most Likely to Base Truth on Feelings," Barna, February 12, 2002, www.barna.com/research/americans-are-most-likely-to-base-truth-on-feelings.

51 Os Guinness, *Prophetic Untimeliness: A Challenge to the Idol of Relevance* (Grand Rapids, MI: Baker Books, 2003), 98.

52 Amy Carmichael, *If: What Do I Know of Calvary Love* (Fort Washington, PA: CLC, 2011), 26–27.

CHAPTER 5

53 A. W. Tozer, *The Dangers of a Shallow Faith: Awakening from Spiritual Lethargy*, ed. James L. Snyder (Ventura, CA: Regal Books, 2012), 15.

54 Matt Walsh, "Jesus Didn't Care about Being Nice or Tolerant," Matt Walsh, April 7, 2014, https://themattwalshblog.com/jesus-didnt-care-about-being-nice-or-tolerant-and-neither-should-you.

55 Nancy Pearcey, *Total Truth: Liberating Christianity from Its Cultural Captivity*, study guide ed. (Wheaton, IL: Crossway Books, 2005), 261. All quotations from *Total Truth* in this book are taken from *Total Truth* by Nancy Pearcey, © 2005. Used by permission of Crossway, a publishing ministry of Good News Publishers, Wheaton, IL 60187, www.crossway.org.

56 Melville Fuller, quoted in William J. Federer, *America's God and Country: Encyclopedia of Quotations* (St. Louis: Amerisearch, 2000), 267.

57 Simon Greenleaf, *An Examination of the Testimony of the Four Evangelists*, (Boston: Charles C. Little and James Brown, 1846), v–vi.

58 Dorothy L. Sayers, "The Other Six Deadly Sins," in *Letters to a Diminished Church: Passionate Arguments for the Relevance of Christian Doctrine* (Nashville: W Publishing, 2004), 98.

59 G. K. Chesterton, *The Everlasting Man, in The Collected Works of G. K. Chesterton*, vol. 2 (San Francisco: Ignatius, 1986), 319.

60 Chesterton, *Everlasting Man*, 320–21.

61 Merilyn Hargis, "On the Road: The Inns and Outs of Travel in First-Century Palestine," *Christianity Today*, www.christianitytoday.com/history/issues/issue-59/on-road.html.

62 Walsh, "Jesus Didn't Care about Being Nice or Tolerant."

63 Matt Walsh, "Dear Christians, Now Is the Time for Intolerance," The Blaze, November 25, 2015, www.theblaze.com/contributions/dear-christians-now-is-the-time-for-intolerance.

64 John Piper, "Should Christians Be Encouraged to Arm Themselves?," Desiring God, December 22, 2015, www.desiringgod.org/articles/should-christians-be-encouraged-to-arm-themselves.

65 A. W. Tozer, "Some Things Are Not Negotiable," in *Man: The Dwelling Place of God* (Chicago: Moody, 2018), chap. 38.

66 Tozer, "Some Things," in *Man,* chap. 38.

67 Joel McDurmon, *The Problem of Slavery in Christian America* (Powder Springs, GA: American Vision, 2017), 53–54.

68 Tozer, "In Praise of Dogmatism," in *Man,* chap. 27.

69 Tozer, "In Praise of Dogmatism," in *Man,* chap. 27.

70 Stephen Tomkins, *John Wesley: A Biography* (Grand Rapids, MI: William B. Eerdmans, 2003), 193.

71 A. W. Tozer, "The Duty of Opposing," in *The Next Chapter after the Last,* ed. Harry Verploegh (Chicago: Moody, 2019), 19.

72 Tozer, "Duty of Opposing," 19.

73 Tozer, "Some Things," in *Man,* chap. 38.

74 Tozer, "Some Things," in *Man,* chap. 38.

75 J. Gresham Machen, "Christianity and Culture," *Princeton Theological Review* 11, no. 1 (1913): 6.

76 Machen, "Christianity and Culture," 7.

77 Machen, "Christianity and Culture," 13.

78 Jim Phillips, Pastor, North Greenwood Baptist Church, Greenwood, MS, quoted in Todd Starnes, "Have Christians Lost the Culture War?," Fox News, February 20, 2014, www.foxnews.com/opinion/2014/02/20/have-christians-lost-culture-war.html.

79 David Hankins, quoted in Paul F. South, "NOBTS: Confront Culture, Hankins Urges," Baptist Press, March 4, 2010, http://bpnews.net/32424/nobts-confront-culture-hankins-urges.

80 Adrian Rogers, "The Sin of Silence, Part 1," OnePlace, www.oneplace.com/ministries/love-worth-finding/read/articles/the-sin-of-silence-part-1-15853.html, emphasis added.

81 Abraham Kuyper, quoted in Charles Colson, *Against the Night: Living in the New Dark Ages* (Ann Arbor, MI: Servant, 1999), 163.

CHAPTER 6

82 Os Guinness, *Prophetic Untimeliness: A Challenge to the Idol of Relevance* (Grand Rapids, MI: Baker Books, 2003), 75.

83 Guinness, *Prophetic Untimeliness,* 11.

84   Guinness, *Prophetic Untimeliness*, 15.

85   Guinness, *Prophetic Untimeliness*, 54.

86   Guinness, *Prophetic Untimeliness*, 57.

87   Guinness, *Prophetic Untimeliness*, 58.

88   Guinness, *Prophetic Untimeliness*, 60.

89   Guinness, *Prophetic Untimeliness*, 62.

90   Guinness, *Prophetic Untimeliness*, 65.

91   Guinness, *Prophetic Untimeliness*, 67.

92   Guinness, *Prophetic Untimeliness*, 77.

93   Guinness, *Prophetic Untimeliness*, 86.

94   Simone Weil, quoted in Guinness, *Prophetic Untimeliness*, 105.

95   "Table 1. Time Spent in Primary Activities," Bureau of Labor Statistics, June 28, 2018, www.bls.gov/news.release/atus.t01.htm.

96   David Hinckley, "Average American Watches 5 Hours of TV Per Day, Report Shows," *New York Daily News*, March 5, 2014, www.nydailynews.com/life-style/average-american-watches-5-hours-tv-day-article-1.1711954.

97   Russ Rankin, "Study: Bible Engagement in Churchgoers' Hearts, Not Always Practiced," LifeWay, January 1, 2014, www.lifeway.com/en/articles/research-survey-bible-engagement-churchgoers.

98   Christopher Ingraham, "Here's How You Spend Your Days, America—in 10 Charts," *Washington Post*, June 27, 2014, www.washingtonpost.com/news/wonk/wp/2014/06/27/heres-how-you-spend-your-days-america-in-10-charts/?utm_term=.726f3f7f9b5d.

99   Frank Newport, "Church Leaders and Declining Religious Service Attendance," Gallup, September 7, 2018, https://news.gallup.com/opinion/polling-matters/242015/church-leaders-declining-religious-service-attendance.aspx.

100 Ingraham, "Here's How You Spend Your Days."

101 "Consumer Expenditures—2017," Bureau of Labor Statistics, September 13, 2018, www.bls.gov/news.release/cesan.nr0.htm

102 "American Donor Trends," Barna, June 3, 2013, www.barna.com/research/american-donor-trends.

103 "American Donor Trends."

104 "American Donor Trends."

105 Juvenal, *The Satires*, trans. Niall Rudd (New York: Oxford University Press, 2001), 10.77–80.

106 Michael Snyder, "34 Signs That America Is in Decline," Economic Collapse, http://theeconomiccollapseblog.com/archives/34-signs-that-america-is-in-decline.

107 Old Deluder Satan Act, quoted in Department of Education, *Report of the Commissioner of Education* (Washington, DC: Government Printing Office, 1868), 327.

108 Nadia Pflaum, "Trump: U.S. Spends More Than 'Almost Any Other Major Country' on Education," PolitiFact, September 21, 2016, www.politifact.com/ohio/statements/2016/sep/21/donald-trump/trump-us-spends-more-almost-any-other-major-countr.

109 Pflaum, "Trump: U.S. Spends More."

110 Abigail Hess, "Here's How Much It Costs to Go to College in the US Compared to Other Countries," CNBC, July 13, 2017, www.cnbc.com/2017/07/13/heres-how-much-it-costs-to-go-to-college-in-the-us-compared-to-other-countries.html.

111 National Center for Education Statistics, *Education Expenditures by Country*, 4, https://nces.ed.gov/programs/coe/pdf/coe_cmd.pdf.

112 Anne Rondeau, "The True Value of a College Education," Huffington Post, March 29, 2017, www.huffingtonpost.com/entry/the-true-value-of-a-college-education_us_589ce13de4b0e172783a9a2a.

113 Malcolm X, "(1964) Malcolm X's Speech at the Founding Rally of the Organization of Afro-American Unity," BlackPast.org, October 15, 2007, www.blackpast.org/african-american-history/speeches-african-american-history/1964-malcolm-x-s-speech-founding-rally-organization-afro-american-unity.

114 Sonia Sotomayor, quoted in Jeff Blumenthal, "Sotomayor Receives Philadelphia Bar's Diversity Award," *Philadelphia Business Journal*, March 11, 2011, www.bizjournals.com/philadelphia/blog/jeff-blumenthal/2011/03/sotomayor-receives-philadelphia-bars.html?ed=2011-03-11&s=article_du&ana=e_du_pub.

115 Michelle Obama, quoted in David W. Chen, "Michelle Obama Denounces Donald Trump in CUNY Commencement Speech," *New York Times*, June 3, 2016, www.nytimes.com/2016/06/04/nyregion/michelle-obama-city-college-new-york-commencement.html.

116 Charles Rangel, "Advancing the Dream through Education," Huffington Post, April 4, 2013, www.huffingtonpost.com/rep-charles-rangel/mlk-assassination-anniversary_b_3014441.html.

117 Dick Cheney, "Full Text: Dick Cheney's Speech," BBC, September 2, 2004, http://news.bbc.co.uk/2/hi/americas/3620486.stm.

118 Horace Mann, "Report for 1848," in *Annual Reports on Education* (Boston: Lee and Shepard, 1872), 669.

119 Horace Mann, *Thoughts Selected from the Writings of Horace Mann* (Boston: H. B. Fuller, 1867), 220.

120 "Sample Quotes," National Education Association, www.nea.org/grants/35593.htm.

CHAPTER 7

121 Sproul, R.C. Jr., "Bread, Circuses & the Coliseum," available at https://web.archive.org/web/20150702223055/http://rcsprouljr.com/blog/bread-circuses-and-the-coliseum/. Posted July 2, 2015.

122 Sproul, R.C., Sr., "The Divine Foundation of Authority," online article, available at http://www.christianity.com/bible/the-divine-foundation-of-authority-11600891.html.

123 Sproul, R.C., Sr., "The Divine Foundation of Authority," online article, available at http://www.christianity.com/bible/the-divine-foundation-of-authority-11600891.html

124 Mayhew, Jonathan, "A Discourse Concerning Unlimited Submission and Non-Resistance to the Higher Powers," (Boston, MA: D. Fowle. (1750) 28.

125 Mayhew, Jonathan, "A Discourse Concerning Unlimited Submission and Non-Resistance to the Higher Powers," (Boston, MA: D. Fowle. (1750) 37.

126 Mayhew, Jonathan, "A Discourse Concerning Unlimited Submission and Non-Resistance to the Higher Powers," (Boston, MA: D. Fowle. (1750) 38.

127 Mayhew, Jonathan, "A Discourse Concerning Unlimited Submission and Non-Resistance to the Higher Powers," (Boston, MA: D. Fowle. (1750) 30-31.

128 Mayhew, Jonathan, "A Discourse Concerning Unlimited Submission and Non-Resistance to the Higher Powers," (Boston, MA: D. Fowle. (1750) 54-55.

129 Rutherford, Samuel, *Lex Rex*, Question XXXIV, Obj. 11, Ans. 1 (Edinburgh: Robert Ogle and Oliver & Boyd, 1843), 178.

130 Lea, Penny, "Sing a Little Louder," available at https://www.pennylea.com/sing-a-little-louder.

131 McDurmon, Joel, "The Great Omission," (May 6, 2011), available at https://www.lambsreign.com/mcdurmon/the-great-omission.

CHAPTER 8

132 G. K. Chesterton, quoted in Benjamin Wiker, *Worshipping the State: How Liberalism Became Our State Religion* (Washington, DC: Regnery, 2013), 327.

133 Wiker, *Worshipping the State*, 145.

134 Jean-Jacques Rousseau, quoted in Wiker, *Worshipping the State*, 177.

135 Wiker, *Worshipping the State*, 31.

136 Wiker, *Worshipping the State*, 30.

137 Wiker, *Worshipping the State*, 32.

138 Arthur M. Wright Jr., *The Governor and the King: Irony, Hidden Transcripts, and Negotiating Empire in the Fourth Gospel* (Eugene, OR: Pickwick, 2019), 56–57.

139 Maurice Casey, *Jesus of Nazareth: An Independent Historian's Account of His Life and Teaching* (London: T & T Clark, 2010), 423.

140 Thomas O'Loughlin, *The Didache: A Window on the Earliest Christians* (Grand Rapids, MI: Baker Academic, 2010), 161.

141 O'Loughlin, *The Didache*, 162.

142 Wiker, *Worshipping the State*, 32.

143 Wiker, *Worshipping the State*, 32–33.

144 Francis Schaeffer, A Christian Manifesto, rev. ed. (1982; repr., Wheaton, IL: Crossway Books, 2005), 92.

145 Wiker, *Worshipping the State*, 118.

146 Wiker, *Worshipping the State*, 119.

147 Wiker, *Worshipping the State*, 130–31.

148 Wiker, *Worshipping the State*, 132.

149 Wiker, *Worshipping the State*, 138.

150 Planned Parenthood of Southeastern Pa. v. Casey, 505 U.S. 833, 851 (1992).

151 Ken Ham and Britt Beemer, *Already Gone: Why Your Kids Will Quit Church and What You Can Do to Stop It* (Green Forest, AR: Master Books, 2009), 77–78.

152 William Edgar, "The National Confessional Position," in God and Politics: *Four Views on the Reformation of Civil Government*, ed. Gary Scott Smith (Phillipsburg, NJ: Presbyterian & Reformed, 1989), 181–82.

153 Wiker, *Worshipping the State*, 152.

154 Wiker, *Worshipping the State*, 154.

155 Wiker, *Worshipping the State*, 153.

156 Wiker, *Worshipping the State*, 153.

157 Wiker, *Worshipping the State*, 154.

158 Wiker, *Worshipping the State*, 155.

159 Wiker, *Worshipping the State*, 155.

160 Wiker, *Worshipping the State*, 157.

161 Wiker, *Worshipping the State*, 172.

162 Wiker, *Worshipping the State*, 180.

163 Wiker, *Worshipping the State*, 177.

164 Wiker, *Worshipping the State*, 195–96.

165 Wiker, *Worshipping the State*, 237.

166 Wiker, *Worshipping the State*, 239.

167 Wiker, *Worshipping the State*, 241.

168 Wiker, *Worshipping the State*, 268.

169 Wiker, *Worshipping the State*, 286.

170 Lawrence W. Reed, "Augustine: Searching for Truth and Wisdom," Foundation for Economic Education, March 4, 2016, https://fee.org/articles/an-unjust-law-is-no-law-at-all.

171 John Calvin, "Lecture 30," in *Commentaries on the Book of the Prophet Daniel*, trans. Thomas Meyers, vol. 1, www.ccel.org/ccel/calvin/calcom24.xii.xx.html.

172 Edgar, "The National Confessional Position," 188.

173 See Edwards v. Aguillard, 482 U.S. 578 (1987).

174 Wiker, *Worshipping the State*, 140.

175 Obergefell v. Hodges, 135 S. Ct. 2584, 2594 (2015).

176 Obergefell, 135 S. Ct. at 2602.

177 Wiker, *Worshipping the State*, 305–7.

178 John MacArthur, "Christians and Politics, Part 3," Grace to You, www.gty. org/library/articles/A126/christians-and-politics-part-3.

179 John MacArthur, "Christians and Politics, Part 4," Grace to You, www.gty. org/library/articles/A127/christians-and-politics-part-4.

180 Associated Press, "Los Angeles church can hold indoor services, judge says," Aug. 15, 2020, available at https://apnews.com/article/los-angeles-courts-virus-outbreak-194e76be65f3c85c826a365b78d056fb.

181 Wiker, *Worshipping the State*, 300.

182 Wiker, *Worshipping the State*, 287.

183 School District of Abington Township v. Schempp, 374 U.S. 203, 313 (1963).

184 Wiker, *Worshipping the State*, 287.

185 Wiker, *Worshipping the State*, 189.

186 Russell Moore, quoted in David Roach, "Moore: SCOTUS Will 'Probably' OK Gay Marriage," Baptist Press, February 12, 2015, www.bpnews.net/44212/moore-scotus-will-probably-ok-gay-marriage.

187 Schaeffer, *A Christian Manifesto*, 90.

188 Benjamin Wiker, *Worshipping the State: How Liberalism Became Our State Religion* (Washington, D.C.: Regnery Publishing, Inc. 2013), 145.

189 Os Guinness, *Prophetic Untimeliness: A Challenge to the Idol of Relevance* (Grand Rapids, MI: Baker Books, 2003), 50.

190 Wiker, *Worshipping the State*, 287.

191 Edgar, "The National Confessional Position," 191–92.

192 Edgar, "The National Confessional Position," 194–95.

193 Peter Powers, *"Jesus Christ the True King and Head of Government": A Sermon Preached before the General Assembly of the State of Vermont, on the Day of Their*

First Election, March 12, 1778, at Windsor (Newburyport, MA, 1778), 40, http:// quod.lib.umich.edu/e/evans/N12679.0001.001?rgn=main;view=fulltext.

194 Dorothy L. Sayers, "Why Work?," in *Letters to a Diminished Church: Passionate Arguments for the Relevance of Christian Doctrine* (Nashville: W Publishing, 2004), 131–32.

195 Edgar, "The National Confessional Position," 190.

196 Edgar, "The National Confessional Position," 191.

CHAPTER 9

197 Edwards v. Aguillard, 482 U.S. 578 (1987).

198 School District of Abington Township v. Schempp, 374 U.S. 203 (1963).

199 Lee v. Weisman, 505 U.S. 577 (1992).

200 Child Evangelism Fellowship of Maryland, Inc. v. Montgomery County Public Schools, 373 F.3d 589 (4th Cir. 2004).

201 Charles Colson, *Kingdoms in Conflict: An Insider's Challenging View of Politics, Power, and the Pulpit* (Grand Rapids, MI: William Morrow/Zondervan, 1989), 226.

202 Torcaso v. Watkins, 367 U.S. 488 (1961).

203 *Humanist Manifesto I*, 1933, American Humanist Association, https:// americanhumanist.org/what-is-humanism/manifesto1.

204 *Humanist Manifesto II*, 1973, American Humanist Association, https:// americanhumanist.org/what-is-humanism/manifesto2.

205 Beverly Eakman, "Bushwhacking Johnny," *Chronicles*, August 1, 2002, www. chroniclesmagazine.org/2002/September/26/9/magazine/article/10826474.

206 Colson, *Kingdoms in Conflict*, 213.

207 Ellwood P. Cubberley, *Public Education in the United States: A Study and Interpretation of American Educational History* (Boston: Houghton Mifflin, 1919), 167.

208 Horace Mann, "What God Does, and What He Leaves for Man to Do, in the Work of Education," in *Lectures and Annual Reports on Education* (Cambridge, 1867), 210.

209 Marlin Maddoux, *Public Education against America: The Hidden Agenda* (New Kensington, PA: Whitaker, 2006), 98.

210 John Dewey, *Impressions of Soviet Russia and the Revolutionary World* (New York: New Republic, 1929), 61, 76.

211 Dewey, *Impressions*, 61.

212 John Dewey, "Soul-Searching," *Teacher Magazine*, September 1933.

213 John Dewey, *My Pedagogic Creed* (New York: E. L. Kellogg, 1897), 18.

214 Charles Francis Potter, quoted in

215 J. Gresham Machen, "Christianity and Culture," *Princeton Theological Review* 11, no. 1 (1913): 2.

216 Paul Blanshard, "Three Cheers for Our Secular State," *Humanist*, March–April 1976.

217 John J. Dunphy, "A Religion for a New Age," *Humanist*, January–February 1983.

218 Martin Luther, quoted in J. H. Merle D'Aubigné, *History of the Reformation of the Sixteenth Century*, trans. H. White (London: Religious Tract Society, 1846), 190.

219 Stone v. Graham, 449 U.S. 39, 42 (1980).

220 Voddie Baucham Jr., *Family Driven Faith: Doing What It Takes to Raise Sons and Daughters Who Walk with God* (Wheaton, IL: Crossway, 2007), 201–2.

221 Maddoux, *Public Education against America*, 76.

222 Maddoux, *Public Education against America*, 91.

223 Dan Smithwick, "One Generation to Go, Then the End," Nehemiah Institute, February 21, 2002, www.nehemiahinstitute.com/articles/index.php?action=show&id=18.

224 Smithwick, "One Generation to Go."

225 Dan Smithwick, "Where Are We Going?," Nehemiah Institute, August 1, 2008, www.nehemiahinstitute.com/articles/index.php?action=show&id=35.

226 "Worldview Trend Chart," Nehemiah Institute, www.nehemiahinstitute.com/pdf/TKS-Chart-2.pdf; "The 'PEERS Worldview' Grid," Nehemiah Institute, www.nehemiahinstitute.com/PEERS-Worldview.pdf.

227 Maggie Gallagher, "Banned in Boston," *Weekly Standard*, May 15, 2006, www.weeklystandard.com/banned-in-boston/article/13329.

228 Debbie Truong, "In Fairfax, a Lesson on Why Words Matter, Especially in Sexual Health Class," *Washington Post*, June 23, 2018, www.washingtonpost.com/local/education/in-fairfax-a-lesson-on-why-words-matter-especially-in-sexual-health-class/2018/06/23/bc705114-6ef6-11e8-afd5-778aca903bbe_story.html?utm_term=.b83675b3e559.

229 Truong, "In Fairfax."

230 Tony Perkins, "Against Parents' Wishes, School District on the Radar of LGBT Group Imposes New Sex Ed," Daily Signal, June 29, 2018, www. dailysignal.com/2018/06/29/against-parents-wishes-school-district-on-the-radar-of-lgbt-group-imposes-new-sex-ed.

231 Austin Ruse and Cathy Ruse, "Fairfax County Votes to Tell Boys They Might Be Girls," Stream, June 15, 2018, https://stream.org/fairfax-county-votes-tell-boys-might-girls.

232 Ruse and Ruse, "Fairfax County."

233 Perkins, "Against Parents' Wishes."

234 Maddoux, *Public Education against America*, 203–5.

235 Maddoux, *Public Education against America*, 208.

236 Maddoux, *Public Education against America*, 209.

237 Jeffrey Lord, "When Nancy Met Harry," American Spectator, October 5, 2006, https://spectator.org/46366_when-nancy-met-harry.

238 David Thorstad, "Harry Hay on Man/Boy Love," NAMBLA, www.nambla. org/hayonmanboylove.html.

239 Maddoux, *Public Education against America*, 182.

240 Maddoux, *Public Education against America*, 182–83.

241 George Grant, *Grand Illusions*, 2nd ed. (Franklin, TN: Adroit, 1992), 110.

242 Grant, *Grand Illusions*, 111.

243 Maddoux, *Public Education against America*, 189.

244 James Dobson, quoted in Maddoux, *Public Education against America*, 245.

245 Emphasis added to the verses in this paragraph.

CHAPTER 10

246 A. W. Tozer, "In Praise of Dogmatism," in *Man: The Dwelling Place of God* (Chicago: Moody, 2018), chap. 27.

247 Christopher Ingraham, "Here's How You Spend Your Days, America—in 10 Charts," *Washington Post*, June 27, 2014, www.washingtonpost.com/news/wonk/wp/2014/06/27/heres-how-you-spend-your-days-america-in-10-charts/?utm_term=.726f3f7f9b5d; David Hinckley, "Average American Watches 5 Hours of TV Per Day, Report Shows," *New York Daily News*, March 5, 2014, www.nydailynews.com/life-style/average-american-watches-5-hours-tv-day-article-1.1711954.

248 Os Guinness, *Prophetic Untimeliness: A Challenge to the Idol of Relevance* (Grand Rapids, MI: Baker Books, 2003), 100.

249 Lee Bernstein, "I Love You, You Love Me," Kids Environment Kids Health, https://kids.niehs.nih.gov/games/songs/childrens/i-love-you.

250 Dictionary.com, s.v. "sovereignty," www.dictionary.com/browse/sovereignty.

CHAPTER 11

251 Elizabeth Day, "Jesus Might Have Been Homosexual, Says the First Openly Gay Bishop," *Telegraph*, April 3, 2005, www.telegraph.co.uk/news/uknews/1487002/Jesus-might-have-been-homosexual-says-the-first-openly-gay-bishop.html.

252 Manya Brachear Pashman, "Campus Pastor at North Park University Suspended Indefinitely for Officiating Gay Wedding," *Chicago Tribune*, January 23, 2018, www.chicagotribune.com/news/breaking/ct-met-north-park-campus-pastor-gay-marriage-20180118-story.html.

253 Tony Campolo, "For the Record," Tony Campolo, June 8, 2015, https://tonycampolo.org/for-the-record-tony-campolo-releases-a-new-statement.

254 Joel Osteen, interview by Larry King, *Larry King Live*, CNN, June 20, 2005, http://transcripts.cnn.com/TRANSCRIPTS/0506/20/lkl.01.html.

255 John MacArthur, "Christians and Politics, Part 3," Grace to You, www.gty.org/library/articles/A126/christians-and-politics-part-3.

256 John MacArthur, "Christians and Politics, Part 4," Grace to You, www.gty.org/library/articles/A127/christians-and-politics-part-4.

257 *Encyclopaedia Britannica*, s.v. "John Knox: Scottish Religious Leader," by James Stevenson McEwen, last modified January 3, 2020, www.britannica.com/biography/John-Knox.

258 Quoted in Stanley J. St. Clair, ed., *Prayers of Prophets, Knights and Kings: A Symposium from 2334 B.C. to Date* (St. Clair, 2006), 9.

259 David F. Wells, *No Place for Truth: Or Whatever Happened to Evangelical Theology?* (Grand Rapids, MI: William B. Eerdmans, 1993), 147.

260 John Calvin, *Institutes of the Christian Religion*, trans. John Allen (Philadelphia: Presbyterian Board, 1844), 2:637.

261 Jay Rogers, "Two Views of Civil Government: Puritanism vs. Pietism," Forerunner, May 1, 2008, www.forerunner.com/statesman/twoviews.html.

262 Simon Greenleaf, *An Examination of the Testimony of the Four Evangelists*, (Boston: Charles C. Little and James Brown, 1846), v–vi.

263 Abraham Kuyper, "Sphere Sovereignty," in *Abraham Kuyper: A Centennial Reader*, ed. James D. Bratt (Grand Rapids, MI: William B. Eerdmans, 1998), 488.

264 Allen Wooten, *America, Christianity, and the Forgotten Link* (self-pub., 2013), 58 (citing David Barton, "American Heritage DVD Series," Episode 6).

265 Wooten, *America*, 58 (citing David Barton, "American Heritage DVD Series," Episode 38).

266 Wooten, *America*, 58 (citing David Barton, "American Heritage DVD Series," Episode 36).

267 Wooten, *America*, 58 (citing David Barton, "American Heritage DVD Series," Episode 12).

268 Wooten, *America*, 58.

269 Calvin Coolidge (speech, Jewish Community Center, Washington, DC, May 3, 1925), in William J. Federer, *Treasury of Presidential Quotations* (St. Louis: Amerisearch, 2004), 242.

270 Calvin Coolidge, "The Inspiration of the Declaration of Independence" (speech, 1925), in Jackie Gingrich Cushman, ed., *The Essential American: 25 Documents and Speeches Every American Should Own* (Washington, DC: Regnery, 2010), 228.

271 Wooten, *America*, 61.

272 George Barna, quoted in Michael L. Brown, *Saving a Sick America: A Prescription for Moral and Cultural Transformation* (Nashville: Nelson Books, 2017), 123.

273 Chuck Baldwin, "New Research: Pastors Deliberately Keeping Flock in the Dark," Chuck Baldwin Live, August 7, 2014, https://chuckbaldwinlive.com/Articles/tabid/109/ID/1213/New-Research-Pastors-Deliberately-Keeping-Flock-In-The-Dark.aspx.

274 Baldwin, "New Research."

275 Baldwin, "New Research."

276 David F. Wells, *No Place for Truth: Or Whatever Happened to Evangelical Theology?* (Grand Rapids, MI: William B. Eerdmans, 1993), 108.

277 Wells, *No Place*, 108.

278 Wells, *No Place*, 109.

279 Wells, *No Place*, 131.

280 Dorothy L. Sayers, "Why Work?," in *Letters to a Diminished Church: Passionate Arguments for the Relevance of Christian Doctrine* (Nashville: W Publishing, 2004), 131–32.

281 Wells, *No Place*, 136.

282 Wells, *No Place*, 216–17.

283 Charles Brown, quoted in Wells, *No Place*, 252.

284 J. Gresham Machen, "Christianity and Culture," *Princeton Theological Review* 11, no. 1 (1913): 9.

285 Dietrich Bonhoeffer, letter to Erwin Sutz, September 11, 1934, in *Dietrich Bonhoeffer: A Life in Pictures*, ed. Renate Bethge and Christian Gremmels, trans. Brian McNeil (Minneapolis: Fortress, 2006), 79.

CHAPTER 12

286 Nancy Pearcey, *Total Truth: Liberating Christianity from Its Cultural Captivity*, study guide ed. (Wheaton, IL: Crossway Books, 2005), 47.

287 Pearcey, *Total Truth*, 20–21.

288 Pearcey, *Total Truth*, 93–94.

289 Pearcey, *Total Truth*, 21.

290 Pearcey, *Total Truth*, 22.

291 Michael Goheen, *"As the Father Has Sent Me, I Am Sending You"*: J. E. Lesslie Newbigin's Missionary Ecclesiology (Zoetermeer: Uitgeverij Boekencentrum, 2000), 377.

292 Pearcey, *Total Truth*, 38.

293 Pearcey, *Total Truth*, 38.

294 Pearcey, *Total Truth*, 41.

295 Pearcey, *Total Truth*, 98.

296 Pearcey, *Total Truth*, 35.

297 Pearcey, *Total Truth*, 74–75.

298 Pearcey, *Total Truth*, 75.

299 Pearcey, *Total Truth*, 77.

300 Pearcey, *Total Truth*, 77.

301 Pearcey, *Total Truth*, 77.

302 Pearcey, *Total Truth*, 80.

303 Jacques Maritain, *Integral Humanism: Temporal and Spiritual Problems of a New Christendom*, trans. Joseph Evans (New York: Scribner's, 1968), 22.

304 Pearcey, *Total Truth*, 80–81.

305 Pearcey, *Total Truth*, 82.

306 Pearcey, *Total Truth*, 93–94.

307 Pearcey, *Total Truth*, 118.

308 Pearcey, *Total Truth*, 118.

309 Pearcey, *Total Truth*, 266.

310 Pearcey, *Total Truth*, 278.

311 Alan Wolfe, *The Transformation of American Religion: How We Actually Live Our Faith* (New York: Free Press, 2003), 35–36, 67.

312 Pearcey, *Total Truth*, 323.

313 Pearcey, *Total Truth*, 118.

CHAPTER 13

314 Alvin L. Reid, "Remembering the Haystack Prayer Meeting," Baptist Press, September 22, 2006, www.bpnews.net/24037/firstperson-remembering-the-haystack-prayer-meeting.

315 Os Guinness, *Prophetic Untimeliness: A Challenge to the Idol of Relevance* (Grand Rapids, MI: Baker Books, 2003), 108.

316 Guinness, *Prophetic Untimeliness*, 108–9.

317 Charles Colson and Nancy Pearcey, *How Now Shall We Live?* (Wheaton, IL: Tyndale, 1999), 414.

318 Colson and Pearcey, *How Now Shall We Live?*, 416.

319 Colson and Pearcey, *How Now Shall We Live?*, 417.

320 John Winthrop, "A Model of Christian Charity" (sermon, 1630), Winthrop Society, www.winthropsociety.com/doc_charity.php, spelling modified to modern English.

321 Pearcey, *Total Truth*, 356, emphasis added.

322 Os Guinneszs, *Prophetic Untimeliness*, 71.

323 Caleb Johnson, "Church and Religion," MayflowerHistory.com, http://mayflowerhistory.com/religion.

324 Paul Lawler, "Wesley, Wrath, & the Revival That Changed a Nation," Seedbed, June 16, 2014, www.seedbed.com/wesley-wrath-revival-changed-nation.

325 Joel Osteen, *Your Best Life Now: 7 Steps to Living at Your Full Potential* (New York: FaithWords, 2004).

326 Lawler, "Wesley."

327 Lawler, "Wesley."

328 Christopher D. Hancock, "William Wilberforce (1759–1833): The Shrimp Who Stopped Slavery," *Knowing & Doing*, Summer 2007, www.cslewisinstitute.org/webfm_send/603, 2.

329 Hancock, "William Wilberforce," 2.

330 William Wilberforce, quoted in Hancock, "William Wilberforce," 2.

331 Hancock, "William Wilberforce," 2.

332 Jonathan Edwards, "Sinners in the Hands of an Angry God," in *The Norton Anthology of American Literature*, ed. Nina Baym, shorter 8th ed. (New York: W. W. Norton, 2013), 210–13.

333 Edwards, "Sinners," 211.

334 Edwards, "Sinners," 214.

335 Stephen Williams, quoted in *Jonathan Edwards's "Sinners in the Hands of an Angry God": A Casebook*, ed. Wilson H. Kimnach, Caleb J. D. Maskell, and Kenneth P. Minkema (New Haven, CT: Yale University Press, 2010), 1.

336 Henry Varley, quoted in Mark Fackler, "The World Has Yet to See," *Christianity Today*, www.christianitytoday.com/history/issues/issue-25/world-has-yet-to-see.html.

For more information about

God, Caesar, and Idols
and
Rick D. Boyer
please visit:

www.ChristandCultureMedia.com

Ambassador International's mission is to magnify the Lord Jesus Christ
and promote His Gospel through the written word.

We believe through the publication of Christian literature, Jesus Christ and
His Word will be exalted, believers will be strengthened in their walk with
Him, and the lost will be directed to Jesus Christ as the only way of salvation.

For more information about
AMBASSADOR INTERNATIONAL
please visit:

www.ambassador-international.com
@AmbassadorIntl
www.facebook.com/AmbassadorIntl

*Thank you for reading this book. Please consider leaving us a
review on your social media, favorite retailer's website,
Goodreads or Bookbub, or our website.*

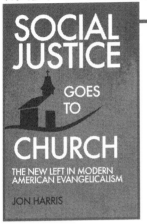
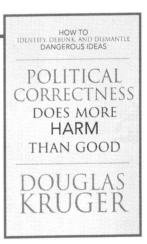
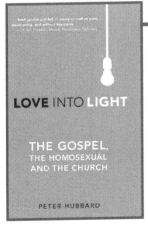

Made in the USA
Columbia, SC
13 June 2022